D1633301

SCANDAL AT
CONGO HOUSE

Cardiff Libraries
www.cardiff.gov.uk/libraries

Llyfrgelloedd Caerdydd
www.caerdydd.gov.uk/llyfrgelloedd

ACC. No: 02905498

By the same author:

Llandudno before the Hotels

Paupers, Bastards and Lunatics: the story of Conwy Workhouse

Walks from Conwy

Walks from Llandudno

Walks in the Conwy Valley

Walks from Colwyn Bay

Scandal at Congo House

Christopher Draper
and John Lawson-Reay

First published in 2012

© Christopher Draper and John Lawson-Reay

© Gwasg Carreg Gwalch 2012

All rights reserved. No part of this publication
may be reproduced, stored in a retrieval system,
or transmitted in any form or by any means, electronic,
electrostatic, magnetic tape, mechanical, photocopying,
recording, or otherwise, without prior permission
of the authors of the works herein.

Published with the financial support
of the Welsh Books Council

ISBN: 978-1-84527-400-9

Cover design: Welsh Books Council

Published by Gwasg Carreg Gwalch,
12 Iard yr Orsaf, Llanrwst, Wales LL26 0EH
tel: 01492 642031
fax: 01492 641502
email: books@carreg-gwalch.com
website: www.carreg-gwalch.com

'European Christianity is a dangerous thing ...
a religion which points with one hand to the skies,
bidding you *lay up for yourselves treasures in heaven,*
and while you are looking up
grasps all your worldly goods with the other hand.'

Mojola Agbebi (1860–1917)
Lagos, 1902

'The hope of Africa is not in Europeans, Americans,
or any other foreigners,
but in the natives of the country themselves.'

William Hughes (1856–1924)
Colway Bay, 1898

Contents

Introduction

Have you ever stayed in a hotel or holiday cottage whose leisure facilities amounted to a bookcase of dusty, discarded volumes that no-one in their right mind would ever wish to read? That's how I first stumbled upon the extraordinary story of William Hughes and his African Institute. Lodged amongst a motley collection of infinitely forgettable paper-backs, an attractively illustrated Victorian binding and intriguing title attracted me to the pages of *Dark Africa and the Way Out.*

As I leafed through William Hughes's 1892 account of his years in the Congo and subsequent attempt to enlighten the 'Dark Continent' by bringing African boys to the north Wales holiday resort of Colwyn Bay I became hooked. Captivated by photographs of Hughes and his African boys, I was frustrated by the lack of a conclusion and was left pondering the ultimate fate of 'Congo House', of the Africans and of William Hughes himself.

I was surprised to find no-one had written a book about the Congo House story although I did manage to track down a few relevant magazine and newspaper articles. After some preliminary research, in 2000 I published a brief account of William Hughes and the Congo House story in a 'Walks With History' guide to Colwyn Bay (published by *Gwasg Carreg Gwalch*). This was followed by a Welsh language television programme, directed by Will Aaron (*Ffilmiau'r Nant*) and broadcast on S4C.

I was invited by an educational organisation to deliver a public lecture on 'Congo House'. Amongst those who attended the talk was accomplished photographer and local historian John Lawson-Reay. Ever since then John has encouraged me to publish a comprehensive account of William Hughes and his African Institute. Eventually I agreed, on condition that Mr Lawson-Reay took responsibility for producing an appropriate collection of photographs to illustrate my text. John's expertise in restoring poor-quality pictures proved invaluable and a further decade of detailed research finally culminated in the publication of this book, exactly one hundred years after Congo House collapsed in scandal. Any remaining imperfections in the following photographs are due to the poor quality of the originals, however shortcomings in the text are entirely my own responsibility.

This book is aimed at the general reader, as well as those pursuing more specific academic or ideological interests. I have therefore blended the dramatic narrative of William Hughes's life with description and analysis of the wider context of the Congo House scheme. To maximise readability I have confined references and supplementary notes to a section at the end of the book that includes details of the locations of original documents and relevant sites of interest as well as an acknowledgement of the help provided by specific individuals and institutions.

At the risk of interrupting the narrative flow I devote chapter nine to the biographies of individual Congo House students for this is also their story. Of necessity these are potted and selective, featuring twenty-six of the eighty-seven students who trained at the Institute. Despite its original name, almost from the outset Congo House admitted students from a far wider area than just the Congo, embracing many parts of Africa and even the Americas. The student biographies featured in chapter nine were selected to illustrate the Institute's geographical diversity. Biographies of other students are included elsewhere in the narrative (for particular reasons).

I have generally retained the names of students and places as they appear in the Institute's official documents, although obvious inconsistencies have been corrected. As readers will appreciate, in the period considered here, Africa was being carved up into colonial states by the major European powers. Ancient tribal groupings were frequently rent asunder or randomly combined according to the whims of the imperial powers. Old Calabar, Lagos, New Calabar and Yorubaland, for instance, were bundled up to create 'Nigeria'. In places I refer to these more recent names where I consider it aids the understanding of the general reader but this doesn't indicate approval of the colonial authority's action in reshaping, redefining or renaming African territories.

The rise and fall of William Hughes is a sad and moving

episode in Welsh history but its importance is international. William's ideas on Africa, his relationships with black Africans and African-Americans, and his influence on his students were all shaped and informed by his own experiences growing up as a Welshman in England's oldest colony. William Hughes once wrote, 'It is a wrong and a blunder to appoint Englishmen as judges, preachers and magistrates over the people of Wales; even were they the best of men they should be in the wrong place…they are ignorant of the Welsh language, unacquainted with the affairs of the Welsh people, their poverty, history, wrongs; they cannot sympathise with the sentiments, hopes and aspirations of a conquered people'.

Hughes was out of step with the age of imperialism and Europe's scramble for Africa but he was in tune and in contact with black radicals shaping a pan-African alternative. A century after Hughes and his African Institute collapsed in scandal and was cast into obscurity it is time to re-examine this much neglected episode in our history.

Christopher Draper
Llandudno
Summer 2012

W. HUGHES, F.R G.S.,

William Hughes, Fellow of the Royal Geographical Society

Chapter One

Farm Boy to Visionary
(1856–1882)

Nothing in William Hughes' childhood suggested he would become such an ambitious, enterprising and controversial character in later life. He was born into a close-knit, Welsh agricultural community on 8 April 1856 at the family home of Bryngraianog, a seventeenth-century stone-built longhouse in Rhoslan, two miles north of Llanystumdwy, north Wales. His father, Hugh Evans, a native of Tydweiliog, worked a tenant farm of 45 acres with the help of his Llanystumdwy-born wife Catherine (nee Jones), their eight children and an additional agricultural labourer.

William's mother registered his birth ten days after the event at Criccieth, inadvertently indicating her own illiteracy by signing the register with a cross. Given the middle name Hugh, after his father, and in childhood officially called 'William Hugh Evans' it is significant that as an adult William consciously adopted a form closer to the old Welsh patronymic, recording his own name as simply 'William Hughes'.

William's early experiences seldom extended beyond the family farm and the local community, where all aspects of social life were conducted entirely in Welsh, and until the age of nineteen, as he later recalled, 'I was unable to understand the simplest English sentence'. As a teenager it seemed inevitable that William would follow his older brothers into a life on the land, until one day in 1873 a few friends persuaded him to accompany them to the annual meeting at Garndolbenmaen Baptist chapel. William was never the same again.

Divine Inspiration

An earnest prayer at the commencement of the service decided me for Christ. The Minister who offered the prayer pleaded for the pastor of the church, who had just settled

Hugh Evans, father of William Hughes

there, that he might be blessed with the salvation of sinners. I felt he was praying for me, for I sat under that ministry. It was then that the joy of salvation filled my soul, and that night I determined to give myself for ever to Christ and his cause.

I did not join the church that night but thought it best to test myself by waiting for six months or so. In a few weeks I found longer delay impossible and felt constrained to give myself to God's people at Capel y Beirdd, a church in connection with Garn, and under the same ministry.

This was William's explanation of the cause that elevated his aspirations from the land to the heavens, as years he later confided in a letter to the secretary of the Baptist Missionary Society. He joined the Baptists at Capel y Beirdd rather than Garndolbenmaen as it was much nearer his home, a few hundred yards rather than the two miles to Garn. It was a fortunate choice as Capel y Beirdd (*capel* = chapel; *beirdd* = poets), as the name suggests, was the centre of a rich literary tradition. Founded in 1823 as part of an active revival of the old Bardic tradition by local farmer-poets David Owen (Dewi Wyn o Eifion, 1784–1841) and Robert Williams (Robert ap Gwilym ddu, 1766–1850), Capel y Beirdd provided influences and inspiration that enriched and extended William's vision of the world beyond Rhoslan. William was baptised by the Reverend Anthony Williams at Capel y Beirdd in 1873, and it was here, two years later, that William's fate was sealed by a second life-changing sermon. As Hughes listened attentively to a lecture on David Livingstone's missionary exploits in Africa, delivered by Reverend Herbert Evans of Caernarfon, he was captivated by the drama of Stanley's famous greeting on the shores of Lake Tanganyika, and inspired by Livingstone's determination to enlighten the Dark Continent. As he walked home that night he felt his commitment to Christ calling him to follow in the footsteps of Livingstone and Stanley and evangelise Africa.

An Alien Culture

Before tackling Africa William had first to experience and overcome the alien culture of England. He couldn't become a missionary without ordination, and admission to the Baptist College required fluency in English, the language of the London-based Baptist Missionary Society (BMS). In April 1875 William left home for the first time and secured a job as a farm labourer near Nantwich, Cheshire. By the end of the year he had picked up enough English to move on to his 'finishing school', a branch of Ryland & Sons drapers' shops in Manchester where he was employed as a sales assistant.

By 1877 William was fluent enough in English to become a Sunday School teacher at Greenheys Baptist Church, in the comfortable middle class suburb of Moss Side, springing up on fields to the south of the city (long-since demolished and overbuilt amidst dense modern urban sprawl). Whilst teaching at Greenheys in September 1877 William was captivated by an article in that month's edition of *The Missionary Herald*, which announced the Baptist Missionary Society's acceptance of Robert Arthington's offer to provide £1,000 for an

Catherine Evans, mother of William Hughes

15

Bryn Graianog, birthplace of William Hughes

Capel y Beirdd, where William was baptised in 1873

exploratory sortie to the Congo to assess the practicality of setting up a BMS mission. A rich Quaker, Arthington was prepared to finance the Baptists as they were already well-established at the nearest British mission station, on the island of Fernando Po. Hughes was struck by the phrase emblazoned, for the first time, across the *Herald*'s front page, 'Africa for Christ'; he would, in future years, make great use of it himself, significantly amended.

In William's mind his trajectory from farm boy to missionary had settled on a final target, he was aiming not only for Africa but for the Congo.

Anxiously Awaiting Developments

In between improving his English-language skills and salesmanship during the week at Ryland's and perfecting his evangelism at weekends at Sunday school Hughes scoured newspapers and magazines for developments in the Congo. On 17 September 1877 *The Daily Telegraph* reported on Stanley's discoveries on finally reaching the mouth of the river Congo at the culmination of a three-year-long transcontinental expedition. By the end of 1877 the BMS felt it had had amassed sufficient information to instruct two of their missionaries in the Cameroons, George Grenfell and Thomas Comber, to visit the lower Congo with a view to setting up and staffing a permanent mission station. The two men arrived at Banana, on the northern bank of the great rivermouth on 23 January 1878, but finding it virtually impossible to travel further inland in the middle of the rainy season they left after a fortnight. Following further explorations by Grenfell and Comber the BMS resolved to set up a permanent base south of the river at Sao Salvador, where they had the support of the chief of the local Bakongo people.

In July 1879 a BMS team comprising Thomas Comber, his wife Minnie, H. E. Crudgington, John Hartland and William Holman Bentley finally established a mission station at Sao Salvador. The following month H. M. Stanley, who had recently contracted to serve the commercial interests of King Leopold II of Belgium, returned to the mouth of the Congo:

Llangollen Post Office, formerly North Wales Baptist College

with the novel mission of sowing along its banks civilised settlements, to peacefully conquer and subdue it, to remould it in harmony with modern ideas into National States within those limits ... justice and law and order shall prevail and murder and lawlessness and the cruel barter of slaves shall for ever cease.

While Comber's group laboured south of the river, Stanley used the northern bank to make rapid progress through various French, Dutch and Portuguese trading posts. By 26 September 1879 he had advanced 110 miles inland to Vivi, on a plateau overlooking the river where, after several days of negotiation with chiefs, he bought land for the first capital of Leopold's future Congo Free State.

In the same month that Stanley secured his capital, William Hughes having followed these events with intense interest and having acquired the requisite skills, began his much anticipated training at Llangollen Baptist College.

A Very Rewarding Education

Llangollen College had opened on 24 August 1862 to train ministers for the Baptist cause in north Wales. Hughes made steady but unremarkable progress during his three years at the college, distinguished only by two factors: his declared aim to become a missionary in the Congo, and his pursuit of the principal's daughter. In the spring of 1881 news reached the college that Bentley and Crudgington had finally reached Stanley Pool, via Stanley's northern route, having failed with thirteen attempts in two years to reach their goal from Sao Salvador. With his final year of studies still ahead of him, in July 1881, Hughes wrote to the BMS in London saying he had resolved to give himself entirely to mission work in the Congo.

Secretary Baynes was not encouraging, informing William that there was no immediate hope of being accepted. The following year, as the end of his studies approached, Hughes made another impassioned appeal to the BMS, writing to Baynes on 18 May 1882:

Little short of twelve months ago I wrote to you about the resolution I had long since taken of giving myself entirely to mission work in Congoland. You then held out no immediate hope of my being received by your Society, nor indeed did my case need an early consideration, but now that my course at this college terminates at the end of July next I am compelled to look around me, and ask how am I to get to the scene of my life work fully equipped?

I have long since been ambitious to get a little medical knowledge, feeling sure that my usefulness would be greatly enhanced thereby and would prefer not leaving this country without it.

I am pleased to say that my mind is unshaken and that nothing would give me greater joy than to have the honour of being one of the two missionaries who you say in the Missionary Herald for this month are needed to make up the staff of ten for Congoland.

To enhance his prospects William enclosed a letter of support from Hugh Jones, Principal of the college and father of Katie, Hughes' fiancée:

I beg to state that I have every confidence in the Christian character of Mr Hughes, and in the genuineness of his missionary zeal. I heard him express his intention and hope of becoming a missionary before he entered the college, and several times since. I paid little attention to it at first because I had heard others say a similar thing at some time or other, who finally gave the thought up altogether. Mr Hughes is not so, and now he will not entertain an application for his services from any church until he has first done his best to enter the mission field.

You may judge in part his proficiency from the enclosed letter, for English was to him a foreign language, and his knowledge of English has been acquired since he has grown up; and from the College report which I send by post. His term of three years will be up next July. Mr William Hughes is not one of our brightest students in every respect: we have had students who have mastered the niceties of language and subtleties of syntax better than he, so that I think he might do well in Congo whereas I might hesitate to recommend him for service in India or China where the peoples are literary nations. Nevertheless I think he might master a foreign language and be able in due time to preach with acceptance in it.

He is a young man of sound health, I believe, and well able to endure hardness in the discharge of his duties. His case is somewhat urgent and I trust you may be able to attend to it soon.

Appealing to Alfred

William Hughes' whole future lay in the hands of the General Secretary of the BMS. Alfred Henry Baynes (1838–1914) had risen through the ranks of the BMS, originally seconded as an accountant in 1860. In December 1878 he was appointed General Secretary. The Congo mission was Baynes' pet project and he was anxious to appoint only dependable ministers to that particular field. After weighing up Hughes' appeal he duly listed him as a potential candidate and dispatched a twelve-point questionnaire for him to complete.

Writing on 2 June 1882 Hughes described his dramatic conversion to the cause at Garn, his work as a Sunday school teacher at Greenheys and his preaching since 1877:

During the past winter I found great pleasure in distributing tracts and New Testaments amongst the destitute children in this locality and in addressing them. I have reason to believe that my work was blessed. My fellow labourers and myself at last succeeded in commanding over one hundred children every week. During my career as a Sunday school teacher I had the pleasure of hearing three of my scholars declaring that I had been a means of turning them to their Saviour. And now, when I go here and there to preach the Gospel as an occasional supply from this college, I have often occasion to rejoice in the fact that my poor words have been blest to rejoicing souls. Nothing has ever given me greater delight than

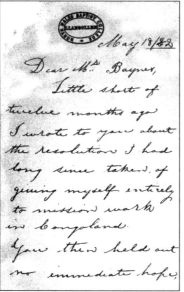

*William Hughes's Letter to Alfred
Baynes, May 1882*

the thought that I shall one day preach Christ to the poor heathen. I feel I am better adapted to this work than any other. I seem to have had very little thought of any country other than Africa…and during my stay in this college my love for Africa has ever increased.

Asked about his health, Hughes said he had never felt the need for medicine and had never suffered from the heat of the sun, 'even when during the harvest, toiling in its scorching rays throughout the day'.

Asked for references, William provided Baynes with the names of four referees: Reverend Anthony Williams, Ystrad; Reverend Dr Hugh Jones, Llangollen; Reverend Gethin Jones, Llangollen and the Reverend Benjamin Humphreys, Greenheys. Gethin Davies had been classics teacher at Llangollen College since 1872 (and succeeded Hugh Jones as Principal in 1883) and Anthony Williams was the man who had baptised Hughes at Capel y Beirdd in 1873.

Reverend Anthony Williams, Ystrad, Rhondda

In his testimonial, dated 9 June 1882, Williams confided:

> I have known Mr William Hughes for the last ten years. He was baptised by me in 1873, commenced to preach in 1877 and entered Llangollen College in 1879… I am happy to be able to bear the best testimony to his unblemished moral and religious character. I always found in him the zealous and ready worker in every department of the Christian vineyard. Taking into consideration that his knowledge of the English

language was so very limited before he entered college, owing to the locality in which he was brought up being so Welshified, I am of the opinion that his progress in the different branches of education speaks highly of his mental ability and aptitude for learning. I have heard him preach more than once, and that to the entire satisfaction of the churches. He has been inclined to the mission field for several years and as far as I am able to judge, he possesses many qualities conducible to render him a successful missionary of the Lord Jesus.

Reverend Dr Hugh Jones, Llangollen

On 12 June Principal Jones wrote to Baynes referring to his earlier letter and adding:

Mr Hughes is a very acceptable preacher, especially in Welsh; several churches thought of inviting him to become their pastor but he has discouraged all such intentions so far, in hopes that he may be accepted as a missionary. He preaches also very creditably in English, especially when it is remembered that the English language is to him an acquired language and that he had not been in the habit of speaking it till he was about 20 years of age. I believe that the acquisition of the English language is a fair criterion of a man's ability to acquire any foreign tongue.

I have every confidence in Mr Hughes' Christian character and in the purity of his motive and the genuineness of his missionary zeal. I should be inclined to regard his abilities as respectable though not of a high order; but I believe him to be possessed of what is essential to a missionary – an enthusiastic zeal which will issue in unreserved devotion to his work.

Mindful that Hughes was hopeful of being invited for interview before the BMS Candidate Committee at their 18 July meeting, Principal Jones forewarned them of a peculiarity of speech:

He feels a difficulty in some connections in pronouncing 'sh' it becomes, imperceptibly to him, 's'. This is, I believe, the result of habit, and I think he will ultimately get over it. I believe his case deserves the earnest consideration of the committee and I trust that the Lord will lead them to the right decision.

Reverend Gethin Davies, Llangollen

Gethin Davies was similarly supportive and equally blunt, writing on 17 June 1882:

Mr William Hughes is a splendid fellow and eminently fitted for the work in Congoland. Did one not know his antecedents it were easy to fall into a very wrong estimate of his worth but when it is remembered that he was nearly 20 years of age before he learnt a word of English and that all he has since acquired by way of fitting him for the master's service has been gleaned during the last five years of his life, his progress must be pronounced marvellous. Spiritually – he is one of the humblest and most devoted of the young men I have known – full of faith and good works – flinching at nothing if, by any means, he may save souls.

Mentally – slow, but very sure and grandly persistent. I have said slow but mean comparatively so. He has been outstripped by young men here but he was far behind them at the start. Really it is a slowness born of early disadvantages a defect which is more than amply compensated by the admirable persistence, the sleuth-hound doggedness with which he pursues his task.

Temperament – bright, buoyant, quite joyous. One of the most happy Christians. Always wears a smile. I have often heard it said his brightness is contagious. The Churches love him and I know of three at this moment that would gladly invite him to their pastorate did they not know he was espoused to another cause.

Physique – full, firm and well-built. Chest – bold and full, with the muscle of a lion. In a word SEE this man and you will LIKE if not LOVE him at once. I have had long talks with him about Congoland – I have pointed out the dangers and deaths incident to the climate – in vain.

He MUST go. I trust you will not refuse him but if you do William Hughes will be found in Congoland before many years are past or I have greatly misread the man.

Reverend Benjamin Humphreys, Greenheys, Manchester
Humphreys was last to submit his letter of testimonial. Addressed from 22 Greenhill Street, Greenheys and dated 4 July 1882, Reverend Humphrey's wrote:

Mr Hughes has for many years been a member of the church of which I am pastor. Though he had left a few months before I commenced my ministry here I have had considerable personal acquaintance with him during his several visits here and my numerous visits to Llangollen College. I have not the least hesitation in saying Mr Hughes's moral character is untarnished and his piety above suspicion. In the house of business where he was employed during his several years stay in this city he is looked upon by all as a pious young man and when he now visits the place he is respected and esteemed both by employer and employed. With this coincides the testimony of my people who have had full proof of him among them. I have heard them say over and over again that he was the best young man they ever knew and whenever his name is mentioned they speak in commendable terms of his zeal, character and piety. I consider this testimony all the more genuine and precious as it was spontaneous and unsolicited.

When this church was without a pastor previous to my settlement here, Mr Hughes was a very valuable member indeed, in the week-night services, especially in the 'Society' – the weekly social gathering of church members – over which he very often presided. Equally valuable and zealous was he as a Sunday School teacher and superintendent. I cannot personally bear testimony as to his ability to preach as I have never had the pleasure of hearing him but I have been told, here and elsewhere, by friends in whose sincerity and judgement I have every confidence, that he is a very powerful preacher. I am of the opinion that Mr Hughes has many of those good qualities which are essential to success in the work of foreign missions.

It was a strong application but as Hughes arrived in London on Saturday 15 July 1882 to spend the weekend with a friend in Porchester Road he awaited his forthcoming interview with considerable trepidation.

Interview at Mission House
On the Monday Hughes made his way to the Mission House in Furnival Street, off Holborn, and was ushered into the green-carpeted ground floor office in which the formidable Mr Baynes was firmly ensconced behind his desk, flanked by the intimidating portraits of C. H. Spurgeon and other Baptist worthies. After a rigorous interrogation Hughes was directed to undergo a medical examination at the Harley Street rooms of Dr Frederick Roberts.

The following day William was cross-examined by members of the Candidates' Committee, who had before them Dr Roberts' medical assessment:

> I have examined Mr Hughes, a candidate for mission work in the Congo river. He is in all respects satisfactory, except that his arteries are somewhat changed, probably as a result of working on the farm in his early days. There are some risks connected with this condition but I think he may be accepted.

Hardly a ringing endorsement, and it was essential for Hughes to perform well before the Committee. His obvious sincerity and passionate enthusiasm won over the waverers, and the members agreed to forward his name to the following day's meeting of the BMS General Committee for final approval. At the conclusion of the General Meeting his appointment was endorsed by General Secretary Baynes and exactly one month later William Hughes embarked for the Congo.

Chapter Two

Steaming Up the Congo
(1882–1885)

Embarking on the greatest adventure of his life William Hughes sailed from Liverpool on 19 August 1882, accompanied by fellow novice missionary, H. K. Moolenaar. It was a slow, uneventful and leisurely voyage aboard the steamer SS *Benguela* down the west coast of Africa as it completed the monthly mail run. Near the end of the journey Hughes disembarked briefly at the old Portuguese slaving port of Cabinda, in Landana, where for nine years the French Catholic Holy Ghost Fathers had been running a self-supporting agricultural settlement. The community's model of combining spiritual evangelism with practical training left a profound impression on him.

A little more than a month after leaving Liverpool, Hughes and Moolenaar finally stepped ashore at Banana, a northerly creek at the mouth of the great river Congo. They were met by Frederikus de la Fontaine Verweij, the local representative of the African Commerce Association of Rotterdam, a Dutch trading company that acted as agents for the BMS. When introducing the new and idealistic reverend missionaries to the oldest European trading post on the Congo, Frederikus neglected to introduce his pregnant black mistress, whose mixed-race offspring, Ernestina, would later share most of her life with Hughes; she now lies buried in Colwyn Bay.

After a brief rest in Banana, Hughes and Moolenaar were collected by Reverend Henry Butcher. Together they travelled 93 miles up river, by steamer, to the Underhill BMS base, at Matadi, established a few months earlier by Butcher and H. E. Crudgington. Underhill was ironically a hill-top station named after Dr Edward Underhill, BMS Secretary from 1849 to 1876. During a brief period of instruction on the finer points of mission work in the Congo, Hughes befriended an eleven year-old native

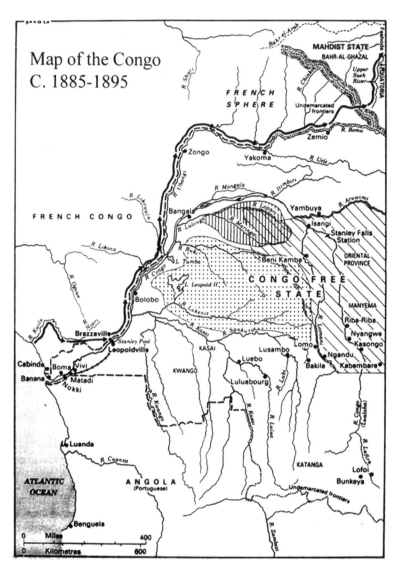

Map of the Congo Basin; circa 1885–1895

boy named Kinkasa. It was a relationship that would eventually lead Kinkasa to Colwyn Bay. Soon Hughes was separated from Moolenaar, sent further up-river and given charge of Bayneston settlement at Vunda.

A Disturbing Death

After a few weeks instruction from a senior missionary I was left in charge of what we had named Bayneston (sometimes 'Baynesville') station, which included a tent, the stores made of grass, a few fowls, some coloured servants from the coast and one Congo boy, Kinkasa, whom I had found about a hundred miles nearer the coast... I was to have a colleague in a month or six weeks but alas he died from the terrible African fever in sixteen days after landing on the Congo and he was buried at Underhill Station. Thus I had to do the best I could for eighteen months alone on the solitary peninsula. The Mission station was on a fertile plot of land, stretching into the River Congo, about forty acres in area and almost surrounded by water, which was felt to be a safeguard against fear of attack or plunder.

No suggestion of any manpower shortage, isolation or despondency appeared in the *Missionary Herald*, whose December 1882 issue reported that Hughes and Moolenaar had safely arrived at the Congo, where all their colleagues were 'well, hopeful and in good spirits'.

In the 91st Annual Report of the BMS, for the year ending March 1883, Thomas Comber, resident minister in charge of the Congo mission, recorded, 'Moolenaar is at Wathen, assisting (John) Hartland ... and Hughes is rapidly gaining influence at Baynesville [sic] station, of which he is now in charge.' In April Hartland was struck down by malarial fever and transported to Bayneston, where he was tirelessly nursed by Hughes until he passed away on 12 May 1883. It was a bitter blow to William, who had been close to Hartland and had corresponded with his family, but as Hughes himself was then struck down by fever it was weeks before he could express his sympathies to Hartland's mother.

On 4 October 1883 William wrote to Mrs Hartland, apologising for his previous indisposition and explaining:

> I can assure you that your dear son was a loving brother to me from the first and that I, with the greatest pleasure, did my best to [*sic*] him, day and night, for about three weeks, during his illness. I was quite worn down seeing my dear Hartland getting worse. You all have my deepest sympathy and I pray that our Heavenly father may console your hearts.

Hughes added a touching footnote to his letter of condolence:

> P.S. I have put a fence around his grave and a white cross on it and now a wreath from his betrothed is placed there. It looks clean and it will be kept so as long as I live, if my life will be spent at this place.

Isolation at Bayneston

Despite Hartland's death and ever-present feelings of isolation Hughes was encouraged by the trust he began to share with the natives. Eschewing force and bribery, he concentrated on winning over individuals with kindness and respect for their own beliefs and feelings:

> Experience teaches us that it is a primary duty of every African missionary...to make friends of those around him and win their confidence...We never bribed children to attend school, which has been the bad policy pursued by some African teachers. We endeavoured to make school life attractive...One of the most important steps is to teach the native boys to read and write in their own language...We found it to be unwise in any way to attack and denounce native customs, prejudices and habits...On one occasion, when visiting a native village, I pointed to a charm I saw there, and made a few kind remarks about it. At this the natives were surprised as well as pleased, and one of them said to my native boy: *The white preacher does not attack our charms; he is not*

unkind and foolish like a missionary who came here the other day and took hold of our charm and dashed it to pieces.

In three or four months we had won over to our side eighteen native boys who were placed under our charge at the Mission station.

One of the boys, Nkanza was brought to Hughes by his old chief because his feet were severely infested with 'jiggers', a burrowing parasite (*Tunga penetrans*) that lodges under the skin of the soles of the feet, eventually making walking extremely painful. Jiggers, or 'chigoe fleas' flourish in the hot soils and sand of Africa and feed intermittently on passing warm-blooded hosts such as cattle or humans. 'Nkanza could hardly put his feet on the ground, only just the toe, the heel being completely honeycombed by these jiggers.'

William washed the boy's feet and extracted the parasites and as a consequence: 'He acted towards me as a child to his father. He had perfect confidence in me.' William assumed the chief was Nkanza's father and was shocked to learn that Nkanza wasn't the chief's son but his property – his personal slave.

Besides the eighteen boys under the direct charge of Hughes' mission station at Bayneston, 'thousands of the natives became very friendly. They, during that period [1883], went down about a hundred miles to Underhill and brought up the whole of the steamer *Peace* in seven hundred sections'. Hughes' 'friendly natives' were part of a long chain of bearers transporting the disassembled steamship 260 miles overland from the mouth of the Congo for eventual reassembly and launching at Stanley Pool (now Malebo Pool).

Peace and Death
Surrounded by uncharted and almost impenetrable jungle inhabited by dangerous wild animals and hostile natives, steamships were vital to the success of the Baptist's Congo mission but direct passage from the river mouth to Stanley Pool was barred by over 200 miles of cataracts, rocks and rapids. The solution devised by the BMS was to commission their own vessel

William Hughes' Mission School, Vunda (Bayneston), Congo, 1883

that, once built, could be easily dissembled, shipped to Africa and carried in crates overland to Stanley Pool. This was the vessel whose overland transportation William Hughes helped organise. Designed by senior BMS Congo missionary Reverend George Grenfell, the steamship *Peace* had been fabricated by Thorneycrofts at Chiswick and tested on the Thames in September 1882 before being dismantled, packed into hundreds of crates and shipped to the Congo for reassembly. Each section, weighing around 65 pounds, was sewn into a canvas sack and numbered, with the idea that if one element was lost during the long journey a duplicate could be easily ordered and shipped out from England. Unfortunately W. H. Doke, the young engineer sent out to accomplish the reassembly, was struck down with fever and died within weeks of arriving in the Congo. Two replacement engineers died on their way upriver from Banana, as did two further replacements. It wasn't until 7 July 1884 that a scratch team of missionaries and natives, including a blacksmith and a carpenter, under the direction of George Grenfell, finally managed to assemble and launch *Peace* onto the River Congo. By then Hughes had moved on.

New Best Friends

On 30 October 1883 William's feelings of isolation temporarily lifted when he was joined at Bayneston by his old companion from the voyage out, Reverend Moolenaar. Unfortunately, after an all-too-brief period working together, Hughes was sent back downriver to Underhill in 1884, taking Kinkasa with him. Although Hughes retained charge of Underhill for the remainder of his time in the Congo, he meanwhile undertook a brief mission upriver to establish a new station at Ngombe, which the Baptists called Wathen. On his way back William called in at Bayneston for a chat with Moolenaar and discovered they shared some critical opinions about operations in the Congo. He also sought out the old Vunda Chief and after a degree of bargaining managed to secure Nkanza's freedom in exchange for a bale of grey Rylands' cloth worth four pounds and ten shillings! 'I shall never forget the way he started on the path before me when leaving his village in the little red coat which I had given him for fear the old Chief would get hold of him and retain him as well as the bale of grey baft.' Nkanza, like Kinkasa, remained ever loyal to Hughes and accompanied him back to Underhill.

On 11 March 1885 Moolenaar wrote to London from Bayneston citing cases of cruelty to native blacks by white missionaries and specifically requesting that his complaints be laid before the BMS General Secretary, Alfred Baynes. No hint of this appeared in the BMS report on the Congo mission presented to the 93rd annual meeting in July 1885:

> The work at Bayneston has been carried on alone by Mr Moolenaar. It has suffered much in consequence of his solitariness but he bravely holds on ... At Underhill Mr Hughes has just been joined by our new brother Mr Macmillan. The beautiful wooden house sent out from England is complete and the station is in good working order. Mr Hughes will now be able to gather round him a large school from the many towns within easy reach ...

Unfortunately by July 1885 Mr Hughes' morale was already too depressed to be revived by the arrival of either 'brother Macmillan' or a 'beautiful wooden house'.

A Fateful Decision

Despite Hughes' desperate efforts to inform the BMS of his intentions in time for the July 1885 gathering, their annual report ignored his communication, despatched on the 15 May 1885 downriver mail run of the Congo Free State's *SS Viva*, which was timed to meet the Portuguese mailboat at Banana. In his letter Hughes informed Baynes:

> I have one thing to raise with you that has caused me a lot of anxiety and weariness for more than a year. As you know I am engaged to Miss K H Jones, daughter of my late teacher, Dr Jones. She has set her mind on coming to the Congo and her wish is to spend her life with me in the big work. But because my health is so poor; because so many deaths are taking place among the missionaries; because of the many discomforts one has to contend with, together with the fact that the Mission is so far only opening the way so that none of us can refer to a station where we can establish and do missionary work, cause me to believe it would not be reasonable to take such a step. Besides this, the manner in which the Committee is preventing our having a voice among our elder brothers in the operation of the Mission is weakening our interest in it and causing one to feel less at home in the work.

The last point was dynamite, Hughes was not only opting opt of his avowed mission but laying part of the blame for his decision at the door of the London leadership of the BMS. Like Moolenaar, Hughes empathised with the Africans and wanted to win them over with love rather than force and fear. He had reluctantly come to the conclusion that the BMS was constitutionally and ideologically authoritarian.

His letter continued:

> I believe, my dear Mr Baynes that I have fully considered this

matter. I have thought about it for several months and at last have reached the decision to leave the Mission and on my return to set up home. I know that I am going to leave work in a field of which I care a lot and in which I expected to spend a long time. I know too that I shall be leaving my brothers at a time when so much support is needed and when they are so lonely; and that I shall be leaving the poor Africans who are in such darkness and so much in need of enlightenment and leadership to the Saviour [sic]. But my absence from the Congo will not prevent my working for the Congolese and the whole nation. My mind is made up on this. And if you consent I will bring with me two boys whom I will train at my own expense in my own home in a way that they can be sent out for the benefit of their own people. These boys are eager to be with me and desire four years of training. Both are free (i.e. not slaves) and perfectly at liberty to stay as long as they wish. They have now been with me for about 2 ½ years. One, Nkanza, is from a village near Bayneston. I saw his chief and his parents recently while coming down from Ngombe and they assured me that he was perfectly free to go with me to my own country and stay as long as he wished. The home of the other, Kinkasa, is in the village nearest to this station. He has been with me since November 1882 and he is a very good lad. He is equally free as the other. I will pay the passages of my friends and if necessary maintain them afterwards.

Despite his public refusal to acknowledge the difficulties of the Congo mission, Baynes could hardly claim ignorance. Right from the first, when he directed Grenfell and Comber to make an initial sortie on behalf of the BMS to the Congo in 1878 he was informed of the negative effects of intervention. Comber reported back coruscating criticism of the white man's cynical trading of rum, gin and gunpowder in the region: 'Oh! It is awful the amount of corruption and filth introduced by Europeans', he wrote. Comber's colleague, the Reverend George Grenfell, was hardly above a bit of filth and corruption himself, and had to resign mid-expedition when it was discovered that his black 'housekeeper' was pregnant with his child, although Baynes was happy to readmit Grenfell to the missionary fold once the pair got married.

Perhaps, back in London, Baynes was too busy to attend to complaints from missionary minions when he had a slap-up celebration to organise! In June 1885 the BMS hosted a sumptuous dinner at the Cannon Street Hotel in honour of Henry Morton Stanley who was presented with an address in recognition of his help and cooperation in the Congo Basin. Obviously Baynes didn't realise that Stanley was soon to write to his boss Sir Francis de Winton (Leopold II's Congo agent), about, 'those miserable Baptists' who prevaricated over whether to lend him their steamship, *Peace*. Stanley solved the problem by simply seizing it for himself.

Scrambling for Africa

Hughes' hopes and dreams had run up against an unpleasant reality. William's want of health, society and support in the Congo was exacerbated by political developments for he had inadvertently become part of the 'Scramble for Africa'. The major European powers were tearing the continent apart, grabbing land and raw materials and parcelling Africa up into colonies run by political puppets. At Bismarck's Berlin Conference of 1884–5, Britain, Belgium, France, Germany and Portugal agreed, in theory, to an orderly, imperial share out of Africa, but in reality conflict continued on the ground.

In 1884 German troops attacked and formally annexed the Cameroons, the Baptists' longest established settlement on the West Coast. With the support of the Royal Navy the BMS attempted to maintain their mission station with the result that the Baptists were reported to Berlin as, 'the worst agitators against German ascendancy'. During one punitive German raid against the natives the BMS church at Hickory Town was burnt to the ground and, finally, after two years of continuous harassment the English-speaking BMS capitulated and sold its land, buildings (and converts!) for £4,000 to the German-speaking Basle Missionary Society (Swiss Lutheran Reformed), who were later to become an implacable opponent of William Hughes' African Institute.

The consequences of the Berlin Conference for the Congo were immediate and disastrous. The region was officially declared Leopold II's own private fiefdom. For a decade the King of the Belgians had cannily established himself in the Congo through forming the International African Association, and engaging Stanley to map the area and inveigle native chiefs into accepting exploitative treaties. Leopold had appointed Sir Francis de Winton to manage this whole dubious enterprise. Following the Berlin Conference, Leopold's ambitions were no longer confined by the International African Association which he converted to the Congo Free State with himself as absolute sovereign. Guaranteed unfettered control, Leopold demanded his agents extract ever-increasing profits from his African fiefdom without regard to the interests of the natives. The Congo descended into unspeakable horrors of cruelty and colonial exploitation, but in 1885 the reality of the Congo was little understood in Britain.

William Hughes had inadvertently involved himself in forces far beyond his control and by 1885 his personal discomfiture was compounded by a growing awareness of the context in which the BMS was operating. He resolved to pursue his original mission by other methods.

Faithful Companions

In August 1885: 'When the time for leaving Africa drew near I was again attacked by fever and nearly lost my life.' Hughes feared he was about to join colleagues buried in the small BMS cemetery that is all that now remains of the Underhill station.

> I had endured many previous attacks but this was the worst. For thirteen days I had been confined to my bed and felt it would be necessary to postpone my departure; but Mr Stanley's doctor who had attended me for three days and nights said that the voyage home was my only chance of life.

Throughout his illness he was faithfully nursed by Kinkasa. When

William was sufficiently recovered both Kinkasa and Nkanza insisted on accompanying him downriver:

> the hour arrived for our departure … I told the boys to put our flag at half-mast, that being the signal for the State's steamer to stop in the river Congo. As the steamer was approaching my serving-men brought a hammock to my bedside and placed me therein as I was too weak to walk. While the two men were doing this the two boys who wanted so much to come to this country hurriedly shouldered their little packs, which they had previously made up and slipped out of the house before the men took me towards the boat. Lying on my back in the hammock I could see the boys in the front all the time. When we got to the beach the small boat was ready to take us to the steamer in the river and I noticed before the hammock men could place me in the boat the two little fellows had jumped in with their packs for fear I might be placed in first, the boat shoved off and they left behind in Africa.
>
> I continued weak and very bad on the State's steamer, under the care of Sir Francis de Winton, whence I was transhipped to the mail steamer along with my faithful companions.

It was to be eight years before Hughes would see Africa again – and by then both boys would be dead. For the next month on the voyage William had ample time to contemplate alternative ideas for evangelising Africa, but first he needed to recuperate.

Madeira: a Suitable Site for a College?
'As soon as we cleared the river and got into the ocean the sea breeze revived me', William wrote, and by the time the steamer tied up for re-coaling at Funchal, Madeira his health was back to something like the normality he had enjoyed in his youth. Hughes thoughts were beginning to crystallise around the idea of founding a missionary college based outside Africa with Kinkasa and Nkanza enrolled as his first two students:

For a long time I thought the island of Madeira would be a suitable place for a training college, the climate being mild and healthy to both white and coloured residents. In Central Africa the missionary cause has suffered irreparable loss from the unhealthiness of the climate, the best men being struck down in their ripe experience, necessitating changes in teachers and plans, with consequent expense, disappointment and failure. After several of these sad deaths of missionaries I noticed that the converts and pupils returned to their villages, and it took a long time to revive interest in new men, new ideas and new plans. Much of the good done by white missionaries is undone by these climatic calamities.

In Madeira I thought the difficulties of the premature death of the missionaries would disappear and they might labour there in health for as many years as at home, while African students would thrive as well as in their native land. But something more than the climate of Madeira had to be considered.

It was the fact that Madeira was a Portuguese island that in Hughes' judgement weighed most heavily against it. Hughes considered Portuguese colonisers he met in Africa exceptionally racist and immoral and as Madeira was overwhelming Catholic, religion was an issue too:

Madeira is inhabited by Portuguese, who consider themselves to be a civilised people, yet their morals are awful and this contaminating influence would imperil any educational institution. There are other reasons against selecting Madeira as the site of the Congo Training College but the moral objection was strong enough of itself to dismiss the idea of beginning the work in that beautiful island.

Remembering Landana

Having rejected Madeira as a suitable site, Hughes' thoughts drifted back to the Landana training scheme he'd witnessed three years earlier on the voyage out. Whilst the climate there, on the

African mainland, was undoubtedly unhealthy, Hughes admired the practical aspects of the self-supporting agricultural community, with its own school, run by the French Catholic Holy Ghost Fathers:

> Though not of the same faith, the plan of working at Landana is excellent, and the results of their lines of operation are the most effectual and most successful on the whole coast.
>
> The sensible plan adopted at Landana ought to be followed elsewhere ... There are at Landana native craftsmen – carpenters, blacksmiths, gardeners etc – who were redeemed from slavery in the interior and have been trained for some part of each working day in these much needed trades and during the rest of the day and the evenings are instructed in school studies and the faith of their teachers.

Before the voyage ended William Hughes had settled on the Landana model for his intended institute but where should it be sited?

There's No Place Like Home!

Hughes' thoughts turned to Wales, the land that had inspired and nurtured his own spiritual development: 'I was afraid that the climate of Britain would be too cold in the winter for African students.' Despite initial reservations about the weather, Hughes felt, with some justification, that there was, 'no country on Earth with such religious surroundings as little Wales', and after weighing up the options concluded, 'Wales seemed to be the best place in regard to health, religious influence and economy.'

Chapter Three

William, Nkanza and Kinkasa in Wales
(1885–1890)

Arriving in Liverpool in September 1885 William Hughes, Nkanza and Kinkasa transferred to one of the vessels of the Liverpool & North Wales Steamship Company for the two hour trip to Llandudno pier. From Llandudno, the trio took a five mile train ride to Colwyn Bay followed by a two-mile hike to Hughes' sister's farm at Llanelian.

William's sister, Sydney and her husband, Owen Williams, accommodated Hughes and the boys at their Llanelian farmhouse for the next few months. Colwyn Bay railway station proved an invaluable transport hub for visiting Hughes' parents at Rhoslan, his fiancée in Llangollen, and assorted Baptist contacts scattered across Wales.

The First 'Congo House'

William's trip back to his old family farmhouse certainly left a lasting impression on Rhoslan. Stepping off the train at the village railway station, that William's brother David had help construct in his youth, the trio's arrival was received with great interest by a community raised on folk memories of Jac Blac Ystumllyn, who in about 1742 had been kidnapped in West Africa by a member of the Wynne family of Ystumllyn and brought back to Cricieth. Thought to be about eight years old when captured, during his time at Ystumllyn he learnt fluent Welsh and English

Sydney Williams, Llanelian

Fund-Raising Carte-de-Visite (Kinkasa & Nkanza, June 1886)

and was employed as a gardener. In 1768 he married a local girl, Margaret Griffith from Hendre Mur, Trawsfynydd , with the son of the vicar of Cricieth acting as his best man. The couple had seven children, and after Jac died in 1786 an englyn was inscribed on his gravestone at Ynyscynhaern:

Yn India gynna'm ganwyd – a nghamrau
Yng Nghymru'm bedyddiwyd;
Wele'r fan dan lechan lwyd
Du oeraidd y'm daerwyd.

To mark the visit of William and his young African companions it was decided to name the new village grocers' shop in their honour: 'Congo House', a name duly recorded on the 1888 Ordnance Survey map.

An Unholy Alliance

Back in London, Baynes and the BMS were reluctant to recognise Hughes' 14 May letter as a resignation. The October issue of *The Missionary Herald* (edited by Baynes) blandly stated:

> We are glad to report the safe arrival in England of the Reverend William Hughes of Underhill Station, Congo River. Mr Hughes left Africa in a very sadly broken state of health; the voyage home, however, greatly benefited him and he is now fast recovering his usual strength.

Hughes was kept on the BMS payroll and employed on what was described as 'deputation' work. This was standard practice for junior missionaries on home-leave and obliged Hughes to travel around the Baptist chapels of Wales collecting money for the BMS, but it was an unholy alliance that couldn't last forever. Hughes was intent on establishing an independent African Institute in Wales, and the BMS were equally determined to send him back to the Congo.

William was content to bide his time and remain on the BMS payroll whilst he finalised plans to marry his fiancée, Katie Jones, the following spring. By the end of 1885 Baynes was becoming increasingly impatient and subjected Hughes to alternating threats and promises. If he agreed to return to the Congo he could choose his own station and be promoted to senior missionary with an increased salary. If he refused to return he was warned by a fellow Baptist minister that he would be 'suppressed'. When Hughes prevaricated in January 1886 a colleague advised William, 'You must either go back to the Congo or send the Committee a medical certificate that you are not fit to bear the climate, otherwise they will crush you, my brother, as sure as your name is Hughes.'

Under intense pressure William and Katie submitted themselves for medical examination and to their great relief were formally declared physically unfit for service in Equatorial Africa.

A Temporary Truce
In response to a letter from Baynes acknowledging these results, offering sympathy and promising to report this development to the Society's Annual Meeting in May, Hughes replied from Llanelli on 1 March 1886:

Many thanks for your kind letter which came to hand at Llangollen (where Hughes was visiting his fiancée, Katie Jones) ... I am exceedingly obliged for your kind expression of sympathy. I wish to continue my allowance only as long as I serve this mission. I have sent a letter to Mr Myers (joint secretary of the BMS) of churches to be visited on behalf of the mission as far as the end of April. I have received several invitations as well from May. Do you wish me to visit these churches on behalf of the Society?

Myers and Baynes were anxious not to provoke a public split with Hughes. They knew that discontent in the Welsh Baptist Union (WBU) over its lack of representation on the BMS continued to bubble away beneath the surface and might easily be fanned into full-blown rebellion. Myers had already been forced to attend special conferences at Swansea and Rhyl in order to dampen down demands for direct WBU representation on BMS committees. There was a rising tide of nationalism in Wales, and some Welsh Baptists were beginning to suggest that they abandon the English-dominated BMS and set up their own WMS. Baynes feared that the forthcoming Aberdare conference might opt for a WMS if encouraged by the eloquent, experienced and alienated Welsh missionary William Hughes. Baynes temporised whilst he effected a cunning plan.

Love in Llangollen

Whilst he awaited the decision of the BMS, Hughes attended to matters of the heart. On 5 March 1886 William married Katie, his sweetheart from college days, at Bethel Baptist Chapel, Castle Street, Llangollen. The bride, Miss Katherine Jones, the daughter of the late principal, Reverend Hugh Jones, was one of thirteen brothers and sisters. Born in Llangollen in 1861, Katie was the second-oldest child of the Jones family. After the wedding William and Katie moved into their first home, Tudor House, Llangollen together with constant companions, Kinkasa and Nkanza.

After settling into Tudor House, and awaiting further instructions Hughes and the boys continued their tour of the

Baptist chapels, until they received Baynes' shockingly definitive response. As Baynes subsequently reported to the May meeting of the BMS, at Exeter Hall; 'The Reverend W Hughes, of the Congo, in pursuance of medical advice, will not resume foreign mission work and his official connection with the Society has therefore terminated.' Hughes was sacked!

Katie (left) and Claudia Hughes

Outmanoeuvred by the BMS

Whilst the potentially divisive Hughes toured the chapels in March and April 1886 with his well-advertised *Bechgyn Duon* (black boys) Baynes had wasted no time organising an alternative, loyalist Congo missionary to supplant his role. As soon as the returning and utterly dependable Congo missionary Reverend Thomas Lewis landed at Liverpool on 5 April 1886, he was ordered to accompany Baynes on one of his rare visits to Wales and both addressed the 1886 annual meeting of the Welsh Baptist Union at Aberdare. Baynes had chosen carefully, for Lewis was not only a BMS loyalist through-and-through, he was also Welsh and had returned from Africa with his own little black boy!

As William, Kinkasa and Nkanza continued to tour the chapels of Wales they were shadowed by the official BMS roadshow, starring Lewis and his own *Bachgen Du*. Whilst Lewis obediently handed over his collection money to the BMS the now otherwise unemployed Hughes relied on his touring income to feed his ad hoc family and to amass sufficient capital to one day establish his own independent Congo college. Fortunately, William proved an attractive speaker and audiences were both charmed and entertained by his talks, and by the boys singing in not only English and Welsh but also their own native language. As people filed out Kinkasa and Nkansa supplemented funds with the sale of photographs (illustrated) of themselves at a shilling each.

Letter from Wrexham

Searching for more secure employment, whilst continuing to solicit funds for his projected African institute, in September 1886 William moved to Wrexham, the largest town in north Wales. It was from there that he renewed contact with BMS Secretary Baynes on 7 October 1886, with a letter accusing white missionaries of cruelty against the black people of the Congo. Baynes suppressed it, though he probably sent a copy to Thomas Comber, who had received and ignored a similar complaint seventeen months earlier from Moolenaar. All this added to the tension that culminated in Comber's interception of a letter that Hughes sent to a boy named Nzinki, at Underhill, together with £10 to enable him to pay his fare to Liverpool. Hughes had taught the boy to write and speak English and had promised to continue his education in Britain. Writing from Underhill on 9 March 1887, Nzinki said that while both his mother and father agreed to his going, the 'white men' (of the BMS station) had refused to send him, saying that if he went to Wales he would be lost and that his friend Kinkasa would never return to the Congo. That was regarded by Hughes as his final breaking point with the BMS, although fortunately his £10 was handed on to missionaries of the American Baptist Union, who put it towards the passage to Wales of two more Congo boys. In future years Hughes was to enjoy a more fruitful relationship with the American Baptists than the BMS.

That spring, however, in Wrexham, William's immediate concern was the birth of his first child, Katherine, on 27 March 1887.

Congo Guest House, Colwyn Bay

In June 1887 Hughes was appointed pastor of the Baptist chapels at both Old Colwyn (Calfaria) and Llanelian (Ebeneser) with the promise of founding a new, Tabernacl, chapel at Colwyn Bay. The cause at Llanelian was then at a very low ebb with its Ebeneser chapel in a pitiful state, but William rapidly set about reinvigorating the local Baptist movement with his characteristic energy and enthusiasm. William, Katie and the boys moved from Wrexham to rent a large terraced house in Bay View Road, Colwyn Bay, which they renamed Congo House. For propaganda purposes William referred to this Bay View building as The Congo Institute but in reality it was run by Katie and the boys as a commercial guesthouse catering to visitors to

Congo Guest House, Bay View Road, Colwyn Bay

the rapidly expanding seaside resort. Whilst William preached at Llanelian and planned the imminent opening of Tabernacl, Colwyn Bay, he was still focused on his main aim of establishing a fully-functioning Congo College. Despite the immediate demands of his professional duties Hughes continued to give public lectures to publicise the project and solicit funds and support.

In February 1888 William was encouraged both by the commencement of building work on his new Colwyn Bay chapel and by the arrival of a third Congo student, Frank Teva, sent to Wales by the American Baptist Mission. Frank was soon joined by Daniel Harvey, another student despatched from the American's Congo Mission. Hughes' confidence really needed a boost at that time, as his claim that the health of African students wouldn't suffer in Britain was bluntly rejected by Baynes' loyal spokesman, Thomas Lewis, whose BMS-sponsored lectures warned Baptist audiences that, 'Experience has taught us all better ... these poor lads looked in despair at the snow covered country of the white man.'

Tabernacl, Colwyn Bay

William must have begun to wonder whether Lewis might have a point after his original student and faithful friend Kinkasa fell seriously ill in March 1887. Throughout the following year Kinkasa's health never fully recovered and on 5 May 1888 he died, aged only twelve, and was buried three days later in Old Colwyn Cemetery, his grave marked by a sandstone memorial.

Before the year-end William's spirits were lifted by the completion of Tabernacl chapel and the birth of Claudia, his second child.

Historic Meeting at Llandudno
In March 1889, William:

delivered a most interesting lecture entitled *Stanley and the Congo*, to a large and appreciative audience at the Baptist Chapel, Sussex Street, Rhyl. Mr Hughes was accompanied by two native boys he is training for the mission work in this wide field of Central Africa. By means of a large map the lecturer pointed out the different routes of H M Stanley's travels, the means of transit, difficulties with the natives, their manners, religion and language; giving an account of his own experience on the Congo, the encouragement to proceed with the work of enlightenment and evangelising the dark continent, and the labours Mr Stanley is still pursuing. Mr Hughes brought his lecture to a close after speaking for nearly two hours, during which the audience frequently applauded the lecturer. Mr K M McEwen proposed a vote of thanks to the lecturer and chairman (W R Williams, Esq.) Mr Lanceley, Colwyn Bay, whose brother lost his life in the Congo Mission field, seconded.

On 4 April 1889, years of tireless determination came to fruition with the first meeting of the Committee of the Congo Training Institute, under the presidency of Cardiff coal baron Alderman Richard Cory. William Hughes was formally appointed secretary, and together with the eminent individuals identified below these seven members constituted the Institute's founding committee at that historic meeting in Colwyn Bay:

- Thomas T Marks, Llandudno's Chief Civic Engineer
- Principal Gethin Davies, of Llangollen College
- Simon Jones, 'Master Confectioner' and Baptist preacher of Wrexham
- W. S. Jones of Chichester Street, Chester
- Reverend W. Ross, ex-Congo missionary who, like Hughes, had returned to Britain after 'his health had broken down'

'A Serious Accident'

In August William's best-laid plans were disrupted by a tragic event recorded by the local newspaper:

About 2.30pm on Tuesday 27th a most shocking accident occurred in Abergele Road, near to Mr Blud's shop. It appears that the nurse of the Revd W. Hughes, Congo House, was near the above shop in charge of two children, one in a perambulator [Claudia], the other [Katie], a little girl about two years of age, running about. Unseen by the nurse the little mite running across the street, just as a carriage belonging to Mr Jones, Royal Hotel, was being driven past, was accidentally run over. The wheels passing over her chest, undoubtedly caused internal injuries. Medical assistance was procured, and we hear that the little one is progressing favourably. Great sympathy has been displayed towards Mr and Mrs Hughes in their trouble.

Little Katie Hughes seemed to respond well to medical treatment and apparently made a rapid recovery but later events indicate all was not well. Nevertheless the family were reassured and throughout 1889 William played an ever-increasing role in Colwyn Bay's civic society as well as its religious life. He was particularly outspoken on the Local Board's scheme to construct an underpass under the railway to connect the newly-developing town to the seafront.

At Tabernacl Chapel, Hughes not only conducted both English- and Welsh-language services, but also ran weekly Sunday Schools and occasional musical entertainments in which the two new students Frank and Daniel performed songs in their native language.

By the end of 1889 William's committee were confident enough of their organisation and finances to authorise him to look around for a larger, permanent home for their Institute. In the spring of 1890 William settled upon the ideal building.

Chapter Four

Early Days at Congo House
(1890–1893)

In April 1890 William's dream became reality, just a year after the founding committee had first met, the Congo Training Institute acquired a permanent home. Myrtle Villa, a large detached Victorian house, set in two acres of grounds with ample space for William's ambitious expansion plans, still stands at the head of Nant-y-glyn Road, overlooking the beautiful bay of Colwyn. After preparing the villa for its new educational function William, Katie, their two young daughters and the African boys moved in over the summer of 1890. Despite being heavily pregnant, Katie continued to operate the guest house in Bay View Road until the end of the tourist season.

Comings and Goings at Congo House

Katie's baby was born late that summer at Congo House, as The Congo Training Institute was then more familiarly known. The couple's first boy, Stanley was named in honour of the famed explorer, who back in William's boyhood at Capel y Beirdd provided his original inspiration. Stanley was the couple's third child, their first, Katharine, having been born in 1887 when they were lodging in Wrexham and Claudia, their second, born in 1888 at the Bay View Road 'Congo Guest House'.

That summer was an emotional time at Congo House where Stanley's appearance was echoed by the arrival of another African student, the sixteen year old Kofele M'besa, a native of the Cameroons. Kofele wanted to train as a medical missionary but was willing to learn any useful craft. His arrival was matched by the departure of one of the Institute's trained students, Daniel Harvey, to Africa, an event comprehensively reported by the local *Weekly News and Visitors Chronicle*.

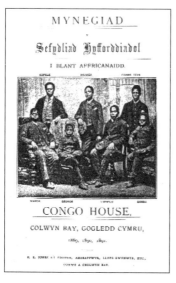

Cover of the first Congo House *annual report*

King Leopold II, Patron of the Congo Institute

Congo Institute (Myrtle Villa), *Colwyn Bay*

'A Valedictory Missionary Meeting'

On Monday evening, 14 July, an interesting meeting was held at the Colwyn Bay Baptist Chapel in connection with the Congo House Training Institute, a valedictory missionary meeting being held to bid farewell, on his departure to Africa to a native student known as Daniel Harvey who has been apprenticed in a Colwyn Bay carpenters shop, where he has thoroughly learnt his trade. The President of the Institute (Alderman R Cory, JP, Cardiff) presided and after a portion of scripture had been read followed by the singing of a hymn 'From Greenland's Icy Mountains' and by the offering of prayer, fulfilled the duties appertaining to the office of chairman admirably explaining very lucidly and felicitously the objects of the Institute to the meeting. He then informed the meeting that Messrs Elder Dempster and Co. of Liverpool, agents for the British and African Steamship Company Limited had written expressing their sympathy with the objects of the Institute and had kindly consented to make arrangements for Daniel Harvey to work his passage back to Africa.

William Hughes then gave a brief outline of the aims of the Institute followed by contributions from other worthy speakers. Presently:

The Chairman addressing Daniel, after having complimented him upon his satisfactory progress and conduct whilst in Europe and having exhorted him to take to his people who had never heard of the *Englishman's God*, the knowledge of the Gospel called upon him to give Gospel discourse:

Daniel (who was received with great applause), spoke as follows: – 'My speech is not a long speech. I thank you all, Welsh and English, for all your kindness, bodily and spiritual, since I have been in England [sic]. Pray for me that I may be able to tell my own people of the Gospel of Christ.'

The Chairman then said that there was very little use in clapping hands, let the audiences give a practical illustration of their goodwill by a good collection. Any gifts of joiners tools or agricultural implements would be welcome, if they were sent to Congo House.

The collection having been taken up and the customary votes of thanks having been heartily passed and suitably responded to, the proceedings were brought to a close by the audience all joining in singing the doxology.

Two weeks after the official farewell at Tabernacl William, Frank and Nkanza accompanied Daniel on the short sea voyage on the *St Tudno* from Llandudno to Liverpool, where they disembarked before seeing him safely aboard *SS Nubia* bound for the Congo. The trio then returned to north Wales.

H. M. Stanley to Visit Colwyn Bay?
In the summer of 1890 Henry Morton Stanley was back home in Britain and there was speculation, encouraged by the local press, that he might visit Colwyn Bay:

> The idea is being warmly taken up in Colwyn Bay and the Local Board at a special meeting decided to undertake the responsibility of the cost of entertaining the great Welshman should he come to deliver a lecture in aid of the Revd Mr Hughes' Training Institute for African Children and nearly £40 was subscribed in the room towards the cost of erecting a pavilion to seat 7,000 people and the Chairman of the Board, Mr Porter, offered to place the Pwllycrochan Hotel at Stanley's disposal during his visit.

The *Weekly News and Visitors Chronicle* devoted a lengthy leader to the projected Stanley visit:

> The news recently received that the greatest traveller and explorer of modern times is probably about to visit Colwyn Bay has aroused intense interest not only among the residents in, and the visitors to, that popular and rising watering place, but throughout north Wales, and more than one busy and

pretentious nobody, on the strength of some chance acquaintance with Mr. Stanley has endeavoured to gain a fleeting notoriety by trying to secure a visit from that great Welshman *en passant*...However, from recent reports, it seems that Stanley's visit in aid of the Revd Mr Hughes Training Home for African Children is pretty certain to come off ...

As the likelihood of the anticipated visit ebbed away William Hughes set about organising an inscribed gift to be presented on behalf of local Baptists at Stanley's forthcoming wedding at Westminster Abbey. As subsequently reported in the press:

The simplicity of their testimony of the great explorer's sterling moral character are the words of presentation in a Jamieson's Family Bible from the Colwyn Bay Baptist Churches whose pastor, as is well known, became intimately acquainted with Mr Stanley years ago out in Congoland. The volume, magnificently bound in levant Morocco by Messrs Virtue and Co. Limited, has an inscription stamped in gold on purple watered silk, inside the cover and facing the flyleaf, as follows:

PRESENTED
AS A TOKEN OF THE HIGHEST ESTEEM
AND REGARD
BY THE
English and Welsh Baptist Churches
OF
COLWYN BAY, NORTH WALES
AT THE DESIRE OF THEIR PASTOR
REV. W HUGHES
TO
HENRY M STANLEY, ESQ.,
ON THE OCCASION OF HIS MARRIAGE
TO
MISS DOROTHY TENNANT
WISHING THAT THE UNION MAY BE LONG, MOST
HAPPY, USEFUL AND PROSPEROUS

Thomas Lewis Johnson   *James Spinther James*

William and Institute Students, 1892

'A Yarn Permingled with Fictions'

Soon after Stanley's wedding his name was again linked by the press with that of William Hughes, but this time with an even more fanciful story. In August 1890 the following appeared in the *Liverpool Echo*:

> At a time when the Anglo-American [sic] explorer started for Africa Mr. Stanley was presented with a ring on which was engraved his name, the name of the expedition and the date. Mr Stanley wore this ring whilst exploring the lakes in Central Africa on his first march across the Dark continent, when the ring was missed being either stolen or lost. After eight years it came into the possession of a Welsh missionary to the Congo, the Revd W Hughes, now Principal of the Congo House Training Institute, who bought the ring from a native at Vivi and brought it home. On Stanley's recent return the other day, the missionary forwarded the ring to Mr Stanley as a wedding memento.

Hughes wrote to the newspaper and whilst disclaiming responsibility for the original story submitted an amended version:

> Mr. Stanley lost, probably at Vivi (his first African camping station) a massive silver ring, on the outside of which was engraved *Stanley Anglo-American Expedition 1874-77*. In 1885 the Revd W Hughes, Principal of the Congo Training Institute at Colwyn Bay, who was then a Baptist missionary in Congoland, went from his residence, Underhill Mission Station. Tunduwa, situate on the south bank of the river Congo, on an evangelistic tour through the surrounding district and at a desolate village, about ten miles from Vivi and about the same from Underhill, a native African man came to him and said, *White man will you buy something from me?* In response to the coloured man's request that Mr Hughes should consent, to use a vulgarism, *to buy a pig in a poke*, that gentleman flatly told the ebony skinned individual that he

would not *buy a cat in a bag*. The native was ultimately induced to show and finally to sell for a piece of Turkey-red cloth, value (in London) 3s 6d, Mr Stanley's ring (originally worth more than a British sovereign). The native's story and said Mr Hughes *he obviously had a guilty conscience* was that some time previously he had bought the ring from one of Mr Stanley's servants. Mr Hughes' object in purchasing the ring was to present it to his friend the great explorer when he next met him face to face, but although correspondence on other subjects passed between them they never had the opportunity of meeting. Meanwhile the ring was resting in Mr Hughes' safe, first at Wrexham and then at Colwyn Bay. At length, on Stanley's return, the missionary forwarded the ring to the great explorer as a wedding memento. Mr Stanley in acknowledging the receipt of the ring expressed great surprise and delight that it should have followed him from the darkest regions of Africa.

Such Sweet Sorrow

Following the disappointment of Stanley's failure to visit Colwyn Bay and Daniel's return to the Congo, William felt rather deflated. Installed in his fine new Institute he was left with only three students, Nkanza, Frank and Kofele to train, and with insufficient funds to maintain more. Even the birth of his new son failed to lift his spirits. As he later reported to the Committee, it was:

in my opinion, the darkest time in the history of this work. As you are aware, we had then three students, and though I had been pleading on their behalf and knocking on the door of our churches seeking help for five years, it was as much as we could do at the end of that period to support *three* ... sometimes I was inclined to do with the Institution as Moses did with the stones at Sinai ...

At least William's involvement with the Bible Society, of which he was the local secretary, was encouraging: 'The issue of the Bible, Testaments, or portions thereof amounted in 1889–90 to

3,790,000 copies, an increase of 115,059 copies over the previous year'; but it was small consolation.

More consoling was news from the Royal Geographic Society in November that, on the proposition of Sir Francis de Winton, William had been elected a Fellow of the Society. The letters FRGS meant a lot in those days: even King Leopold was impressed.

New Year's Resolution, 1891
An extremely positive article written by Marianne Farningham and published in *The Christian World* opened the New Year with good publicity for the institute. After outlining the aims and history of Congo House she informed her readers that:

> I spent a very pleasant evening with Kofele, Nkanza and Frank, who sang, recited and prayed, both in their own language and in English and whose black faces shone with pleasure as they talked of Africa…there is no town in the kingdom, nor any single individual who may not help with subscriptions and be sure that the money will be wisely used.

In March the students' varied contributions to a local Baptist entertainment produced further positive publicity. Nkanza offered a recitation intriguingly entitled, *Where Do You Live?*, Frank Teva played several musical airs on his tin whistle, whilst Kofele's singing in his native tongue, Dualla, proved so popular his audience demanded an encore!

Support for Congo House, both moral and financial, was increasing even before Hughes learned that arrangements were finally in place for H. M. Stanley to deliver a fund-raising speech in June at Caernarfon on behalf of the Institute. Confidence restored, Hughes looked forward to accepting more students but of the six expected, two were delayed, and when *SS Benguela* docked at Liverpool in May 1891 four Congo boys disembarked and took the steamer across to Llandudno. Thomas Wamba, William Lufwilu, Samba and George Fraser were warmly welcomed at the Institute, raising the total number of students on the roll to seven.

William Welcomes 'The Philanthropic Hero'

Besides William's personal adulation of H. M. Stanley, he was acutely aware that publicity was the lifeblood of the Institute's fundraising and Stanley was publicity personified. Hughes described Stanley as 'The Philanthropic Hero – the Apostle of the Dark Continent', but apparently the Caernarfon public weren't entirely convinced, as a quarter of the seats in the enormous eisteddfod Pavilion remained unfilled at his 15 June 1891 lecture, although 4,000 did attend, after paying what many complained was a rather expensive admission charge. Seated on the speaker's platform alongside H. M. Stanley were representatives of the Congo House Committee, William Hughes, Nkanza, Kofele, Thomas, William, Samba, George and Frank. It was probably the proudest day in Hughes' life.

From the platform, Hughes formally welcomed the guest speaker:

We, the Committee of the Congo Training Institute for African Children, Colwyn Bay, North Wales, who reside in various parts of the principality, on behalf of ourselves and our numerous friends, beg to be allowed to offer you a most cordial Welsh welcome on this occasion of your first public visit to North Wales.

We would also like to express to you our most sincere appreciation of the honour conferred upon our Institution as well as North Wales in general, by your visit to the ancient town of Caernarfon on behalf of a work which is so closely connected with the wonderful country you have explored and where you have accomplished some of the highest purposes of the nineteenth century.

We thoroughly understand your Philanthropic achievements in Central Africa and we are fully aware that you have been the chief instrument in opening up that vast country for the entrance of commerce, civilisation and the gospel with their universal benefits to the millions of Ham's sons who will some day with their rich country liberally respond to their benefactors.

We sincerely hope that you together with Mrs Stanley, will spend the remainder of your days in Gwalia which we trust and pray will be the most pleasant and happy of your useful lives.

'Luminous and Picturesque Language'

Mr Stanley then rose and was received with tumultuous cheering the audience rising *en masse* and waving their handkerchiefs for several moments. The great explorer then proceeded with the lecture which was an interesting narrative of perils and escape…
Mr Stanley described in luminous and picturesque language his march across the *Dark Continent* with its sensational adventures, desperate encounters with savage tribes, toilsome marches and hairbreadth escapes.

Accompanied by a number of the natives they arrived at length at Ujiji on Lake Tanganyika and fired a glorious salute. Two black men met them with shining faces and said *Good morning*, Sir. Astonished at hearing the welcome sounds of English in the middle of Africa he asked them sharply who they were. They said in reply that they were servants of Dr Livingstone. Before Mr Stanley's party could quite realise that their ardent search was at an end they were in the presence of an aged European wearing a consular cap with a gold band around it. Doubtful of the temper he would receive him in, Mr Stanley said, addressing him, *Dr Livingstone, I presume?* [Applause] …

After an amusing account of his dealings with Ngalyema, Chief of the Stanley Pool district and of the terror which he inspired by his gong which the chief believed to be a powerful fetish Mr Stanley said that by August 1884 he had established regular communications between Stanley Falls and the sea and the following December he was present as technical counsellor at the Berlin Conference and two months later the European Powers organised the independent Congo Free State, with the King of the Belgians its sovereign …

On Lake Tanganyika they had several adventures, some very laughable and others of a serious nature. They were subsequently greeted by a grand flotilla sent to them by Mtesa, the King of Uganda, who had dreamed a dream and the king's mother had also dreamed a dream, this last dream being to the effect that there was on the way a boat with white wings and having on board a sad-faced white man. They found the Mtesa and his Court encamped picnicking at Merchison Bay. Mtesa wanted to know many things – among others how well a white man could shoot. This Stanley demonstrated by shooting a baby crocodile. The next wish was to know about angels ... the next wish was to be told the story of Christianity, in which the King and his Court showed the deepest interest, refusing to allow Mr Stanley to depart until he had translated the Gospel of St Luke ...

There were children in that town (Caernarfon) who would live to see the day when the millions of Central Africa would have learned to love the summons of the Christian church bells joining joyfully in the beautiful anthem which was first heard under the stars over Bethlehem – *Glory to God in the Highest and on Earth Peace and Goodwill Towards Men*. (Enthusiastic applause, during which the lecturer resumed his seat).

A Royal Patron

It was announced after Stanley's lecture that he had not only agreed to become a Patron of the Institute but also agreed to use his influence to secure the patronage of King Leopold II. Stanley wrote, obligingly, to Leopold, from London, on 7 July 1891 commending to him as sovereign ruler of the Congo the work of William Hughes. A week later, on 14 July, the Chief of the King's Cabinet, Borchgrave D'Altina, replied to Stanley from the Palace at Brussels, acceding to his request and granting to Hughes Leopold's official patronage.

With its publications boasting the patronage of H. M. Stanley, King Leopold II and Messrs. Elder, Dempster & Co, and its Director, an elected fellow of the Royal Geographical Society, the respectability and solidity of Congo House was highly evident to all potential supporters.

Welcome Arrivals

In July 1891, Roul van der Most arrived at the Institute from St Paul de Loanda, Angola, along with George Steane from Victoria,

Cameroons. George had been expected since May but was delayed when his ship, *SS Soudan II*, was wrecked off the coast of Africa on its voyage to Liverpool. In August Congo House gained its first female student, with the arrival of Ernestina Francis from Banana on the Congo. Both Roul and Ernestina were the illegitimate offspring of the union of black African women and white Dutch traders.

With their arrival the number of African students on the roll at Colwyn Bay increased to ten, with most having come via the American Baptist Missionary Union rather than the BMS. This prompted Hughes to observe, 'Our American friends seem to appreciate this idea more than some of our friends nearer home.' And as if to illustrate his point, despite a hectic 1891 tour schedule, celebrated American evangelist and hymn-writing duo Dwight Lyman Moody and Ira David Sankey still managed to squeeze in a visit to Congo House.

William illustrates a more enduring link with 'American friends' in the Institute's 1889–91 Report, where he describes parallels between Congo House and the Wayland Seminary, Washington DC, which, he reports, had recently admitted six Congo boys for training. Wayland college had been founded in 1867, just after the American Civil War, to provide education and training for freed slaves who wanted to enter the Baptist ministry. William Hughes went on to explain that the African boys at Congo House corresponded with the youngsters at Wayland.

Colwyn Bay Eisteddfod

Somehow, despite his duties at the Institute and Tabernacl, William still found time to involve himself in civic society in Colwyn Bay. In 1891 he was President of the town's Eisteddfod Committee whose, 'list of subjects' (according to the local newspaper):

> is an attractive one, including stanzas (*englynion*) *The Subway*, essays on, *Colwyn Bay*, *Bazaars* and *Total Abstinence*; a Shorthand competition held in public; a fine art competition, the subject for an original watercolour painting being the

Pwllycrochan Hotel; competitions in knitting, fancy work and blacksmith's work; and a multitude of musical competitions, vocal and instrumental. In fact the events are too numerous to specify in detail.

'Dark Africa and the Way Out', 1892

In March 1892 William sent the manuscript of his book *Dark Africa and the Way Out* to Stanley's publishers, Sampson Low. The title was an inspired play on a theme of the period. Stanley's *In Darkest Africa* appeared in the summer of 1890, quickly followed by General Booth's Salvation Army handbook *In Darkest England and the Way Out*. Hughes' book was described as 'a scheme for civilizing and evangelizing the Dark Continent' and was dedicated to King Leopold, H. M. Stanley and the Elder, Dempster shipping company.

Comprising 156 pages, illustrated with photographs and organized into sixteen chapters, Hughes' book interweaves an account of the personal journey that led him to found the Congo Training Institute with an implicit, extended appeal to readers to lend their support, moral and financial, to the project. Attractively produced with gold-blocked, pictorial covers, available in blue or red, 5,000 copies of *Dark Africa and the Way Out* were printed, but the Institute had to pay the £239 11s 8d cost of publication.

The Christian World review was very positive:

> At a time when pretty well all the Missionary Societies are recognising the fact that if a way out of Dark Africa is ever to be found it will be by native agencies, the appearance of Revd W Hughes' *Dark Africa* is opportune. The scheme he propounds is being tried at the Congo Training Institute, Colwyn Bay, and the book is a long and intensely interesting argument in favour of widened effort on similar lines.

The Institute naturally pushed sales of the book:

> Many favourable remarks have already appeared in the Press concerning it. Every friend of the work should procure it by

sending 2/4½ without delay to the Secretary (price 2 shillings, postage 4½ pence). PS. We should be greatly obliged if our friends in different localities would endeavour to make it known to others and thus increase the interest in the scheme.

An old friend of Congo House in the locality of Liverpool, Sir Alfred Jones, passed a copy of *Dark Africa* to the famous African-American Baptist and ex-slave, Thomas Lewis Johnson, as he was passing through the port en route to Liberia. Johnson was so struck by Hughes' scheme that he delayed his trip in order to visit Colwyn Bay to see the Institute in action. Afterwards he wrote:

Cover of Dark Africa and the Way Out, *1892*

> Mrs Johnson and I received a very hearty welcome on our arrival … We were gratified and delighted with all the arrangements and purposes of the Institute. The book, which I had read, and the course pursued by the Institute agreed in the high aim of blessing the people of Africa spiritually and materially, through her own children trained in the Truth and in necessary trades. Mr Hughes was enthusiastic in his work and Mrs Hughes was a real mother to those children of Africa. The Institute and its work made a great demand upon the time and resources of these two devoted friends of Africa and they not only give themselves heartily to the cause but stirred up interest and secured the co-operation of those in a position to help. It was very clear concerning *Darkest Africa* that the way taken by Mr Hughes was the *Way Out* and I advised my brethren in America and Africa to co-operate with Mr Hughes in his splendid work.

Support from the BMS?

The 1892 publication of *Dark Africa and the Way Out* coincided with the centenary celebrations of the BMS, and for a moment it appeared that the even the Baptist Missionary Establishment had been converted to Hughes' scheme. Leading BMS missionary George Grenfell advised the committee, 'It is quite clear to us familiar with the work that Central Africa is not going to be evangelised by white men. The toll in lives is against us...and we feel more and more that most of the work must fall on people of the country itself.'

Whatever the committee's private response there was no policy volte-face from General Secretary Baynes who continued to treat Hughes as an implacable enemy. Addressing a meeting in Aberystwyth in October 1892, Baynes once again expressed his whole-hearted opposition to the Colwyn Bay Institute.

Nationalism or Colonialism?

Running throughout Hughes' book is an implicit Welsh nationalism that occasionally surfaces:

> It is wrong and a blunder to appoint Englishmen as judges, preachers and magistrates over the people of Wales; even were they the best of men they would be in the wrong place ... They are ignorant of the Welsh language, unacquainted with the affairs of the Welsh people, their poverty, history, wrongs; they cannot sympathise with the sentiments, hopes and aspirations of a conquered people ... The English Church has failed in Wales because it came here with an English cloak upon it, attempting to teach in an unnatural way, preaching in another tongue to people who spoke Welsh.

Hughes implicitly claims insight into the predicament of natives colonised by invading powers and foreign missionaries; ignorant and unimpressed by indigenous cultures these colonisers arrogantly impose their own. Hughes' contrasts this approach with his Institute's commitment to train natives to work with their own people, in their own way:

Our idea in training Africans as missionaries is that in all points they are like their brethren, of the same blood, the same colour, the same humour, the same language, the same in everything excepting in education and training.

Hughes's own nationalism was echoed by other advocates of the Congo House scheme. Addressing the Institute's 1892 Annual Meeting, Revd E Rowe Evans, Merthyr, claimed:

The great advantage that the Society gave to those it instructed was that it took the young Congo men from their native surroundings and gave them the advantage of living in a civilised country. The civilisation of England was not much to boast of but a great deal of good was done by bringing those young men over from Africa and showing them what Christianity had done for that assemblage's own country, Wales.

'In the Midst of Life'

The positive achievements of the early months of 1892 were sadly counterbalanced by the deaths of two more students in Colwyn Bay. Samba died on Wednesday 9 March 1892, after falling and injuring himself whilst playing on the field outside the Institute. A short memorial verse subsequently appeared in the local newspaper under the initials of 'DG', probably David Gamble, a Manchester business-man and Institute supporter who had retired to Colwyn Bay:

IN LOVING MEMORY OF SAMBA

Rest to the little sleeper,
On earth he'll wake no more;
Safe in the arms of Jesus,
And all his sufferings o'er.

'His will be done'. Who ordered
How all this sorrow came,
He gave, and He hath taken,
And blessed be His name!

Less than a month later followed the death of Nkanza, who had been with William for a decade, since his early missionary days in the Congo. Nkanza's death was diagnosed as acute heart failure caused by congestion of the liver. Both of William's original students had now died in Colwyn Bay.

In August William's spirits were revived by the birth of his third daughter, Edith, named in honour of her mother's sister, who had passed away the previous year aged only twenty-five. With tragic irony, little Edith survived for only six months, dying on 13 March 1893. It was a difficult time for William and his wife but, outwardly at least, he remained positive, preparing plans for new links with Africa.

Preparatory Schools for Congo House

Congo House relied on friends in Africa sending their most promising students to Colwyn Bay to enable the Institute to continue its work as a 'finishing school' for native missionaries. Hughes realised the importance of maintaining and developing links with existing African mission stations, but was contemplating founding new Industrial Training Institutes in Africa to serve as 'feeder' schools for Congo House. This more direct relationship with African training missions offered great potential for regularising recruitment to Congo House, but for Hughes and his Committee to take on the additional responsibility for finding finance and personnel to maintain branches thousands of miles from Colwyn Bay was extremely ambitious. Undaunted, in August 1892 the local newspaper reported:

> On Monday 15 August a very interesting and important Committee Meeting was held at the Congo Training Institute, Colwyn Bay, for the purpose of selecting two white Missionaries to go to the borders of Zululand, South Africa, to superintend and conduct an Industrial and Educational Institution for the Natives. The Institution is to be on the lines of the Lovedale Institution and is to be a Branch of the Congo Training Institute at Colwyn Bay.

The Revd H T Cousins (late Vice-President of the Transvaal Baptist Association), who the last thirteen years, has been labouring in South Africa, and who is now on a visit to Colwyn Bay, was unanimously elected Superintendent of the Foreign Branch, the Revd L Ton Evans, Cadoxton Barry, Cardiff, being chosen his colleague. The Revd Mr Cousins, who has accepted the appointment from September 1, 1892 will before leaving for South Africa, visit the larger cities and towns of England and Scotland and will be accompanied by two of the Native Students, for the purpose of making known more fully the important work carried on in Colwyn Bay by the Revd W Hughes, F.R.G.S.; and also enlist sympathy and help for the all-important and aggressive work among the South African heathen.

'Three Congo Students Returning Home'
On Tuesday evening, November 15, a farewell meeting was held in the Baptist Chapel, Abergele Road, Colwyn Bay, in connection with the departure of three of the African Students (Frank Teva, Willie Lufwilu and Kofele M'Besa) to their native land. The meeting had been well advertised and public interest seemed to have been thoroughly aroused for the occasion...the Revd W Hughes introduced the Revd Joseph Clark, for fourteen years a missionary in Central Africa ... he also stated that this was the gentleman who had sent to the Institution several of the students now undergoing their course of training, in that place, amongst whom were two (Frank and Lufwilu) who were then going back with him to assist in his work. Mr Clark then gave a soul-stirring address on missionary work in general and paid a very high tribute to the noble and practical work now being done at the Congo Institute. He said that there was room for hundreds of such Institutions, and that he earnestly hoped that the Committee would soon see their way opened to extend their work by establishing like Training Schools on some of the healthier parts of the African Coast, a course which was already their purpose as soon as funds would allow.

Visiting Missionaries at the Institute, 1893

Plans to expand the Congo House scheme began to take shape in 1893. In May alone, three influential missionaries visited Colwyn Bay and spoke in support of the Institute. As described above, the ex-slave, Revd Thomas L Johnson, arrived after reading *Dark Africa and the Way out*. The Revd W. Powell of the American Baptist Missionary Union:

> testified to the Congo Institute Method ... ascribing his great success in the Indian mission field to his having largely made use of, and worked by means of, natives whom he trained as pastors. Upon that same principle, he understood the Congo Institute was working ... Educated at Pontypool Baptist Theological College, the Revd W Powell went thence to America (after having been refused by the Baptist Missionary Society, London), and was accepted by the American Baptist Missionary Union, and by them was sent to India.

Described as 'An Eloquent Coloured Missionary' by the *Weekly News*, the Revd Theophilus Scholes' lectures, delivered at the Colwyn Bay Baptist Chapel on the invitation of William Hughes. On the subject of the, 'Dark Continent, were heard with the intensest interest by crowded congregations.' On Tuesday 10 May 1893, Johnson and Scholes both spoke at a Colwyn Bay tea party 'in aid of the funds of the Congo Institute' with Scholes regaling his audience with tales of the racial prejudice endemic in his own country:

> When the shackles of slavery were removed, people imagined that all that could be needed had been done for the African race, but it was not so, for the masters, unwillingly forced to give up their slaves, were determined still to oppress them and in the island whence the speaker came from [Jamaica], and it might be taken as being a representative case, the owners of land refused to sell it to coloured people to build houses on it. The speaker's father wished to send his own daughter to a good school but solely on account of her colour, she was

refused admittance. In New York to this day, continued Dr Scholes, there are many places where I could not dine ...

Around the same time, two directors of the Elder Dempster shipping line, 'visited the Congo Institute and gave a handsome donation towards the enlargement of the Institute.' Following their visit the *Weekly News* also reported that:

Gossiping Guide Map of Colwyn Bay Showing *Congo Institute*

The Revd Theophilus Scholes, not withstanding his colour [sic!], has been appointed medical-officer on one of Elder Dempster & Co's African steamships, for twelve months commencing next August, and has been given permission to hold missionary services on board. Subsequent to the termination of this engagement, Dr Scholes will be working in Africa on behalf of the Congo Institute.

Network of Supporters

By 1893 Hughes was despatching 12,000 copies of the Institute's Annual Reports to all parts of Britain, West Africa and America; 8,000 of these Reports were published in English and 4,000 in Welsh. Already Hughes had built up an extensive network of supporters including sixteen prestigious patrons and a management committee with over 150 members. Besides H. M. Stanley and King Leopold, the official patrons included an American doctor and evangelical minister, Levi Daniel Johnson of Iowa. After serving as an Institute Patron for several years Levi

Johnson stood for election to the United States House of Representatives on a Prohibitionist ticket, with a spectacular lack of success.

Another interesting supporter of the Institute in this period was the influential Jamaican Joseph Jackson Fuller, who had been the senior BMS missionary in the Cameroons until the BMS sold out to the Germans in 1888. Living in London in 1893 he could hardly have been entirely ignorant of the BMS establishment's opposition to the Colwyn Bay Institute when he sent Hughes 7s 6d to support his work.

A contribution of two guineas was sent by Quaker philanthropist and chocolate magnate George Cadbury, who famously developed the recipe for Dairy Milk.

Supporters from all over Wales, from Wrexham to Fishguard and Pontypool to Holyhead, constituted a representative management committee. The Presidents of Bangor College and Cardiff College were both members, as was Samuel Valentine, quarryman and Baptist preacher of Llanddulas, north Wales, and father of Lewis Valentine, a founder member of Plaid Cymru, who himself became a great admirer of William Hughes.

'More Students than Ever Before'

The Institute's expanding network of supporters was matched by an increase in the number of students to fifteen. To accommodate them a brick-built extension was erected alongside Myrtle Villa incorporating 'a schoolroom with classrooms and dormitories'. A carpenter's workshop was planned and two printing presses were installed. One was donated by Messrs John Watton and Son, proprietors of *The Shrewsbury Chronicle*, whilst the other was provided by William 'Zulu' Smith, who had published *The Llandudno Advertiser* before selling up to work as a jobbing printer. 'Zulu' Smith was a well-known local character who bore the nickname in reference to twenty-four years he'd spent in South Africa. After settling in Llandudno he famously regaled guests with displays of native souvenirs and tales of his previous life in Africa and he assured Hughes, 'I shall for ever feel grateful to the Africans for many kindnesses extended to me, so that any little help I can offer the Congo Institute will only be to repay in part a debt I owe some of the natives of the Dark Continent.'

Spreading the Word

With an eye to further widening support for Congo House, in the early summer of 1893 Hughes published what amounted to a 'popular edition' of *Dark Africa and the Way Out*. Shorter and cheaper than the original, it bore the spectacularly turgid title: *Congo Training Institute, Colwyn Bay, North Wales; Reasons for Training the Most Promising of the African Converts in This Country, etc.* Nevertheless, at a third of the length and an eighth of the price of the original, it outsold *Dark Africa*'s 5,000 print-run four times over.

The local newspaper published an extensive review of the booklet that favourably compared Hughes' scheme to the work of the American abolitionist, educationalist and escaped slave, Frederick Douglass.

> What he (Hughes) is accomplishing would obtain the benediction of that silver-tongued orator, the Hon. Frederick Douglass, in whose thoughtful remarks at the Tuskegee Normal Institute last May, work, *faithful, unflagging, indefatigable,* was eulogised as the stepping-stone to moral and mental glory. Mr Hughes has planted a fruitful idea which will have imitation. Already the Bishop of Sierra Leone, Dr Ingram, has established a technical school on Africa's soil for the benefit of the natives.

Starting a new 'feeder' Institution in Africa and developing links with those already established was very much on Hughes' mind in the summer of 1893, as he planned to return to the 'Dark Continent' for the first time since 1885. Before William's departure, added urgency arrived in the form of a threatening letter from a German missionary incensed by Hughes' continuing success in recruiting students from Cameroon, which Germany considered part of its African empire ...

Not Praying but Dancing

Describing himself as leader of the German Baptist Missionary Society in Cameroon, on 20 March 1893 the Reverend Augustus Steffens wrote to Hughes telling him:

> It is not enough that our churches have had to suffer through the unwise behaviour of the (English) BMS, but now our youth are being stolen from us...We will not allow our children to be sent to a foreign country. This must stop at once. We own the mission and we are responsible for the education of our Africans. We hope, within a few years, to open a school for training young men for the ministry ...We will not employ anyone who has been in a foreign country. We differentiate between those educated in England, Germany and America. We have had plenty of mournful experience of young people returning home, bringing with them corrupt habits, like drinking beer and wine, gluttony, smoking, dancing, etc. Also, they return as gentlemen, dressed and living like Europeans, ashamed of their own language; and they are, to say the least, a disgrace to their parents and to the missionaries.

Steffens' letter continued:

> The people of Victoria give us a lot of trouble because of your school. They rejected a teacher who received his education in a German school, and who is able to teach in German and Dali. They refused, too, to send their 30 children to us for education and training because they preferred to be civilised and educated in England [sic]. I hope you have some sympathy with us, and that you will leave our children alone. If we hear of any more boys and girls going to England we will use other means.

This veiled threat in Steffens' letter only strengthened William's conviction that it was essential to the long-term development of the Congo House scheme that he return to Africa to reinforce and develop that end of operations.

Fond Farewells

A public meeting was held on Friday evening, June 23rd, at the Baptist Chapel, Colwyn Bay, Mr W. S. Jones (of Chester) presiding to bid God-speed to the Revd W. Hughes, F.R.G.S. of the Congo Institute, Colwyn Bay, who was the following morning to leave for a brief visit to West Africa, where he contemplates establishing several branches of the Congo Institute.

The meeting opened with the familiar singing of *From Greenland's Icy Mountain* – a popular hymn at the Institute, the words of which offer insight into the inherently Imperialist world-view of the typical Victorian missionary:

> From Greenland's icy mountains, from India's coral strand;
> Where Afric's sunny fountains roll down their golden sand;
> From many an ancient river, from many a palmy plain,
> They call us to deliver their land from error's chain.
>
> What though the spicy breezes blow soft o'er Ceylon's isle;
> Though every prospect pleases, and only man is vile?
> In vain with lavish kindness the gifts of God are strown;
> The heathen in his blindness bows down to wood and stone.
>
> Shall we, whose souls are lighted with wisdom from on high,
> Shall we to those benighted the lamp of life deny?
> Salvation! O salvation! The joyful sound proclaim,
> Till earth's remotest nation has learned Messiah's Name.
>
> Waft, waft, ye winds. His story, and you, ye waters, roll
> Till like a sea of glory, it spreads from pole to pole;
> Till o'er our ransomed nature the Lamb for sinners slain,
> Redeemer, King, Creator, in bliss returns to reign.

After various tributes were paid, the Reverend James Spinther James contributed a characteristically controversial speech:

Mr Hughes was a man with one idea, one fruitful idea, the training of young Africans in the wisdom of the Cross ... Mr Hughes' idea was to send Christian civilised Africans into the heart of Africa ... The Missionary Societies had departed far from the ideal of Carey (founder of the BMS), which was that missionaries – when in the mission field – should earn their own living and be free from the dictation of committees of drapers, ministers, etc. Paul was not under the orders of a committee, nor was Barnabas, and for the success of the present day mission work, it was needful to keep closer to the Apostolic method.

Like Hughes, Spinther James was a fearlessly independent-minded Baptist, ever prepared to challenge established authority and his support for William was to prove utterly consistent and vitally important in future years.

After more speeches, there followed:

a very pleasant surprise for Mr and Mrs Hughes in the form of a very handsome framed address presented to Mr Hughes by Mr Brackstone, as Secretary, and a most chaste silver tea service, with her initials engraved, to Mrs Hughes by Mr T Evans-Hughes, as Treasurer, from the members and friends of the English Baptist Church, of which Mr Hughes is pastor.

The Reverend E. Jones Davies then invited everyone to join him in prayer and to finally conclude the meeting, 'Mr Davies earnestly commended Mr Hughes to the loving care and keeping of God and besought that Mr Hughes might have wisdom and health to accomplish the object of his visit and at length be brought back in safety to his family and to the Institute.'

Throughout the six months' duration of his West African trip William maintained a diary that he communicated to family and friends back home in Colwyn Bay in the form of a series of thirteen detailed letters. Together these provide such an interesting account of Victorian West Africa and insight into William Hughes' perspective that, slightly abbreviated, they form the whole of the next chapter.

Chapter Five

Letters from the Dark Continent
(June–December 1893)

I sailed from Liverpool on Saturday the 24 June and I can assure you that to leave relatives and friends behind was a very hard task. I made up my mind in the morning when getting out of bed at Congo House that my wife, children or anyone else, would not be allowed to see a tear rolling from my eyes on my departure and in order to keep my decision, I played a cheerful part until I entered my cabin – closed the door and all my friends had left …

We left the landing stage on board the tender about 12 noon and sailed along for about a mile and a half in the direction of New Brighton, where the large steamer the SS *Teneriffe* waited for us. Mrs Hughes, two of my sisters, the Revd E J Davies, R E Roberts and several other friends came with me on board the *Teneriffe* and saw my new lodgings. About half-past one the most difficult task of the day had to be performed – starting the tender back in the direction of Liverpool with all my friends on board. It was indeed an unhappy thing to hear the first bell ring – much worse the second for this meant the separation of the tender from the ocean-steamer as well as myself from my friends. The steps were soon lifted into their place, the doors on the side of the vessel were closed and a gulf was soon made between the two ships – still we kept on looking at one-another though no word could pass between us. We looked and saluted, waving our hats and pocket handkerchiefs.

Voyage to the Canary Islands: June

The SS *Teneriffe* lifted her anchor and began to sail about 2 o'clock. Now I have fairly turned my back on my home and friends and my face to the land of my adoption for the second

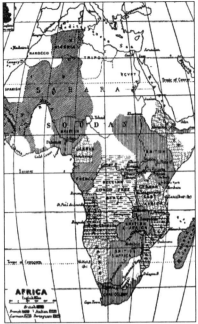

Political Map of Africa, 1892 (from Dark Africa and the Way Out)

time. My heart in one sense is filled with joy but still there is the mixture of sadness and sorrow. I rejoice because I am fond of Africa and the Africans; my spirit has lived there 19 years my body went there for the first time 11 years ago. I shall be pleased to see once more the land I love ... If I happen to die on this journey all will be well for the Lord will provide and the scheme will prosper...

We have now arrived (10 o'clock on Saturday) opposite Holyhead. The wind blows rather hard and I am afraid some of us will be sea-sick by tomorrow morning. Sunday morning came and one of the first things we saw was St David's Point in Pembrokeshire. This is a beautiful morning and no one has any sea-sickness – why even Carnsore Point in Ireland could be seen. After this we may expect to see no more land until the next Saturday when we hope to reach the Canary Islands. We are expecting to hold some kind of service on board during the day. The Captain appears to be a nice man and favours religion. I shall say more about him and others on board to-morrow after I become better acquainted with them.

When Monday morning came I rose early to find my cradle was rocking very much and was persuaded that some of us would be very giddy before the day was over; however I escaped the usual sickness and have by this time become an old sailor. Two of my fellow passengers have lost their breakfast through the troubled waters but they have very little sympathy as we all know that this sickness is not unto death.

We are now in the midst of the Bay of Biscay and it is no surprise that the waves are so playful. I possess one great advantage for my friends, Messrs Elder, Dempster & Co. of Liverpool have secured for me the best berth in the ship, right amidships, so it does not shake about half as much as fore or aft. Let it also be known that my voyage both ways does not cost anything and I shall be at liberty to jump on board of any of the steamers going up and down the West Coast; it's all like Grace – without money and without price …

The sea continues as rough in the afternoon as in the morning and it appears to get worse; it is a dull, rainy and stormy day and the beast we endeavour to ride seems determined to play a donkey's trick with *Teneriffe* and all on board.

Tuesday morning arrives after experiencing a dark stormy night but the *Teneriffe* swims like a duck – the waves do not remain at all on her back. The waves are not quite so rough as yesterday and the firmament is clearing up a little. I hope the worst is over now for my fellow passengers are all thus far in their berths and one of them did not turn up since yesterday morning. There are two medical men with us on board – Dr Griffin, the ship's doctor and Dr Elliot, who is going out to the Coast in connection with the Government. Both of them are Irishmen. There is one young man with us called Captain Matthews from Shropshire; he is going out to Lagos to act as Captain in the English Army. There are two Germans onboard; one of them is going to explore the upper parts of the Niger. This fact, with many others, goes to prove that Germany does not intend to be behind in annexing territories in the Dark Continent. Prince Bismarck said years ago, *England has been stealing in the past and we are now going to follow their example.* Prince Bismarck and his friends have ever since stuck to their determination but the Africans reap the worst benefit from it. English people have not yet opened their eyes to see the value of Africa, though prophet after prophet has been sent to tell them of it … We have arrived this afternoon (12.30) about 581 miles from Liverpool. Nothing of importance takes place for the rest of the day and as the night approaches both wind and storm subside. Our Heavenly Father watches over us; He says, *Peace be still.* We intend leaving the Bay of Biscay, about 12 midnight, to fight with itself.

On Wednesday morning the storm is over. *And He rebuked the wind and the raging of the water and they ceased and there was calm.* There is a nice breeze in our favour and the sailors have unfurled the sails; this may enable us to reach the Canary Islands by Sunday. We should have been there by Saturday had there been no contrary winds. How sweet is the calm after the tempest ... We are by 12.30 pm opposite Lisbon, the capital of Portugal, but there is no land to be seen. We have come by this time 796 miles from Liverpool. Things continue much the same till night and so we retire waiting for Thursday morning.

This is a beautiful morning. The sea is similar to what it was yesterday and all on board are well and happy. Most of my own time is spent in reading and writing...By 12.30 pm we have come from Liverpool 1,034 miles, there are 620 miles yet before we reach the Canary Islands. We are now passing the Straits of Gibraltar and are right opposite the Holy Land, but we cannot see either.

Friday morning is lovely and the weather is much warmer, and the white men on board, throw off their heavy clothing for that of a lighter texture. The Kroo boys too, begin to sing and laugh heartily. This is very natural, and to see and hear them is the source of much amusement – no one can laugh so heartily as a black man. Our distance from Liverpool today at 12.30pm is 1,274 miles, close to the Island of Madeira.

Saturday morning brings weather like the previous day, and by-the-bye it's the 1st of July. At about 4am on Sunday morning, 2 July, we arrived safely at Las Palmas, the Canary Islands, 1,694 miles from Liverpool, *To God be the Praise.*

Sunday at Las Palmas: July

Our steamer anchored by the city of Las Palmas, the capital of Grand Canary. All the houses and buildings are flat-roofed and the place has quite an Oriental appearance. We took a boat and went to the city in order to have a look at it and remained there from about nine o'clock in the morning until 3.30 in the afternoon. We saw its house, palaces, churches etc. There is one large cathedral, the building of which was commenced in the sixteenth century, but it is not yet completed, though to the spectator it appears quite finished and that in a magnificent style; it is the best building in the town.

The inhabitants are Roman Catholic with exceptions and they are much against every form of religion except their own as usual. There was no English Church until about three years ago because the Roman Catholic priests were against them getting land. Now there is an English Church built, and that by the benevolence of the chief friends of the Colwyn Bay Institution, ie Messrs Elder and Dempster of Liverpool. These gentleman during the last six years have accomplished wonderful work here. They purchased much land and a portion of it was given for the purpose of having erected upon it the long-desired English Church so that the Englishman can henceforth worship there in his own language and in accordance with his belief. The other portion is cultivated by some hundreds of natives superintended by an Englishman. In this manner tons of fruit are raised monthly for European markets as well as for the use of some hundreds of ships which call on their way. The remainder of the land is used to carry on two immense works – the engineering and the coaling. The first is for the purpose mostly of repairing all kinds of ships, which had before to be taken all the way to Europe and the other to supply with coal all the ships that call. The coal is brought here from Cardiff and is sold at £1 per ton – ten shillings less than it was sold for at Madeira and similar places a few years ago. The result is that this trade increases rapidly and the poor inhabitants find employment. Between all their businesses at the Canary Islands we are told that Messrs Elder and Dempster employ no less than 2,000 men at the Port Las Palmas and the neighbourhood. The two Companies have 57 ships which run between Liverpool and Africa and there are some running from Hamburg, Rotterdam and Antwerp. It is said in The Porcupine, a Liverpool newspaper, for 24 June that this Company has been one of the most influential means in preventing slavery in Africa and in developing the country as well as life and activity in the Canary Islands.

Goree and the Gambia

We left Las Palmas on Sunday night, 2 July; sailed Sunday, Monday, Tuesday, Wednesday and reached on Thursday morning, 6 July about 9 o'clock a small island called Goree, which stands near the mainland and a little south of Cape Verde, having come 847 miles from the Canary Islands. Goree (and the land beyond it) is a French colony and there is a fort on the island and a man-a-war close by. We are by this time over 2,500 miles from Liverpool and we are of course now on the West Coast of Africa.

William wanted to disembark for a tour of the notorious old slaving centre of Goree but this was prohibited as there had been an outbreak of cholera in some of the French colonies and it was feared that the infection might be brought back to the ship. No passengers from Goree were allowed aboard and goods for delivery were offloaded onto boats and ferried ashore by natives from the town. Twelve hours after arriving *SS Teneriffe* departed for the Gambia.

We arrived at Bathurst by nine this morning (Friday) 7 July. The ship is anchored near the town. This is the capital of the Island of St Mary and of the Gambia Colony. It is an English possession inhabited by 45 whites and 14,221 natives ... We went this morning, by boat, to the town and we saw in three hours everything there is to be seen – very dark people wearing apparel of all colours under the sun, and some without any clothes at all. The houses of the Europeans are

superior to anything we have seen on the West Coast ... We
also saw on our way through the town, the cotton-tree, the
gum-tree, the lime-tree, the cocoanut, the marakusa, the
plantain and many beautiful flowers ... The women carrying
their children on their backs in a piece of cotton tied round
their shoulders so that their hands would be at liberty to carry
something else and in addition to all this a large calabash full
of water is often to be noticed on the top of their heads.

The next morning (Saturday 8 July) *SS Teneriffe* sailed from
Bathurst and after spending an uneventful weekend at sea ...

Sailing to Sierra Leone

We reached Sierra Leone, *Lion Mountain*, about 11 o'clock on
Monday morning 10 July all safe and sound. The city of
Freetown is the capital of the colony. It stands at the foot of
the hills and reaches right to the beach. Some of the houses are
built quite at the top of some of the small hills. The Rockelle
river is to the north of the city. Sierra Leone was taken by Britain
in 1787 by the consent of the native chiefs. The idea in view at
that time was to make it a home for the destitute coloured
slaves who had been set free from their masters in England,
through the noble efforts of Granville Sharp and others ...

The harbour is considered one of the best and large vessels
find it a convenient place for coaling. The length of the colony
is about 185 miles and its area about 4,000 square miles. Its
population in 1891 was 74,835 of whom 210 are white men.
Every Christian denomination is represented in Freetown but
still there are large numbers of heathens and Mahometans.
The inhabitants are mostly traders, acting beyond their
country beyond and the civilised world ...

The natives have a kind of king for themselves to settle
some of their disputes, rather than take them under the notice
of the English authorities, but this native Court is not in any
way acknowledged by the Government, and yet I hear that
they do not in any way interfere with this spirit of *Home Rule*.
This policy must be a wise one, for the more such patriots are

disturbed the stronger, as a rule, the desire for Home Government becomes. One thing is certain, that the hope of the *Dark Continent*, temporarily and spiritually rests upon the coloured people themselves…

We left Sierra Leone about four o'clock on Tuesday afternoon and headed for Liberia.

Liberia, the Garden of West Africa

We reached Monrovia, the capital of Liberia on Thursday afternoon, 13 July. I intended to leave the *SS Teneriffe* here and said goodbye to Captain Perchard and to all the friends I had formed on that happy three week voyage from Liverpool. I hope here to visit *Ricks Institute* as it works on the same lines as our own at Colwyn Bay … I left for the city on Friday morning with the idea of seeing Mr Richardson and going with him to his Institute, which is ten miles upriver and then eight miles inland on the left bank … He and another gentleman named T C Lomax came with me in the boat: we passed through two creeks and then we entered into the St Paul's River. Its banks on both sides are clustered with evergreen trees and shrubs. We had four Kroo men pulling in the boat, with two others with Mr Richardson. We reached the landing at Virginia about three o'clock.

Before visiting Revd Richardson's Institute, Hughes accompanied Lomax three miles further upriver to investigate his independent Baptist Mission at Clay-Ashland.

The population of the village of Clay-Ashland is about 500. They are in great need there of an Institution to train their girls. I hope that the Colwyn Bay Institute may see its way clear to establish one there ere long. We left Clay-Ashland that morning by boat at 11.30 and went down-river as far as Virginia where we landed about twelve o'clock, meeting the Revd R B Richardson, who was anxiously waiting for us.

We discovered on our arrival that the population of Virginia is about 800 and after spending the night we commenced our overland journey of eight miles to the Institute. We walked hard through a country which is rich and fertile. We noticed on our way many houses well-built with bricks and having roofs of galvanised iron, which point out very clearly that the example and industry of the American Negroes are both expedient and beneficial to the natives. We also saw on our way large coffee farms, which is the chief produce of this part of Liberia. We reached the Institute by three o'clock and we felt by this time rather tired. The Institute stands on one of the most fruitful and beautiful spots in Liberia. The coffee is sold for the benefit of the community and it is expected that the Institute will soon be self-supporting. This Institute is exactly the thing we have been advocating for years in connection with the work at Colwyn Bay. The boys work for about four hours every day with the Industrial and are for five hours in school; the evenings and the Sabbath are devoted to the religious training. Every kind of Mission work without the above practical lines fails to be of real use and benefit to the natives ... The Ricks Institute henceforth is to cooperate with our Institution at Colwyn Bay and to send the most promising of its students to us for further training in a similar way to the Glamorgan Institute which is established in the Cameroons and other Industrial Institutions which we intend to establish on this visit to West Africa.

We started punctually at four o'clock, back in the direction of Virginia ... We reached Virginia by six o'clock, jumped in a boat and reached Monrovia, through all the mists and darkness by eight o'clock. I received on my arrival the cheerful news that there was an English steamer at anchor and that I would be able to go on board at six in the morning i.e. Sunday 16 July.

The captain received me on board the *SS Biafra*, which runs between Hamburg and Lagos. I hope to find at Lagos another steamer which will take me further south to Old Calabar and Cameroons where my most important duties on this visit await me.

Ships that Pass in the Night

After calling in at the Gold Coast:

> We reached Lagos late on Wednesday night 26 July. I felt anxious to find, without much delay, a steamer which would take me on towards the south. Early on the following we saw quite unexpectedly the *Teneriffe* coming in, having got free of the quarantine through which she had been detained at Accra. I returned to my old friends with much delight. The *Teneriffe* will go as far south as Opobo River where I hope to find another ship. This place was formerly one of the great centres of the African slave trade. Mohammedanism is in its full bloom here; those who believe in the system are so numerous that a caravan is formed annually to go on a pilgrimage to Mecca in Arabia, 3000 miles away.

William left Lagos on Friday 28 July, reaching Opobo River on Sunday 30 July he transferred to *SS Winnebah* which departed for Old Calabar on Thursday 3 August.

Old Calabar: August

When we arrived at Old Calabar on Sunday morning , 6 August and anchored by the town I noticed some difference in its appearance since I was here before eleven years ago, especially in the houses of the Europeans which seem to be more numerous and of better quality. Still it is one of the most degraded and filthy towns on the West Coast of Africa.

As I had a letter of introduction to His Excellency, Sir Claude Maxwell MacDonald K.C.M.G., and wished to see him particularly about Industrial Missions I left the *SS Winnebah* at the first opportunity but to my great disappointment I discovered that he had gone on a visit to other parts of the Protectorate ... During my four days stay at Old Calabar I paid a visit to the town and saw the parents and friends of two students we have at our Colwyn Bay Institution who had given in my charge books, boots, opening knives etc for their folks. These friends were overwhelmed with joy at welcoming one whom they considered the benefactor of their sons. I also visited village situate in various directions from the town and found that the people are most anxious to have schools established there and to hear the Gospel. This is a vast field for missionary enterprise.

Sir Claude Maxwell MacDonald KPMG

The Cameroons
After sailing from Old Calabar on Wednesday 9 August, William was bound for the Cameroons where the old missionary station, including its converts, had previously been rather shamefully sold for £4,000 to the German-speaking Basle Mission.

> We reached the Cameroons by the *SS Winnebah* on Friday 11 August. I was received very kindly by the Governor and I found he was a nice and reasonable gentleman. I enquired in what direction the Rev. Joshua Dibundu, the native pastor, resided and one of the Germans told me the way to get to his house.

Dibundu was an old friend of William's Colwyn Bay Institute. Experience had led both Joshua and William to share similar opinions on the arrogance and over-centralisation of the BMS and the importance of pursuing their own independent missionary initiatives. The previous year Dibundu had demonstrated his confidence in William's work by sending two of his own sons, Alfred and Samuel, to be trained at Colwyn Bay. Now William relished an opportunity to visit Joshua's Mission

Joshua Dibundu's family & Bethel Chapel, Cameroon

and during his two week stay explored how they might develop their mutually beneficial relationship:

> On Sunday morning, I started at half-past six with Dibundu across the river in a canoe in the direction of Niceory, where he has had a Mission Station and a Chapel built. I saw at this place the land, the house and the schoolroom sold to the Basle Mission. The natives, when they left the Basle Mission had to remove their houses from their land and to build them outside the camp. Joshua Dibundu had to do the same thing in Bethel, Cameroons for his house was built on the Mission land, to start, and the trouble and the expense were great to remove it to the land of freedom, when that Mission was transferred to Basle ... Now the natives have learnt a lesson; they will never again build their houses on the land of other people; all these things are the result of unpractical Parsons at home governing affairs that they know nothing about in Africa.
>
> The present splendid new chapel was built entirely by the congregation and cost about £2,000 though those who sold them over to the Basle Mission thought that they were too worthless to keep the old buildings in repair if they got them –

hence they were sold over, property, principles and all. The Basle Mission was cursed, at once, in the sight of all the people, and they lost their faith, for ever, in them and those who sold them into their hands. The result is that Luther's tree is withered in the Cameroons. There are evident signs that a curse rests upon the bargain struck between the two Missions until this day; and it is no wonder, for it was done without consulting the natives.

The account of building the new Chapel is very amusing. Many of the men determined to make a thousand bricks each and some of the young boys made hundreds of bricks. One of these pointed out to me was named Bikumbuo and he had made fifty bricks though at the time he was no more than nine years of age. The women carried sufficient water for the making of the bricks as well as sand from the river, King Aqua, with Dibundu, went to the forest to hew timber; others sawed them into planks. Some of them went with their canoes for a great distance for stones and lintels required for the building. They bought the glass and roof from England and paid every penny for themselves. Whilst this was going on, the Basle missionaries were mocking their brethren, saying, *Yes, it is begun, but it will never be finished* ...

A little before I left Colwyn Bay, in June last, I received a letter from Dibundu informing me that he had just baptised 200 persons. This morning, Sunday 20 August, I had the happy task of preaching from the Acts ii. 41. and Dibundu baptised, on the profession of their faith, 113 people in the Cameroons River ... I do not remember seeing a Sunday like this anywhere – with so much enthusiasm and reality. At half-past seven in the morning the people were running towards the Chapel from every direction, and, by the time we went in, there was no room to turn in the place; a great many people were looking through the doors and the windows, reminding one of the thousands who used to gather around the chapels to hear Christmas Evans in Wales.

When the service was over the congregation proceeded towards the river, singing beautifully all the time. All the crowd were eager to see the ordinance – some climbed to the tops of the trees, others covered the wharves and the European merchants' boats which were in the water. The crowd continued to sing on the shore for three-quarters of an hour with great warmth and enthusiasm, whilst three local preachers and two old sisters were leading the candidates to and from Dibundu, who stood about 20 yards from the beach, in the water, and there he baptised them, one by one, without moving from the same spot and without any ceremony, in the most happy and easy manner.

Dibundu and his brethren, since the day they left the Basle Mission, have established eighteen Mission Stations themselves, in connexion with the Mother Church, and there is a schoolmaster and a preacher at almost every one of those branches. All this has been done without receiving a penny from any Missionary Society ... Dibundu and all the self-denying friends in the Cameroons are exceedingly thankful to the friends of the Congo Institute for the little help and sympathy shown by them, and for stepping to their rescue when all others had turned their backs on them, *A friend in need is a friend indeed.* I sincerely hope that we shall be able still to help them, and especially the two Institutions established there, – *The Glamorgan* and *The Pembroke* – which will co-operate with us as Branch Institutions of the present one at Colwyn Bay.

Having said goodbye to the Revd Joshua Dibundu, together with his numerous friends, I left the Cameroons on Friday 25 August on board the *SS Benguela*, in which I went to the Congo eleven years ago. I took with me two carpenters, members of Dibundu's Church, for the purpose of constructing the buildings that will be required at the new place. We sailed for about 50 miles and reached on the same day, Victoria, where we remained for a few hours and we took on board there Mr. James Kofele, who was at Colwyn Bay for a period of about 3 years. He will act as a kind of helper at the proposed new Institution.

A New Institution at Old Calabar?

We reached Old Calabar about noon the following day, Saturday 26 August. On Sunday the 27th I visited with Kofele and the two carpenters a small town called Freetown, a place about 3 miles from Duke Town, which is the capital of Old Calabar. I met the Chief of this town, when there some three weeks before on my way to the Cameroons and I had formed a very high opinion of him. His name is Esien Etim Offiorg III, and he is a very intelligent and sensible young man. He preaches every Sunday to his people and many of his youths have been taught to read and to sing hymns. We enjoyed the day immensely in worshipping with him and in speaking to his people. They were all very desirous that we should remain with them and establish our Institution in their district, however we failed to see our way clear to meet their wish this time.

I spent a good part of Monday with the Governor of the Niger Protectorate, Sir Claude Maxwell MacDonald, K.C.M.G. and we entered fully into the scheme of the new Institution. His sympathy is great with our plan and he has promised an annual grant towards the Industrial Branch.

During my stay at Old Calabar I was visited several times by the relatives of the two youths who are at present in the Colwyn Bay Institute, and their presents, with their kindness, are similar to what I received at the Cameroons. There came also many others to see us, – fathers bringing their sons and wishing us to accept them for some years training at home and some of the Chiefs offering to pay a certain sum annually. There are also about a dozen of the young fellows quite anxious to follow us in order to be trained at the Institution now to be established in Africa. We intend this new Institute to be a kind of feeder to the Colwyn Bay one. There will be in it an annual examination and the best two or three will be sent every year from it to Colwyn Bay, in order to receive a further training for, *to him that hath it shall be given*. We have two or three places in view as being suitable for an Industrial school, – Bonny, Opobo and New Calabar.

Having finished our work at Old Calabar we left the place on Monday morning, 4 September in the *SS Cobendu*, with the view of going to Bonny.

A Death on the Ocean Wave: September

We sailed first, as far as the Island of Fernando Po, but had only a few hours to stay there. I landed for a short time at the capital, Clarence Cove, in order to form some idea of the place and also to see some friends – who reside there – from the neighbourhood of Colwyn Bay.

A very sad grievous accident occurred on board of the *Cobendu* during her short stay at Fernando Po. About 8 o'clock in the evening, whilst one of the firemen was returning from the cook with his tea-tin in his hand, he stepped in crossing the ship, on a tarpaulin, thinking that the usual boards were underneath it; he fell, however, through it (or rather with it), a depth of 30 feet, and was found between two casks of palm-oil, right at the bottom of the ship. The poor man was so much injured, especially his back, that he died at one o'clock the following morning, when we were on our way to Bonny. Captain Clarke knocked at my cabin door early that morning and said in a sorrowful tone; *I have the melancholy duty of asking you, will you be so kind as to serve at the burial of the poor man who fell last night? He is to be buried at sea at eight o'clock this morning.* He was buried with deep sorrow in accordance with the Captain's arrangements. He had been in the Company's service for about 8 years and he has left behind him a widow and two children.

I met on the *Cobendu* a man named H A Show, who was with us for some time on the Congo, as a carpenter and blacksmith. He is a thoroughly good fellow and I have engaged him to go with me to the New Institute, where he will erect buildings with the other carpenters and afterwards teach his two trades to the boys.

Suitable Site for an Institute: October

We reached Bonny about one o'clock in the afternoon on Tuesday 5 September. I remained at Bonny, Spying the land, until Saturday and I soon discovered that it was not a suitable place for the proposed Institution. We were informed that there were at Igwarga, a place on the bank of Opobo River, some 50 miles from Bonny, excellent plots, and a convenient place in other respects for the purpose we had in view then I arranged immediately with one of the Bonny Chiefs to give me his boat and 8 men who paddled us off in the direction of Opobo – Kofele, Show, Ralph, one of the Cameroons carpenters and myself.

William and crew spent the following 11 days exploring the creeks and settlements of the Bonny River, until:

On Saturday 16 September we reached, before noon, a place called Bugarra (Buguma), which I understood to be one of the most suitable in the Niger Protectorate to establish the proposed Institution. There is any quantity of good land and a large town of about 8,000 souls where there is no mission station and the creeks are very convenient, running in all directions so that by the aid of a boat, many other towns can be visited. On seeing the locality and the town I soon decided that this should be the spot ... All the Chiefs were called together to King Amachree's house and having spoken, concerning the matter for about an hour and having thoroughly understood each other a piece of excellent land (of about 100 acres) was promised to me, and they agreed to send 20 of their men to cut down and clear some of the dense bush, and to erect there some kind of house for the use of my workforce and afterwards schoolboys, so that they could have some shelter, in order to start our work.

During my stay there we cleared altogether about five acres of a thick forest. Before I left the following buildings were put up, of galvanised iron – a carpenter's shed, a tool-house, a boys' house, a schoolroom and a boathouse. There were about 22 boys in school daily under the care of Kofele and Ralph. About half-a-dozen had commenced to learn a trade already – some with the blacksmith, some with the carpenter and others with the tailor … I remained at Bugarra from 16 September until 30 October on which date I left for Bonny in my boat to meet the ss Nubia, homebound.

Homeward Bound: November

Now I must put aside my pen and think of home once more. I am surprised that I have escaped without a single fever though I have wandered about a great deal and have experienced rather trying times. I have had overland walking, I have travelled in small boats and canoes, slept in all kinds of beds, met all kinds of people and I have eaten all kinds of food. For the last five weeks I worked every day with my hands in the mud, rain and sun from six in the morning until six in the evening but I rejoice in my reward and my satisfaction that my task is completed and that there are established in West Africa five Institutions which are to co-operate with the *Alma Mater* at Colwyn Bay – *The Glamorgan* and *Pembroke* Institutions at the Cameroons; *The Ricks* and *The Russell* Institutes in Liberia; and *The Alfred Jones Institute* at Bugarra, New Calabar.

We left Bonny on *SS Nubia* on Friday 3 November and we are now, 15 November, near Sierra Leone. I sincerely hope to reach Colwyn Bay by Christmas and to enjoy once more the pleasant company of my dear relatives and friends … I can conscientiously say, with regard to my present sojourn in Africa, in the words of Paul: *I have fought a good fight, I have finished my course, I have kept the faith.*

Chapter Six

Days of Hope at the African Institute
(1894–1899)

Having already secured suitable buildings, an enthusiastic committee, eminent patrons and a national network of supporters, Hughes' 1893 West African trip brought new contacts and increased recruitment. Prospects for Congo House looked very promising and the next few years would prove to be a period of dynamism and growth but that wasn't Hughes' immediate concern. As soon as he returned to Colwyn Bay he discovered tricky problems and determined critics were awaiting him

The 'Little Beast' of Old Calabar

Just before William had embarked on his trip an orphaned and impoverished young African prince, Eyo Ekpenyon Eyo II, had despatched a letter to Alfred Jones, Director of the Elder Dempster shipping company, begging to be brought to Britain to be saved from slavery and to receive a decent education, it read as follows:

Pavilion House, Duke Town, Old Calabar, 27th May 1893
Sir – For you honour sir, I beck to inform you I am native of this contry. My father is chief for here, then he die ... and the second time my mother die, I got nobody to look after me, so I am turn a poor boy now. I am thirteen years old now. Since my mother left me I commence to lose what I been learn ... one of my father's brethren want me to be his slave ... One gentleman ask me how you sorry so, then I told him all my trouble since my mother die. He ask me, did you know book or to write. I say yes, then he give me this paper and ink and pen to write to you, and he told me your name and where you are and he began to tell me about you, say you be good master ... Please redeem me; please don't let me die without

BESESEDI BA YEHOVA.

MIEÑGE NA BELOÑGI,

POÑGOBE NA LATABE

JOSHUA DIBUNDU,

ALFRED NA SAMUEL.

J. SPINTHER JAMES, M.A.

BUSIBABE NA:
CONGO INSTITUTE, COLWYN BAY.

Mojola Agebebi, circa 1895

Hymn Book for Cameroon,
Published by Congo Institute,
1896

In Loving Memory of

Katie,

The Beloved Wife of WILLIAM HUGHES, *of the Congo Institute,*
Colwyn Bay,

Who Died August 20th, 1894,

AGED 33 YEARS.

Her Remains were Interred at Old Colwyn Cemetery,
August 23rd, 1894.

" Thy will be Done."

Death notice of Katie Hughes, 1861–94

knowledge ... please send a reply and ticket of passenger and put it in an envelope and registered for me ... I keep watch for any steamer which want to come for Liverpool.

I am yours sincerity, EYO EKPENYON EYO II

Please sir, help the poor boy because I got no silver or gold. I am a little beast.

Alfred Jones was favourably impressed by the letter and arranged for little Prince Eyo to travel to Liverpool from Old Calabar, free of charge, aboard *SS Benguela*. After landing at Liverpool in October, Jones organised and paid for Eyo's travel on to Colwyn Bay and enrolment at the Institute. It seemed a real success story, generating positive publicity for both Alfred Jones and the African Institute, until it turned sour.

'The Shivering Son of Sable Sovereignty'
On his return to the Institute just before Christmas 1893 William was greeted by an unhappy Prince Eyo who presented him with a far from enthusiastic epistle:

Congo Training Institute, Colwyn Bay, 16th December1893. To the Rev W. Hughes.

Dear Sir, – I write this note to inform you that I am in very very pleasure to say no nothing make me to want to go home. I see all of you kindness to me since I have been here, nobody trouble me I got close from Mrs Hughes all what I need she give me. Since I have been here I have my meals every day for good time, when I got fever she look after me, she is very kind to me for everything and about the boys I live among them like my brethren no quarrel, all of them speak kind to me, since I have been here, the reason which I want to go home because I am not feel well about this cold, and I thought in my heart that I will not stand it because now in Africa is warm, that why I want to go home – Yours faithfully, EYO EKPENYON EYO II.'

Within weeks of his arrival in Britain the ungrateful little prince had decided that suffering slavery and destitution in Africa was preferable to enduring an education in Colwyn Bay. He also wrote to Alfred Jones begging to be taken back to Africa ... 'My Lord I don't think I will stand this cold ... I sit beside the fire all day long from morning to evening'. Jones obliged and Eyo sailed home on the 20 December 1893.

The newspapers had a field day, with the *Daily Telegraph* declaring the Prince's protestations of cold provoked 'pity as well as laughter', the *Liverpool Evening Express* described the 'amusing yet pathetic lamentations of this youthful scion of African royalty' and *The Referee* mockingly referred to Eyo as 'the shivering son of sable sovereignty'. *The Referee* was even moved to verse:

OLD CALABAR
A little Black Prince, on a winter's day,
He sat and he shivered at Colwyn Bay
He'd reckoned himself extremely cute
When he came to the Congo Institute

And so it continued for two more verses! The more strident columnists claimed the incident illustrated how the Anglo-Saxon's evidently superior strength and hardy constitution enabled them to endure and survive across a wider range of climes and continents than inferior races! But it was bad news for the Congo House enterprise. Some critics were pleased to see the Institute attract negative publicity and in an attempt at damage limitation Hughes had to assert that the climate alone was to blame when he had previously claimed that it had no negative effect on his African students.

In response, in January 1894, Hughes persuaded current student Joseph Burnley to send a supportive letter to the *Manchester Guardian* claiming Eyo:

> went home through his own foolishness and nothing else: because some of us have been here for three years and we have nothing to complain of the English [sic] winter. I am sure he would have stood it as well as any of us.

Benjamin's Curse

Prince Eyo came and went but Benjamin Evans remained a long-running pain in the neck. When Hughes got back from Africa he learned that arch-loyalist Evans of Gadlys, a Welsh member of the BMS committee had been conducting a vitriolic propaganda campaign against Congo House in the columns of *Seren Cymru*, a Welsh-language Baptist newspaper. 'No missionary belonging to us in Africa, and especially in the Congo, is in sympathy with Mr Hughes and his cause', he claimed in August 1893. Fortunately Hughes' loyal friend and colleague, Revd James Spinther James, maintained a stout defence of Hughes and the Institute before going on to the offensive and publishing Hughes's letters of 1885–6 that had been long suppressed by the BMS. Benjamin was temporarily quieted but the BMS dragon had not been slain.

Viper in the Nest

Benjamin Evans was at least a recognised critic; born in Dowlais, trained at Haverfordwest Baptist College, minister at St David's from 1871–6 and thereafter at Gadlys, Aberdare, he was also based a relatively safe distance away in south Wales; but in October and November 1893 came coruscating criticism from a purported friend. Letters published in *The Liverpool Echo* from 'A SUSCRIBER' attacked the Institute's lack of accountability, challenged its published accounts and questioned the success of its training scheme. D G Lewis countered the allegations against Congo House before the newspaper's editor formally drew the correspondence to a close.

Red Rag to a Baynes

Undeterred, the Institute's supporters rallied to the cause and Hughes campaigned with renewed vigour. At the Institute's Annual Meeting on 24 May 1894 the Committee came out fighting, the chairman, Mr W. S. Jones of Chester, uncompromisingly claiming the Congo House scheme to be the only effective model of missionary work: 'In the course of a few brief prefatory remarks he referred to the great losses the Missionary Societies had been constantly sustaining in Africa, and to the happy issue of

Mr Hughes' recent visit to Africa, and explained that the good work in training native Africans for missionary work among their brethren in their native land. Ninety-nine per cent of that missionary work must be done by the natives, and to Wales appertained the glory of being the pioneer in training natives for this work.' As if that wasn't enough to incense the BMS establishment:

> He must say a word about the relation Welshmen must stand in towards the Baptist Missionary Societies. He saw no reason why Welshmen should not have a Baptist Missionary Society of their own, and he foresaw the day when the Congo Institute would be the nucleus of such a Society.

This was a red rag to Baynes, Grenfell, Bentley and the loyalist lackeys of the London-based BMS, and the challenge to the English Baptist missionary mainstream could hardly have been more boldly stated, but it wasn't at all certain that such a clearly nationalist approach would appeal to the Institute's potential supporters in Wales.

Fanning the Flames

In April 1894 Baptist ministers were instructed to dissuade children from collecting money for Congo House by promising them a tea party if they switched their fund-raising efforts to supporting the BMS. Such animosity from London wasn't surprising but in 1895 when Hughes applied for the church he had established at the Institute to be admitted to the Welsh Baptist Gymanfa (Assembly) he was cold-shouldered by his compatriots. Bitter opposition to the Institute also surfaced at that year's Welsh Baptist Union meeting in Rhyl.

The pretext for the Rhyl dispute concerned a certain John Greenhough, whom Hughes first came across when serving as a Congo missionary in 1883. Greenhough, an African educated at the Cameroons mission, was sent to the Congo by the Baptists to help assemble the steamer *Peace*. He initially spent three months at Underhill with William Hughes, acclimatising himself before moving up to Stanley Pool. When Hughes visited West Africa again in 1893 he was surprised to be intercepted aboard *SS Nubia* by Greenhough, then in the employ of a Dutch trading company, who was accompanied by three young male relatives. Greenhough appeared well-informed about the Congo House training scheme and completely committed to Hughes' approach. According to a booklet published by the Institute, Greenhough said to Hughes:

> Really, you are the only one who is doing any good for our country and I have brought you these three boys to be educated ... Then he placed in Mr Hughes' hand altogether £236 15s saying – Do with this money as you like, but educate these boys. I want this little one to come to Colwyn Bay to be brought up to be a Doctor and be passed through Edinburgh and if this money is not enough I shall go back to the Congo to work and send you more ... It was there and then arranged that Mr Hughes should take the three boys to the Institute that he was just starting at New Calabar, West Africa where they would be trained for some time and thence taken to Colwyn Bay and the youngest of them ultimately be sent to Edinburgh ... These points John Greenhough understood perfectly well and he heartily agreed to the, repeating several times, *Do with the money as you like but educate these boys. I want no receipt from you.*

Once back in Colwyn Bay Hughes handed the funds over to the Committee and an account of the arrangement was recorded in the Institute's 1893–4 Annual Report. Throughout 1894 Greenhough kept in touch with Hughes by letter and appeared completely content, but after leaving Africa and arriving in Liverpool, on 10 February 1895 Greenhough wrote to Colwyn Bay explaining that his plans had changed. He now intended to stay in England and wanted all his money returned to finance his own activities. Hughes wrote back explaining that some of the money had already been expended and until an account could be received from Calabar it was impossible to accurately calculate costs, and inviting Greenhough to explain his claim to the

Committee in person. Unfortunately Greenhough was counselled by 'friends' more interested in destroying Hughes' reputation than achieving a peaceful compromise. Solicitors were consulted and a writ issued before reason finally intervened and a partial refund was agreed (£150 and £21 costs). The matter might have rested there if Hughes' enemies hadn't been so intent on finishing him off.

Open Warfare

Rumours of the Greenhough conflict emerged at the Rhyl meeting and to maximise the damage, an 'anonymous South Wales correspondent', almost certainly Revd Benjamin Evans (Gadlys) reproduced 30 copies of a scurrilous, one-sided account of the dispute which he then circulated by 'button-holing ministers and delegates'. The Institute countered the calumny by publishing its own comprehensive account of the whole affair, penned by Spinther James, and its supporters resolved to attack the dragon in his own lair!

As the *Manchester Guardian* of 22 November 1895 recorded:

At Aberaman, South Wales, on Tuesday evening a meeting on behalf of the Congo training Institute, Colwyn Bay, was held, when the Revd T G Williams, Llandudno, was the deputation. At the close of the meeting the Revd B Evans, Gadlys, who is the local representative of the London Baptist Missionary Society, in opposition to which, it is asserted by some, the Colwyn Bay Institute was established, – asked permission to put a few questions to the speaker; but before Mr Williams had disposed of one-half of the string of questions submitted, the congregation were in a state of frenzy and impatiently denounced the conduct of the questioner and enthusiastically manifested their sympathies with the Colwyn Bay Institute. When Mr Evans endeavoured to gain a hearing the greatest uproar ensued and the meeting had to be terminated in a disorderly manner, a crowd of youths and men following Mr Evans along the Aberdare Road, where the reverend gentleman resides, yelling hideously.

Friends and Patrons

The BMS and their agents had done their worst and the Institute had survived. Although Welsh Baptists clearly didn't all support Hughes his bitterest opponents were those who considered his scheme a rival to the official missionary model and feared the effects of growing Welsh nationalism and estrangement from the BMS. The hostility of London loyalists like Benjamin Evans (Gadlys) and Thomas Lewis (BMS) subsided after 1895 as the Institute expanded and grew ever more influential. William Hughes had apparently faced down his critics and his friends had prevailed but in the shadows embittered and determined enemies continued to scheme against him.

From the hand-to-mouth finance of the early years, by 1896 Hughes had managed to attract an annual income for the Institute of almost £2,000 (approximately £200,000 at 2012 prices). A wide network of formally constituted support committees operated in locations that included Anglesey, Beckenham, Cardiff, Cork, Dowlais, Edinburgh, Frome, Glasgow, Huddersfield, Kingstown, Lagos, Leeds, Llanelli, London, Manchester, Merthyr Tydfil, Pontypool, Pontypridd, Rhonda Valley, St. Helens, Sierra Leone, Torquay, Treorchi, Westbury.

The Institute's Official Patrons now included King Leopold II of Belgium; Sir George Williams, founder of the YMCA; Sir Alfred Jones, Director of Elder, Dempster Shipping Co. and the explorer and adventurer, Henry Morton Stanley. Besides the 'bigwigs' Hughes received encouragement and support from several leading black intellectuals who visited the Institute in this period, but before introducing them it is illuminating to consider the everyday activities and events that took place at Congo House.

Training and Education

Students were offered both academic education and industrial training at Congo House but the content and duration of courses followed at the Institute varied enormously from one student to another. Initially, in outlining his scheme Hughes recommended 'giving about four years thorough training to the most promising

RESULTS OF THE EXAMINATIONS. SESSION 1897—1898.

The marks assigned are to a maximum of 100.   Honours 80.   Pass 50.

Name of Student.	Scripture.	English Grammar.	English Composition	Geography.	Greek.	Latin.	Arithmetic.	Algebra.	Book-Keeping.	Shorthand.	Ambulance.	Average per cent.	Total No. of Marks.
SENIORS—													
Qwesi Quainoo }													
Henry Cobham }													
Ayodiji Oyejola ...	95	80	60	81	92	84	80	60	82			79½	714
Roul Van der Most...	89	63	60	96		69	85	65	72	100		77¾	699
Sujah Dowlah	73	60	72	72		65	80	25	55	100		66⅚	602
A. Wilson		58					80					69	138
JUNIORS—													
J. Boco	45	70		81			75				,	67¾	271
Lawele Tubi		66		86			80					77½	232
Waddy Saggo		62		78			75					71¾	215
Josiah*											:		
INDUSTRIAL STUDENTS													
SENIORS—													
J. R. Ekanem	82									100	100	94	282
J. P. Richards	95		74									84½	169
J. G. Lawson	71		50									60½	121
JUNIORS—													
Mosanya Osota	70	48	42						70	100		66	330
William Ballantyne...	86	60							80			75½	226
Paul Daniels	73	57							78			69½	208
Etim Duke..............	50	51							73			58	174
Latipo Thomas... ...	46	68							60			58	174
Jimsana*													

* Kwesi Quainoo has passed his preliminary Medical Examination in Edinburgh, and Henry Cobham is preparing for the same. Josiah and Jimsana came to the Institute too late for this year's Examination.

African Institute Examination Results 1897–98

of African converts', but in practice most stayed for around three years although some lasted less than a year and a handful remained for a decade. Two female students, Ernestina and Lulu, enjoyed extended stays in Colwyn Bay after they, in effect, became unofficially adopted daughters of the Hughes family as their expatriate Dutch fathers had no desire to acknowledge their illegitimate black offspring, nor return home to Holland with them. Others, such as Ishmael Pratt of Freetown and Ladipo Oluwole of Lagos studied for a decade or so in order to fully qualify as medical doctors. Most other students received a basic academic education, learnt a bit about the Bible and spent two or three years learning a trade such as carpentry, tailoring, printing or shoe-repair. All gained a basic knowledge of first aid and medicine and a few specialised in photography. Tutors were employed to teach the academic subjects and set examinations, the results of which were recorded in the Institute's annual reports. Practical skills were mainly learnt by serving apprenticeships with local tradesmen in Colwyn Bay. Students who demonstrated particular academic ability were encouraged to move on to higher education where their fees were met by the Institute. These students would then live away from Colwyn Bay during university term-time but return 'home' to the Institute for the duration of college holidays. They were also sometimes engaged on 'deputations', visiting chapels and other institutions publicising the work of the Institute.

Printing was the first specialist trade taught within the Institute itself as it not only offered good earnings potential in Africa for trained students but also provided a facility for producing advertising material, reports etc for the Institute. The printing department was developed and lavishly equipped by experienced tradesman Frederick William Bond, who was appointed in April 1899 having been highly recommended by his previous employer, *Robert Gornall & Co.* of South Castle Street, Liverpool. Eventually a thousand pounds worth of equipment was acquired with Congo House not only printing its own regular newspaper, *The Colwyn Bay Times*, but also taking in commercial work.

Garden Parties and Cricket Matches

Situated in a popular holiday resort surrounded by two acres of its own attractively planted grounds, Congo House attracted summer visitors with regular, well-advertised garden parties. Part fund-raising, part propaganda these events took place during the afternoons and early evening in July and August and typically featured a cricket match of African students versus a local school team or a party of visitors. Refreshments were provided and songs and hymns sung. The opposing cricket team, on 23 July 1896 was Plas-y-Coed School who were bowled out for 37 runs whilst 'Congo Institute' batted to an easy victory, scoring 84 runs. The following year the Africans beat Plas-y-Coed again but on that occasion both scores were lamentably poor with a victory of 9 runs to 8! Plasy-y-Coed finally got their revenge in 1898 with a score of 62 runs against the Africans 44. Turning out several times a season against various visiting teams, victories narrowly outnumbered defeats and all matches were conducted in a creditably sporting manner.

The local newspaper invariably depicted events in delightful detail, at one 1897 garden party:

The pretty little lawn which overhangs the romantic pebbly brook dingle contained a nice company of gay and happy pleasure-seekers bent upon doing justice to the festive enjoyments so well and luxuriously catered for them by the genial Director and his band of fellow workers at the Congo Institute … Other diversions help to while away the time most agreeably not the least pleasant perhaps being the balance basket which exhibited some comical freaks the results of the non-maintenance of equilibrium by the acrobatic performers and which elicited hearty roars of laughter. Tea was afterwards partaken of by the visitors, some of whom preferred the quietude of the schoolroom to partake of *the cup that cheers but not inebriates* to the mossy green cloth of Nature's broadland tables.

The North Wales Weekly News noted that at another 1897 outdoor event:

> The variegated head-gears of the ladies gave the onlooker a splendid pictorial view of a real garden-party ... tea was afterwards served on the cricket ground where a sumptuous repast of tea-table delicacies was partaken of with appetising relish. The ladies who presided at the tea-tables were ably seconded by a bevy of young ladies anxious to excel in catering qualities ... A vote of thanks having been accorded all who had partaken in the proceedings a very happy day was brought to a termination by the singing of *God Save the Queen*.'

Concerts and Entertainments

Congo House concerts generally featured a mix of amateur performers including staff, supporters and students. An interesting feature of most shows was the appearance of students not only dressed in their native costumes but also singing and reciting in African languages. In August 1898, for example, James Latayvi Agamazong Lawson, 'with native drum and dress' performed *Gba wa o Emwa* and Kwesi Quainoo sang 'in Fanti tongue and native dress, *Ayeyi* (Praises)'. But native cultures weren't always so sensitively presented: a public entertainment at Congo House in 1899 included a group of students singing The *Darkies' Dream* to a banjo accompaniment, whilst James Latayvi Agamazong Lawson's contribution to a 1897 concert was the 'sad song' *Massa's in the Cold, Cold Grave.*

In a period and place where holidaymakers chose to be entertained at the end of the pier by Troupes of Nigger Minstrels it isn't entirely surprising that Institute entertainments included racist parodies from the slave plantations. Visitors would have been more surprised to see and hear Africans performing in authentic costumes and native languages.

Occasionally professional entertainers held concerts at the Institute as a fund-raising and publicity gesture. In August 1895 The Royal Welsh Ladies Choir, led by its founder, the renowned choral conductress Clara Novello Davies (daughter of a miner

ADMISSION,—From 2.30 to 6.0 p.m., One Shilling ; After 6.0 p.m., Sixpence. Children under
Twelve, Half Price.   547—

THE AFRICAN STUDENTS'

GARDEN PARTY ..

TO BE HELD IN THE

Grounds of the African Institute, Colwyn Bay,

ON MONDAY, AUGUST 14th, 1899, Commencing at 3 p.m.

In the Afternoon a CRICKET MATCH will be played between the African
Students and Visitors, also Solos and African Hymns at Intervals.

TEA ON THE TABLES FROM 4.30 TO 6 P.M.

IN THE EVENING FROM 7 TO 8 P.M., AN ENTERTAINMENT WILL BE GIVEN,
When several well-known Friends will take part, as well as some of the African Students.
Accompanist : MR. J. BURWELL.

Admission to the Tea and Entertainment, One Shilling.   Pay at the Gate.

Several Useful and Fancy Articles will be on Sale in the Schoolroom, under the supervision of a
number of Ladies, and an interesting selection of African Curiosities will be exhibited by the Students.

PROCEEDS IN AID OF THE INSTITUTE.

Weather not permitting, Tea and Entertainment will be held in the Lecture Hall.

All who wish to spend a Pleasant Afternoon and Evening are cordially invited.

548—1

IMMENSE ATTRACTION.

African Students' Garden Party, August 1899

African Students'

ENTERTAINMENT

WILL BE HELD IN THE

Institute's Lecture Hall,

On Wednesday, December 6th, 1899, at 7 p.m.

A Varied and Attractive Programme has been provided.

Several well-known Friends, with the African
Students, will take part.

Accompanist - - MR. R. H. WILLIAMS.

Tea will be provided at 5 p.m., in connection with the Ladies'
. . . Sewing Meeting. . . .

Admission to Tea and Entertainment, 1/6;
Entertainment only, Front Seats, 1/-; Second Seats, 6d.

Pay at the Door.   Proceeds in aid of the Institute.

All who wish to spend a Pleasant Evening, are
cordially invited.   564—1

African Students' Entertainment, December 1899

and mother of Ivor Novello), gave an al-fresco performance:

> The stage, which was draped in scarlet and green and adorned
> with ivy boughs and sprays of mountain-ash in berry, had for
> background the dark green foliage of oak trees closely massed
> together. The members of the Choir were attired in their
> picturesque Welsh national costume and many of them were
> engaged in knitting scarlet stockings whilst solos were being
> rendered.

In 1898 The Treorchi Male Voice Choir performed at the
Institute delivering excellent, 'renditions of some of the most
classical musical compositions including, The Destruction of
Gaza and The Fall of Pompei. They also sang with splendid effect
Lead Kindly Light and *Beth sydd i mi yn y byd* to the tune of
Aberystwyth'.

Not the Nigger-Minstrels!
August 1898 witnessed the very acme of Institute entertainment
with the arrival of the African-American Fisk University Jubilee
Singers. The troupe performed several concerts of 'negro-
spirituals' in Colwyn Bay's Public Hall (now Theatr Colwyn), 'in
connection with the Congo African Institute'. An advertised
feature of one particular concert was a lecture delivered by the
group's director Frederick J Loudin.

As a young man growing up in America, Loudin had suffered
systematic race discrimination because of the colour of his skin.
Denied a place at the local college he trained as a printer only to
find white printers wouldn't work with him; even the local
Methodist church refused to let him join their choir. After the
civil war opened up new opportunities, as an adult he secured a
place at the all-black Fisk University in Nashville, Tennessee,
where he gained a reputation as an outstandingly popular and
talented member of the University's choir. Severely under-
funded, the university encouraged the choir to adopt a
commercial approach and charge for entrance to its concerts.
These proved so financially successful that the Fisk Singers were

soon touring internationally, introducing the world to the 'religious folk-songs of African America'. With introductions and explanations of the songs presented to the audience by Loudin these concerts were a world away from the seaside shows of the blacked-up 'nigger minstrels' more familiar to Colwyn Bay's Victorian holidaymakers.

Bazaars

Concerts often raised ten or twenty pounds, but bazaars featuring a variety of attractions and sales stalls brought in the serious money. Generally spread over a couple of days the usual venue was Colwyn Bay's Public Hall.

The ambitious target set for the September 1894 bazaar was to clear the Institute's accumulated £400 debt and when the bazaar opened at:

> half-past two on Tuesday afternoon selling proceeded very briskly for some time, so briskly, indeed, through the attractiveness of the articles on sale and through the capabilities of the bevy of ladies attached to each stall that the various stalls (six of which bore an African name) had considerably changed in appearance by the end of the first hour after opening. Not only were the various departments of work well organised but the Hall presented so attractive an appearance that those who merely came to look remained to buy.

Unfortunately the African names attached to the stalls had only the most surreal connection to the bizarre mix of items on offer:

> On the right of the Hall ... the visitor came to the *Congo Stall*. At this stall the principal features were a magnificent dressed doll which could say *Mamma* and *Papa* and a fine selection of Japanese and other oriental china.
> Adjacent was the *Cameroons Stall*. Noteworthy here were an exquisite worked wool lamp-stand, ladies shawls and other woolwork, glass model ships and a nice assortment of

macramé work.

Next came the *Calabar Stall* with the refreshment counter attached... Here almost everything good and tempting in the way of refreshments could be obtained, from poultry and ham to grapes, cakes, jellies, bread-and-butter and tea. [Doubtless, this was considered traditional fare in Old Calabar!]

The *Liberian Stall* displayed a fine selection of children's dresses and some beautiful netted work done by an old lady aged over eighty.

At the *Lagos Stall*, which came next, a great attraction was a beautiful canary and among other articles very tastefully displayed were some handsome hand-painted umbrella-stands, fancy tables, vases and a good selection of useful and fancy articles.

In the centre of the Hall cut flowers in great variety interspersed with fruit, all very tastefully arranged, were displayed at the *Accra Stall*.

As if that concatenation were not peculiar enough, 'Between the *Lagos Stall* and the door, the intervening space was devoted to a Rifle Range'.

Visitors interested in genuine African culture might, perhaps, have sought inspiration in the 'African Curiosity Room (under the charge of the African students) ... on the left side of the Hall and fronting the refreshment room' but here, apparently the main item of interest was:

the missionary-quilt sent by Mrs. T Evans, Temple of Fashion, Pontypridd, many people leaving a shilling to have the privilege of having their initials worked on some still vacant square of the quilt, which when completed will be treasured as a memento at the Congo Institution. The quilt's worked centre, a portrait of Livingstone and the names of a number of deceased African missionaries, all surmounted by the words *Africa for Christ* and surmounting the words *These all Died in Faith.*

What it lacked in progressive educational content the 1894 *Congo Institute Bazaar* also lacked in financial success. Useful though the two days proceeds of £125 proved, the takings were a mere quarter of the initial target. Still everyone seemed to enjoy themselves and it was an interesting experience for the students.

Undeterred, Hughes had another go the following year at the same venue and with a similar format. In 1895 the financial target had increased to £500 but the two-day takings only slightly increased to £150 despite the inclusion of a *Sierra Leone Stall* 'attractively draped in art muslin ... very pleasing to the beholder'. All the old favourites were there, the shooting gallery, Calabar tea-room etc, and African student, Ernestina Francis, also enterprisingly operated a bran-tub. In 1895 the *African Curiosity Room*, at least, offered some ethnographic authenticity with:

> three native Africans – Alfred Dibundu, Revd Dr Agbebi and George Fraser taking in turns the pleasing task of explaining the various curiosities from the *Dark Continent*, these curiosities including an *ndinga*, or native fiddle; an idol (*Musango*, the god of love) from Old Calabar; a tailor-bird's nest; an oxtail used as a musical conductor's baton and an enormous carved nutshell, serving the purpose of a lady's workbox.

One Death after Another

It wasn't all fun and games at Congo House and the year following William's return from Africa was the worst ever for deaths at the Institute. George Steane, student from Victoria, Cameroons passed away on Thursday 17 May 1894. Just three weeks later, on Saturday 9 June, Albert Johnstone of Sierra Leone died. Reeling from the shock of these deaths and under attack from the Baptist establishment within a further two months William Hughes had to confront the loss of his own dear wife, Katherine, aged only thirty-three. It was indeed an *annus horibilis* for all concerned.

George Steane had been at the Institute for nearly three years when he caught a severe cold that developed into pleurisy and other complications that caused his death. He was buried with due ceremony in Old Colwyn cemetery on Saturday 19 May.

Albert W. Johnstone had been advised by doctors that his health was suffering from exposure to the Welsh climate and arrangements had been made for him to return to Africa on 23 June but he expired before his due departure. Post-mortem examination revealed that 'his death took place very suddenly from obstruction in the stomach with heart disease'. Albert was buried the following Monday 11 June at Old Colwyn cemetery and like George he lies in an unmarked grave.

As reported in the Colwyn Bay newspaper, William's wife:

who never appeared to be very strong, became seriously ill some few weeks, after which she seemed partly to recover, but on Tuesday 14 August unfortunately a relapse took place when she began to gradually sink and she passed peacefully away early on Monday morning 20 August 1894. Her death can only be regarded especially by those immediately connected with the Institution as a great calamity. Her quiet disposition and gentle influence – which gave to all that she did a charm and powers that others could not have given, – will be sorely missed by her large circle of friends, but by none so much as by the family and relatives and the young African students to whom she has indeed been a mother in a strange land ... On Thursday afternoon, August 23, all that was mortal of Mrs Hughes, Congo Institute, was interred in the old Colwyn Cemetery ... The large number of letters and telegrams of condolence which came to the Institute from all parts of the country speak louder than any words of the universal respect and high esteem in which the departed was held by her very many friends, some of whom pay her memory a tribute such as few indeed obtain in this world. A large number of floral offerings, which were also sent to the Institute, bear the same testimony. Noticeable among these floral tributes of sympathy and respect was a magnificent Welsh harp (with a broken string) from the English Baptist Church.

Saddened but Supported

Many a man would have buckled at the vicious criticism and personal tragedies that Hughes faced in 1894 but determination and strength of character enabled him to push ahead with plans for extending and expanding the Institute. Whatever fate threw at him Hughes continued undaunted, ever-confident. His personal enthusiasm inspired everyone around him. Both at home and abroad knowledge of, and support for, Hughes and the Colwyn Bay scheme continued to expand at a rapid rate.

In 1894 a new support group was convened in Sierra Leone at the chambers of barrister and civic leader, Samuel Lewis, the son of liberated African slaves. In declaring its support for Hughes Lewis' committee resolved, 'to take some definite step in shewing the world our appreciation of this noble work which already is in earnest progress with beneficial results to Africa'. Although Lewis appeared to many people an Empire loyalist he carefully maintained his financial and ideological independence from the Crown. His integrity caused conflict with the governor, Colonel Frederick Cardew, whenever Lewis refused to tow the imperial line on land issues. When the imposition of a 'hut tax' in 1898 erupted into violent opposition Cardew sought to blame Lewis for the rebellion. Although this was a malicious exaggeration, Lewis might well have been responsible for apprising William Hughes of the injustice of the tax and on 7 May 1898 Hughes responded with a letter published in the *Liverpool Daily Post*:

As one who has travelled a great deal along the West and South Coasts of Africa and who takes a deep interest in every African question, I am sure you will allow me to express my opinion about the present disturbances caused by imposing on the natives the hut tax. It is, without a shadow of a doubt a great mistake to force anything against the universal feeling of the people, especially such an unreasonable thing as a tax on a hut which is of no more value than the tax itself. It is to be feared that some of our Governors are much too ready to resort to force …

Hughes' continuing contact with Africa was slowly bringing home to him the reality of colonialism – but he would soon have a more pressing problem to deal with.

Another Flaming Difficulty

'At about two o'clock yesterday (Thursday 20 October 1898) morning, a cabman named Thomas Jones was driving from (Old) Colwyn to Colwyn Bay when he observed dense volumes of smoke issuing from a large out-building standing in the grounds of the Congo Institute', reported the *Weekly News*.

> Jones immediately gave the alarm and the Fire Brigade (in command of Captain Roberts), together with Acting-Sergeant Jones and P.C. Thomas were promptly on the scene. It was discovered that the outbreak had originated in the hayloft, where a large stock of hay was stored, and that the flames were spreading rapidly. Fortunately, there was a copious supply of water, but, although the Brigade and police worked unremittingly, the building was practically destroyed, as well as its contents, which included several tables. The extent of the damage is estimated at over £100, which is partly covered by Insurance. Too much praise cannot be given to the firemen and police for their promptness and the manner in which they worked. It is unfortunate that one of the firemen had his arm broken.

Public Lectures and Sermons

Besides training and educating its students, Congo House offered lively, stimulating sermons and lectures to a wider public. In October 1895, for instance, fiery political activist and eminent historian of the Welsh Baptists, Revd James Spinther James, delivered a detailed, thought-provoking and unashamedly intellectual lecture (subsequently published in booklet form) entitled, 'Early Christianity in Africa'. Spinther's analysis asserted the primacy and antiquity of African Christianity and challenged the whole validity of the European missionary model. He claimed Africans would win back Africa from Islam, concluding:

from Abysinnia – not from any part of Europe, – will come the conquerors of Arabia and the destroyers of the Holy City of Mecca. May this not be taken as representing the fact that the power of Islam will disappear in Africa under the influence of African Christians led by African teachers?

Spinther James' talk provided a useful historical underpinning for the Congo House approach.

Some speakers took a more populist approach to their lectures. In June 1898 African-American preacher, Revd John H Hector 'popularly known as *The Black Knight*' delivered a series of well-attended sermons:

> By his eloquence, humour and pathos he gained a very warm place in the hearts of the congregations. Mr Hector as a preacher is characteristically himself; his teachings parabolic and his style Spurgeonic. His denunciatory remarks on the sins of the age which were sandwiched in between his witty sayings and pathetic anecdotes were as pure as the free air of his native mountains and as healthy as his own superb physique ... On Monday evening, the Revd J Hector delivered a most interesting lecture entitled, *The Thrilling Story of my Early Life*. The chair was occupied by the Revd W Hughes ... The lecture itself was well fitted to the title as thrilling indeed was the tale told of his parents' bold dash for liberty from the bonds of slavery and how when pursued in close proximity by a pack of bloodhounds they found refuge in a hay-stack and were providentially preserved, in answer to prayer, until they reached Canada, the land of liberty and freedom under the British flag. The eloquence and descriptive powers of the lecturer were marvellous.

William Hughes occasionally gave public talks himself, such as that delivered at the Institute on 2 November 1898 when:

> The subject of the lecture which was illustrated with lime-light views was *African Travels and Experiences*. In the course of his

interesting remarks the lecturer drew upon his three years experience of life on the Congo and the description of his travels into the interior were also very interesting. Admirable photographs were exhibited of Dr Livingstone, Dr Moffatt, Bishop Crowther, Mr H M Stanley, General Gordon, the Sirdar, the Khalifa, Neufield (for thirteen years a prisoner of the Khalifa), Cecil Rhodes and his great railway scheme, President Kruger and other notabilities connected with the Christianising and development of South Africa. Mr Hughes had much that was instructive to say about the English and French at Fashoda, Rhodes' railway from Cairo to Cape Town and President Kruger's treatment of the English.

An Intellectual Hub

The Institute not only supplied industrial training to students but exercised a wider role in linking institutions and individuals involved in developing radical ideas on African education. Conveniently located, close to Liverpool, the key maritime inter-change of traffic from both America and West Africa, the Institute attracted interested black activists from both sides of the Atlantic. Numerous African and African-American intellectuals included visits to Congo House in their trips to Britain and several enjoyed extended stays at the Institute. Foremost amongst them was Mojola Agbebi, who spent six months at the Institute in 1895 and whose relationship with Hughes extended over two decades. A descriptive eulogy to Agbebi was published in *The Lagos Standard* just prior to his departure for Colwyn Bay.

Among the intellectual, moral and religious creations of the Colony of Lagos the above named gentleman holds a prominent place ... He is well known as an author, poet, writer, preacher, lecturer, patriot ... Dr Agbebi is well known in the United States as a writer on the Race Problem and as an advocate of the African Exodus. He has come in personal and epistolary contact with most of the late great minds of his race in Africa and America. He belongs to the Ekiti tribe and was born of poor parentage in the interior of Yorubaland on 10

117

April 1860.As a reformer and patriot he has been most
practical, determined, aggressive and exemplary. As a Poet he
has written one of the most phenomenal pieces ever
attempted in West Africa. As a Lecturer he has been most
observant and philosophical. As a Preacher he does not take a
back rank among the preachers of the colony. As a Public
Writer and an unflagging supporter of the press, he wields a
trenchant pen and his composition is delightful. He seldom
writes in vain; his arrows tell. As a Religionist he has organized
independent churches and schools and is not weighed down
by denominational cant or sectarian bias. Of late years and in
keeping with his published ideas and utterances he has
(having been formerly known as David Brown Vincent)
assumed his original and native names of Mojola Agbebi and
adopted a costume more eastern and African in style and
character.

Agbebi, like Hughes, was an evangelist who rejected the racism
and hierarchy of the Baptist establishment and created alternative
organisations better suited to promote 'the essentials of
Christianity'. In 1888 Agbebi, with Moses Ladejo Stone, had
founded the first independent African church in Lagos in
response to Stone's unwarranted dismissal by arrogant expatriate
senior missionary Revd W. J. David. In 1889 Hughes had formally
constituted the *Congo Institute* having been effectively dismissed
by the BMS for his refusal to return to Africa. The close and
enduring relationship between Hughes and Agbebi reflected the
shared vision of the African education and Christian mission both
had arrived at by 1895 and the degree to which Hughes' own
ideas had developed since his initial response to hearing tales of
Stanley's exploits in the little chapel at Capel y Beirdd twenty
years earlier. Chastened by his physical and intellectual
experiences of serving with the BMS in the Congo and
enlightened by a further decade of sharing his life and home with
a 'family' of Africans Hughes had arrived at a mature, respectful
yet challenging attitude to Africa and its native cultures. Hughes's
continuing conflict with fellow Baptists was no mere 'personality

clash' or rivalry over missionary funding, he saw Africans differently. The prevailing British view of black people at the time is authoritatively summarised by the 1911 edition of the *Encyclopaedia Britannica*:

> The Negro in certain characteristics ... would appear to stand on a lower evolutionary plane than the white man, and to be more closely related to the anthropoids ... Mentally the negro is inferior to the white ... a less voluminous brain, as compared with the white races ... the arrest or even deterioration in mental development is no doubt very largely due to the fact that after puberty, sexual matters take the first place in the negro's life and thoughts ... the mental constitution of the negro is very similar to that of the child, normally good-natured and cheerful but subject to sudden fits of emotion and passion, during which he is capable of performing acts of singular atrocity, impressionable, vain, but often exhibiting in the capacity of a servant a dog-like fidelity which has stood the supreme test.

In contrast, Hughes considered Africans as intellectually equipped and capable as any European, as he explained in *Dark Africa and the Way Out*:

> Not only do we think of Africa as a rich and valuable county but we think highly of her people. The Africans only need knowledge, proper treatment and opportunity. Africans as a rule, are keen, deep and sharp; they are also of a genial nature and have any amount of patience, which is no small virtue. They have their full share of good qualities.

Hughes was no revolutionary, but to colleagues schooled in the racist ideology of the British Empire his approach appeared challenging and subversive.

Agbebi had read *Dark Africa* and shared Hughes' rejection of racist ideology but as a black man his criticism was more heartfelt and direct, with less reluctance to lay the blame:

The African is no big child, no child-race, according to the current expression of some Europeans; but a fully fledged man, in the eternal providence of God. He may be a child in terms of European greed and aggrandisement, European subtlety and guile, European trespasses and sins; but he is not a child to his creation or to the law of his being.

As early as February 1885, in a debate at the Lagos YMCA, Agbebi had attacked the rapacious European 'Scramble for Africa' and he scorned the spurious 'scientific' justification for racism yet, like Hughes, Agbebi retained his faith in the liberating power of the Christian mission:

It was adventurous Europe, under the title of *Anthropological Society* that placed us, the inhabitants of this good land, in the category of the brute creation; but it was Missionary Europe that proved us men.

Mojola Agbebi (1860–1917)

Mojola Agbebi left Africa aboard the *SS Bonny* on 12 April 1895. Arriving at Congo House in early May he addressed the Institute's Annual meeting at the Public Hall, Colwyn Bay, on the evening Monday 27 May, dressed 'in his native African attire'. This, like the rejection of his old European name the previous year, was a consciously political act as he once explained to a white missionary in Lagos:

Every African bearing a foreign name is like a ship sailing under false colours and every African wearing a foreign dress in his country is like a jackdaw in peacock's feathers.

Agbebi, who 'addressed himself to (as he prefaced his remarks by saying) not 'Ladies and Gentleman' but 'Brothers and Sisters', said that:

far away in West Africa they had heard of the Congo Institute in Wales ... He wished that he could make his audience realise the difference there was between the way people lived in Africa and the civilisation in Colwyn Bay and how the people of West Africa rejoiced to hear of the foundation of Mr Hughes' Institute. There had been in West Africa missionaries sent forth by the Church of England, the Wesleyans, the Baptists and the Presbyterians but in the Christianity nourished by these bodies of Christians there seemed something wanting and that something seemed supplied in the Congo Institute's missionary scheme – and by the turning back again to the Apostolic plan of combining industrial work and the preaching of the Gospel – by the establishment of Industrial Schools. And so the Africans looked to Wales for the Christianisation of Africa – Wales the land which had come to the forefront at the moment when the other agencies were being found wanting. On behalf of the brethren in Africa the speaker besought help given through the Institute founded by Mr Hughes who in West Africa was regarded as a hero.

Before resuming his seat, Agbebi sang, in Yoruba, a hymn from Africa that voiced the devotion of the Africans themselves and not one that merely rendered in an African language some of the religious sentiments of Europeans.

Mojola's presentation was a miniature masterpiece of black consciousness-raising and his enduring relationship with Hughes underlined the radical approach of the Congo House Scheme.

Although Agbebi frequently delivered well-advertised talks during his stay at the Institute he also visited other parts of Britain. In June he delivered a lecture to the Swedenborg Society in London, reminding its members of the pioneering industrial education practiced by its early missionaries and regrettably since abandoned and recommending their 'unstinted support and sympathy for the African Institute at Colwyn Bay'.

He also spoke at Manchester and Birmingham, and during a week spent attending the annual Keswick Convention, in the Lake District, he was able to meet many of the most thoughtful British Christian thinkers of the era.

In August he was back again preaching in Colwyn Bay and on one particularly fine Sunday afternoon, accompanied by some of the African students, Agbebi held an open air prayer meeting alongside the fountain that stood at the top of Station Road. The irony of the event didn't escape the *Weekly News*: 'it was touching to hear these Africans from that far Dark Continent pleading with the privileged English to come to Christ'!

A farewell meeting for Agbebi was held at the Institute on 1 October and on 12th he left Liverpool on the *SS Batunga* 'laden with gifts and good wishes' and accompanied by John Ricketts and returning student Henry Cobham.

John Edward Ricketts (1857–1908)

Prior to his departure, outspoken Jamaican missionary John Edward Ricketts (1857–1908) had been staying at Colwyn Bay and sharing a lecture platform with Agbebi. Like Hughes, Ricketts had previously served in the Congo, having, in 1887, been posted by the ABMU to Mukumvika, a small village located at the mouth

Mr and Mrs Ricketts, 1896

of the Congo river. His co-worker at Makumvica was Theophilus Scholes but the pair soon violently disagreed over the running of the mission station. After publicly assaulting each other in front of the congregation each wrote to the ABMU secretary complaining of the other's intolerable behaviour. The village elders supported Ricketts and begged for Scholes to be replaced but, in early 1890, it was Ricketts that requested a transfer and was accordingly posted 300 km inland to Lukunga. After a period peacefully cooperating with Reverend Hoste, head of the Lukunga mission, the relationships deteriorated and in 1893 Ricketts was dismissed by the ABMU because of an, 'inability to avoid serious disagreements with his fellow-workers' (although Katja Fullberg-Stolberg suggests the ABMU's increasingly racist outlook is a more likely explanation). Despite his controversial reputation Ricketts bonded well with both Agebebi and Hughes and relationships forged in Colwyn Bay endured for many years with both continuing to correspond with the Institute, and Agbebi returning for another extended stay in 1904.

On the three-week voyage out to Africa Ricketts studied Yoruba under Agebebi's tutelage. Arriving in Lagos on Saturday 8 November 1895 Agbebi encouraged Ricketts to start an industrial mission in the southwestern region of Nigeria. With the support of the local ruler, Prince Ademuyiwa Haarstrup, Ricketts found a suitable place in the little town of Agbowa, where he rapidly erected a house and church and perfected his knowledge of Yoruba. On 1 February 1896 Ricketts was able to open the doors of the *Agbowa Industrial Mission* and accounts of his progress were despatched to Colwyn Bay where they were occasionally printed in the *Weekly News*.

Ricketts, Agbebi and Hughes were united in their advocacy of 'practical salvation' through the propagation of industrial missions. Rickett's mission raised a variety of crops; bananas, coffee, sugar and cocoa, not only for the community's own consumption but also for sale at markets as far away as Lagos. The Congo House philosophy was reflected at Agbowa where in Rickett's own words (as published in the *Lagos Standard*):

The people will be converted to the Lord and the children of the Land will be able to receive an Elementary education and at the same time be trained to become better farmers, carpenters, and in other useful arts. The object of this mission is to become self-supporting as early as possible so as not to depend on foreign support. And in order to effect this, beside teaching the people Christianity I also teach industry in the way of both scientific and practical agriculture and carpentry and joinery.

Ademuyiwa Haastrup, Prince of Jebu Remo, West Africa

Ademuyiwa Haastrup

In August 1896 Ricketts' Nigerian sponsor, Prince Ademuyiwa Haarstrup of Jebu Remo, Yorubaland visited the African Institute to inspect and support the Colwyn Bay model of industrial education:

On Thursday 20th August 1896 the African students' garden party at the Congo Institute was more than ordinarily attractive. The town turned out to greet the exotic visitor. A large crowd gathered at the railway station where the Prince was met by the Revd W H Hughes who

TELEGRAPHIC ADDRESS:
"PATRIOTISM." LAGOS.

Edwin Jones, Esq.,
Carriage Proprietor.
COLWYN BAY.

My dear Sir,

TANIMEHIN HOUSE,
WEST COAST OF AFRICA

COLWYN BAY,
August 27th, 1896.

I am exceedingly grateful to you for your great kindness and attendance which you have shown me in driving me backwards and forwards by your four-in-hand coach during my visit to Colwyn Bay for the good of the Congo Institute established in this town. In assisting me, you have been assisting Mr. Hughes and my country--Africa. Personally, I am not in want of any assistance, but, nevertheless, I feel it is for me inasmuch as it has been done for the good of my country.

I have been highly pleased with the conduct of your servants, and with your beautiful horses and coach.

You have the liberty of using my coat-of-arms.

I remain, dear Sir, yours faithfully,

ADEMUYIWA, PRINCE of Jebu Remo, West Africa

Letter from Haastrup, Lagos thanking Edwin Jones, Colwyn Bay

conducted him to the well-horsed four-in-hand coach *Ye Olde Times*, a handsomely yet quietly liveried coach-conductor being in close attendance. The Prince, who wore a dark red head-dress adorned with gold lace and a cream-coloured robe richly embroidered in gold and other colours, one of the devices being a peacock in natural colours, mounted to the box-seat alongside Mr Edwin Jones ... In front of the coach marched the Penrhynside Band playing appropriate musical selections and the streets were lined with the visitors and residents in acknowledgement of whose hearty cheers his Royal Highness graciously bowed.

At the Congo Institute the Revd W Hughes said that the Prince had come with one errand to North Wales and had cancelled all his engagements till the following Tuesday to give his support to the Institute ... at about six o'clock the announced address was given by HRH who said that he was eighteen when he went to school first and he had five years schooling; he therefore begged his hearers to pardon him if he murdered the Queen's English. He urged them not to be weary in well-doing and explained that he was the result of missionary enterprise. In that Colwyn Bay Institute they were doing good work for the Africans and whatever they gave willingly he knew they would receive tenfold in return. The Welsh were doing well in training the Africans to be independent ... He urged his hearers to give more than moral support to the missionary enterprise of the Revd Mr Hughes.

During his stay at Colwyn Bay Prince Ademuyiwa Haastrup, accompanied by Hughes, made official visits to Rhyl, Llandudno, Bangor and Holyhead where he spoke, at each place, in support of the African Institute. At the conclusion of his stay Haastrup wrote thanking Edwin Jones for his generous provision of coaching facilities and granting the use of his royal warrant.

Robert B. Richardson (b.1851)

As well as the trio of Nigeria-based contacts that visited Colwyn Bay in 1895–6 came Revd Robert B Richardson, President of The

Ricks Institute, Liberia. William Hughes had visited Richardson at the *Ricks Institute* in 1893 when a friendship developed around their shared interest in the value of industrial training for Africa. Richardson attended the *African Institute*'s Annual Meeting at Colwyn Bay's Public Hall on Tuesday 2 June 1896 where he explained, 'that he had a very pleasant duty which he felt it an honour to perform and that was to convey to the Revd W Hughes, FRGS, Principal of the Congo Institute, Colwyn Bay, the following message from the President of the Liberian republic, West Africa:

> Department of State, Monrovia, April 29, 1896. Sir, – The President of the Republic (Joseph James Cheeseman), who has followed with much pleasure your efforts for the spread of education, civilisation and religion in West Africa, has directed me to transmit to you, through the Revd R B Richardson, a Diploma appointing you a Knight Official of the Liberian Order of African Redemption, in recognition of your labours, which I am to express the hope will be crowned with abundant and ever increasing success – and I have the honour to be sir, your obedient servant, Arthur Barclay, Secretary of State.

Describing the diploma as 'a work of art', the *Weekly News* saw it as a sign of the 'appreciation with which the Africans themselves regard the noble and un-wearying efforts which Mr Hughes is making on behalf of their long neglected land'.

Throughout the summer of 1896 Robert Richardson was a frequent and enthusiastic speaker at both the Institute's Public Hall sermons and garden parties held in the grounds of Congo House, and after he returned to Liberia in August he kept in contact with Hughes.

John Augustus Aboyami-Cole (1846–1943)

Following the visit of M. T. G. Lawson, Honorary Secretary of the Institute's Sierra Leone support committee, to Colwyn Bay in 1897 came fellow committee member John Aboyami-Cole

(1846–1943), one of Sierra Leone's most challenging and original thinkers. Priest, politician, author, agriculturist, herbalist and administrator, John Augustus Aboyami-Cole was educated in Freetown, Sierra Leone and ordained in America before qualifying as a medical doctor and becoming an affiliate of the National Association of Medical Herbalists of the United Kingdom. Returning to Sierra Leone in 1887 he was appointed superintendent of the Maroon Chapel, before fashioning his own brand of religion and founding an

Dr Aboyami Cole and his Gospel Banner Hall, *Sierra Leone*

independent African Church at the Gospel Mission Hall, Freetown, where a variety of ethnic groups congregated to worship. Fluent in Arabic, sympathetic to Islam and well-versed in the beliefs and rituals of all sort of esoteric secret societies, his

127

piety prompted some amused sceptics to refer to him as 'Jesus-passing-by'.

Dr Aboyami-Cole combined his scientific medical knowledge with a life-long study of the traditional use of herbs, roots and leaves. This unique understanding of both European and African approaches enabled him to offer a variety of highly effective treatments and gained him widespread admiration amongst both his peers and his patients.

His practical skills famously included the commercial farming of ginger, cocoa, corn, cassava and yams as well as the production of sugar, palm oil, soap and the distillation of spirits. These interests prompted him to found the Sierra Leone Farmers Association in 1909 and the Agricultural Society in 1922.

He was a regular contributor to the *Sierra Leone Weekly News*, and the *Dictionary of African Christian Biography* (DACB) notes 'that his name is to be found associated with almost all the major political movements of his day'. Dr Aboyami-Cole was fearless in defending the rights of fellow Africans against the racial arrogance and injustice of the Colonial administration and the DACB records that documents 'in the Public Record Office (National Archive) in London are full of complaints by the British authorities about his activities'.

Aboyami-Cole had written to Congo House on 9 January 1898 from Freetown arranging his anticipated trip to Colwyn Bay, complimenting Hughes on his missionary scheme and denouncing the work of the missionary societies:

> You are working on God's plan ... I must confess boldly, that the method in which the Christian religion is introduced and sustained in Africa for the past 300 years is false and unapostolic. It is a trade system. It is a method by which the Negro is detained in spiritual slavery, he cannot propagate nor sustain the religion because it is not his own. Churches are retained as landed property by the Missionary Societies, under a system of religious speculation. Africa looks to you for her future leaders in independent thought and the simple religion of Christ without priestcraftism, despots – and gorgeousness

... I am an eclectic medical doctor – I make my living practising organic medicine so that I can preach free of cost to anyone, I enjoy it. It is Pauline and I am exceedingly happy to believe that you are struggling to make many of my countrymen to be so also. If there is any way I can assist your work- either in Europe or America – as a lecturer – count on me.

Dr Aboyami-Cole stayed with Hughes at Congo House from July 1898 until September, delivering regular public sermons and lectures and a couple of times contributing 'An African Marriage Ceremony' party-piece to the Institute's evening 'entertainments', 'which caused a great deal of hilarity and amusement'.

Hallie Quin Brown (1850–1949)
On 10 November 1899, the *Weekly News* reported:

Miss Hallie Q Brown, the justly celebrated Afro-American lecturer and reciter has been paying Colwyn Bay a very welcome visit. After speaking at the three services at the African Institute on Sunday, Miss Brown addressed a meeting at Engedi CM Church. There was a large congregation, representative of nearly all the Free Churches in the town, prominent amongst them being many well-known old friends of the Institute. Dr Roger Edwards the Hon. Surgeon to the Institute occupied the chair and a big pew was occupied by the African students. After a brief introduction by Dr Edwards, Miss Brown delivered a very eloquent address, describing the rise and progress of Wilberforce College, an American institution erected principally for the education of coloured people. After the address, a collection was taken, the proceeds to be divided between Wilberforce College and the Colwyn Bay African Institute. Miss Brown, by the way, spoke with admiration of the splendid work and noble work for Africa which the Revd W Hughes is carrying on. Miss Brown also rendered a slave melody and gave a recitation, her powers as a singer and elocutionist being of a rare order.

Extensions to the Institute erected alongside Myrtle Villa

Hallie Brown also spoke and performed at the Institute during the following week allowing the students and Colwyn Bay public further opportunity to gain a rare insight into the ideas and experiences of a black feminist activist of the Victorian era.

Born in Pittsburgh, Pensylvania, the daughter of two former slaves, after graduating from Wilberforce College in 1873, Hallie Brown (1850–1949) went on to teach on the Senora Plantation in Mississippi. Teaching at a series of plantations her main concern was raising the literacy levels of black youth denied a proper education by slavery and prejudice. In 1892 she was appointed Dean of Women at the Tuskegee Institute where she worked with Booker T. Washington.

Hallie Brown's feminist commitment to black education and civil rights extended into the wider political realm. She was the prime mover of the Colored Women's League of Washington DC and the founder of the National Association of Colored Women. She also participated in conferences abroad, including: Convention of World's Women Christian Temperance Union (London, 1895); International Congress of Women (as US Representative – London, 1899) and African Methodist Conference (Edinburgh, 1910).

The Future Looks Promising
Thomas Lewis Johnson and Theophilus Scholes also made lengthy return visits to Colwyn Bay during these dynamic and influential days of the African Institute, when future growth seemed unstoppable. Over the previous decade Congo House's annual income had increased from £80 to almost £2,000, student numbers had gone up from two to around twenty, the physical size of the college had doubled with the erection of an adjacent building, the Institute's list of Patrons had grown in both length and pre-eminence, and Congo House's field of operations had expanded from just the Congo to include the Gambia, Sierra Leone, Liberia, Ghana, Nigeria, Cameroon, Congo, Angola, South Africa and even 'African-America'.

Business was booming, but it was also a decade during which five students had perished in Colwyn Bay and William Hughes had suffered the traumatic loss of both his infant daughter and his dear young wife Katie. Fortunately, as the end of the century approached William could draw some comfort from the fact that there had at least been no further loss of life since Katie had died in 1894. More likely he was preoccupied planning his imminent marriage to a lady from Ashton-under-Lyne.

Chapter Seven

'Afric's Sons Welcome You Both'
(Autumn 1899)

Five years after Katie's death the Reverend William Hughes, founder and director of the African Institute confided to close family and friends in Colwyn Bay that he was about to remarry. His intended, Bessie Hutton Clarke, conducted a modest 'missionary' enterprise in the Manchester area where she taught classes at the Mission Room, York Street, Charlestown, Ashton-under-Lyne. A quiet Church of England ceremony was organised in Ashton, but back home in Wales, the staff and students of Congo House planned a spectacular reception.

The Bride-to-Be

News of William Hughes' marriage to Bessie came as a complete surprise to the townsfolk of Colwyn Bay. Usually William arranged advance publicity for any event likely to attract public attention and increase interest and support for Congo House. On this occasion he only tipped off the newspapers after the event. Only invited guests were informed beforehand and the bride-to-be hadn't so much as set foot inside the Institute before she married its director.

Aged fifty-one, Bessie Hutton Clarke was eight years older than William Hughes and unlike William, she hadn't been married before. Born in 1848 in the Horton district of Bradford, England, to a John Hutton, master tailor and his wife, Hannah, she was the elder of two little daughters who were separated and adopted by different families as young children. Bessie went to live with gas fitter David Clarke and his wife Ann and two young sons, David and William, in Oldham, Lancashire where she attended school. As David Clarke ascended the ranks of the fledgling gas industry the family moved from Oldham to Glossop and on to Ashton-Under-Lyne. In 1881 Bessie was a domestic

Stanley, Claudia and Katie, August 1899

servant, still living at home with David in Ashton, where he was manager of the local gasworks. David's wife Ann, who was fourteen years older than him when they married, had since died, and the other children had left home. Bessie's surname at this stage was still formally recorded as Hutton and David, then aged forty-six, was described as her step-father. The two of them then lived at Handel Place, Fraser Street, Ashton-under-Lyne.

By 1899 Bessie's step-father, David, was dead and out of respect for his memory she had added his surname to her own. On 30 August 1899 she signed the marriage register as 'Bessie Hutton Clarke, 51, spinster, of Fernlea, Taunton Road, Ashton'.

'Marriage of the Revd W. Hughes, Congo Institute'

On 1 September 1899 the *Weekly News* brought news of the ceremony to the residents of north Wales:

A wedding of great interest to Colwyn Bay took place at Christ Church, Ashton-under-Lyne, on Wednesday morning, the ceremony being performed by the Vicar of the parish. The contracting parties were the Revd W Hughes, FRGS, the well-known Director of the African Institute, Colwyn Bay, and Miss Bessie Hutton Clarke, daughter of the late D Clarke Esq, for many years a prominent and respected citizen of Ashton-under-Lyne. The ceremony was witnessed by many friends, prominent among whom was the Revd Mark C Hayford, who attended as the representative of the black race, in whose midst Mr Hughes has been instrumental in doing such good and noble work. The bride was attended by five bridesmaids – Miss Lizzie Williams, Tanllan, Llanelian; the Misses Claudia and Katie Hughes, daughters of the bridegroom, and his adopted daughters, the Misses Lulu and Ernestina Hughes, all wearing dresses of cream and leghorn hats and looking exceedingly pretty. Dr Hugh Jones, Festiniog, brother-in-law of the bridegroom, acted as best man. After a *recherché* wedding breakfast, the Revd and Mrs W Hughes left for their honeymoon tour ... It is noteworthy that Mrs Hughes has at her own expense carried on Home Mission work on a very extensive scale at Ashton-under-Lyne and has evinced keen interest in mission work generally and especially in the African Institute, so that she will prove a worthy help-mate to the respected Director, who is himself so full of missionary zeal.

Details of the wedding arrangements reveal a lot about William and his new bride. Whilst the ceremony took place on Bessie's home ground, her side of the wedding party are notable by their absence. If she had friends accompanying her they were neither mentioned by the press nor registered as witnesses (all five of whom were William's associates). Though the pair shared a devotion to missionary work, Bessie's brand of Christianity was restrained, unemotional and pious, while William's approach was daring, adventurous and celebratory. She was respected, William was loved.

William's choice of bridesmaid was heart-warmingly inclusive, with the African girls, Lulu and Ernestina, dressed and treated in identical fashion to his birth daughters and niece. The 'prominence' accorded Mark Hayford as 'representative of the black race' was similarly distinctive and daring (within the context of the period).

An Interesting Guest

One of the wedding guests was Mark Christian Hayford, an enigmatic character whose fascinating career would eventually find uncanny parallels with the fate of William Hughes, but in 1899 both their futures looked rosy. Born in the Gold Coast in 1864, Mark and his two brothers, Casely and Ernest, all achieved a degree of fame and success. Casely was a barrister and dedicated pan-African, Edward a medical doctor, whilst Mark pursued a religious career with the Baptists.

Having been baptised, ordained and heavily influenced in Africa by Mojola Agbebi, in 1898 Mark Hayford founded the first independent African Church in Ghana. In 1899 Hayford was visiting Britain not only to attend Hughes' wedding but also to raise funds for the erection of a grand church for his Ghanaian congregation. In contrast to the basic shelters constructed from local materials that satisfied most promoters of independent native churches, such as Aboyami-Cole, Hayford aspired to a grand European-style gothic edifice. This seemed a little at odds with William Hughes' generally self-sufficient approach but it wasn't for William to decry his African friend's ambition. Whilst in England Hayford also befriended Alfred Jones, whose sponsorship facilitated his voyage to Canada. From there he toured the United States, before returning to Britain. With ready cash collected and future funds assured by donors, Hayford placed orders for building materials and in 1902 returned to Africa in triumph.

As Hughes would later learn, everything didn't quite go according to plan.

'For the Benefit of the Readers of the *Weekly News*'

Although Hughes kept quiet about his nuptials before the event, once married he rapidly returned to form and 'for the benefit of the readers of the *Weekly News*' he despatched details of the progress of his honeymoon tour back to Colwyn Bay, for as he obsequiously observed, 'we exist for the sake of others':

We left London – Holborn Viaduct – on Saturday September 2nd, at 8.30 am, reached Queensborough by 10 am and crossed the channel to Flushing in Holland by 5 pm. On landing we immediately started by train, through Holland and parts of Germany for Cologne, which is situated on the banks of the Rhine. Holland presented a beautiful site [*sic*] as we passed through. It was a cool clear evening, after a heavy shower of rain. Everything was in its full bloom. It is a flat, but fertile country, and it was interesting to notice the small country houses, which were all very neat and tasty [*sic*]. Their houses, farms, together with their personal appearances, confirmed my previous idea and knowledge of the cleanliness and industry of all Dutch people. We must confess as in visiting America that their mode and conveniences of travelling are before ours, for we had a corridor train with every comfort all the way from Flushing to Cologne. We reached the latter place after a long but interesting journey, by 12 o'clock at night. Cologne is a beautiful town and has a long and intensely interesting history. But, as this is only a very brief account of our journey, I cannot mention more than two or three matters.

'An Eyesore to Every Frenchman'

The two things which make Cologne famous and popular are first the beautiful spot on which it stands, namely the bank of the Rhine; therefore it is the attraction of thousands continually, especially in the summer months. The Rhine is the sea of the Germans and their chief watering-place. The second thing that makes the place so well known is its Cathedral, this being a magnificent building. It is much higher than St. Paul's in London and I believe more beautiful than the Lichfield Cathedral. It was built in its primitive form in the ninth century but was destroyed by the Normans. It has been built and destroyed several times from that period until the present century. The events of the Reformation, the severe defeats of 30 years of war, all combined to draw the town and the Cathedral from the pinnacle of their glory, till finally in 1794 the French put an end to its independence, confiscating its property and wealth. Many valuable antiquities were destroyed by them and the bronze tombs of the Archbishops were melted. The Church was turned to the use of storing provisions for the French and later prisoners of war were kept there, but in the Franco-German War of 1870-71; the Germans repaid their foes. The Emperor remembered the melting process of 1794 and ordered some of the cannons captured from the French to be melted and formed into the most magnificent bells of the Cologne Cathedral, which are there in use at the present moment, and are an eyesore to every Frenchman. Every Emperor has taken interest in this Cathedral and thus it has become the pride of the nation. Grants have been given by the Government for its restoration and building until it has now reached its present completeness and glory. It was enjoyable to watch the Germans worshipping in this Church on Sunday, most of them singing as heartily as Welsh people do, and that without hymn books. The tunes, one would say, must have been well known to them. They also appear to be very homely and sincere. The population of Cologne is half a million. Their gardens, galleries and other places of amusement are numerous and attractive. The main industries are the *Rhine Wine* and the well-known perfume *Eau de Cologne*.

'Berlin is a Lovely City'

We left Cologne on Tuesday at 12.40 for Berlin, and reached the latter place by 10.30 at night, after a long but pleasant journey. This afforded an excellent opportunity to see the country, which like Holland, is very flat, with the exception of a small hill here and there. There is much similarity in the scenery, the customs of the people and the buildings. Oxen are found in both countries, working in the fields, as often as horses, and the women cultivating, mowing and gathering the crops as numerically as the men. Their cottages are small, built, I believe, that way by the men on purpose to prevent the women having an excuse for house work, in order to have their assistance in the fields. I fear that our farmer brothers in Germany approach too much in this respect the uncivilised countries and that they are inclined to be too severe on the weaker vessel. We noticed some women cutting the corn with a scythe and others mowing the second crop of hay, sharpening their instruments as skilfully and consequentially as any man. We saw others carrying heavy loads and a man sometimes walking quite near without any. The towns of Germany approach the English towns in appearance, some more than their farmers and country those of ours. My feeling, after an interesting inspection is that the farmers and workmen need more education and attention. Berlin is a lovely city which has a wonderful history. Her palaces and monuments are very valuable and famous. We have seen here a great many wonders which cannot be mentioned in a short article of this description. We visited the graves of the two last

Emperors and Queens, and had the privilege of going through the grand palace of the present Emperor. Their works-of-art in their *National Gallery* are beyond anything we have seen before in this respect. My conviction is, after my visit to Berlin and other parts of Germany, that the German nation is industrious and ambitious. Their developments in various ways during the last 30 years have been amazing. Great Britain must be on the alert, otherwise she will be surpassed by Germany and America. Where have we been so long in making the proper use of electricity and other modern inventions? London is still without even the electric tram. I am glad that our modern and rising Colwyn Bay can soon boast of its electric light and tram, with its Pier and Pavilion. The victory of the Germans over the French, in 1870-71, who had kept them down for centuries, has created in them a new union and energy. Only to refer to France and the last war, brings out sparks of fire from the eyes of even the children who were not born when that struggle took place. The monuments of this victory in Berlin are impressive and costly. We met in this city, friends of Africa, who are carrying on an Institution similar to our own, by training the natives in Germany and sending them back to their Colonies. With these we exchanged thoughts and the information both sides, was very acceptable. The progress of Protestant religion is on the increase in the land. We visited one Church of 1,200 members in the city. We left Berlin on Friday, and after three hours arrived at a place called Heidelberg, by the sources of the Rhine. We have crossed the rivers Ems, Wiser, Elbe, Main and Rhine.

Tomorrow (Tuesday 12th September) we hope to sail down the Rhine again to Cologne, then to Antwerp, Brussels, Holland and home.

'Home-coming of the Revd and Mrs W. Hughes'
On Monday 18 September 1899 the newly-weds returned:

to Colwyn Bay (and the columns of the *Weekly News*) from

their honeymoon tour on the Continent, and were given a most hearty *Welcome Home*. They were met at the railway station by the Reverend E Jones Davies and the Revd T G Williams, of the Institute, and driven to their home. On arriving there they discovered that the whole of the grounds had been highly decorated in their honour. Spanning the two entrance gates was the motto, *Welcome Home*, whilst over the threshold of the house was another very striking greeting, *Afric's Sons Welcome You Both*. The lawn and garden were gay with streamers and bunting and everywhere was there to be discerned an air of joy and welcome and festivity…As Mr and Mrs dismounted from their carriage a hearty cheer went up from the throats of the staff and students, and the beloved Principal and his wife were deluged with showers of confetti.

'Within the Cosy Lecture Hall of the Institute'

At six o'clock, a large crowd of invited guests assembled within the cosy lecture hall of the Institute, where a *conversazione* was given with the object of welcoming Mr and Mrs. The interior of the hall was most tastefully decorated with flowers and evergreens, whilst on the walls were mottoes, *Welcome Home* and *Long Life and Happiness*. The effect produced by the various colours was pretty in the extreme. The gathering was an exceedingly happy one and as Mr Hughes entered this scene of some of his labours, together with Mrs Hughes, he was naturally affected by the cheery welcome.

After this hilarity the bridal pair held a reception. A most enjoyable repast was provided and thoroughly enjoyed. The chair was taken by the Revd Benjamin Evans, chairman of the Institute Executive Committee, who in the course of a short address, said it was as a successful missionary they all knew Mr Hughes, he having spent some years on the Congo, and also as the man who conceived of the idea of training native missionaries in this country for work in Africa. With regard to Mrs Hughes, they were very pleased to know she was in full sympathy with the work that was being carried on in that place. It was very important that Mrs Hughes should be in full harmony with the work to which the Institute had been consecrated. They had heard of her philanthropic work in Ashton-under-Lyne, and her readiness to help the needy, both spiritually and temporally. They wished both Mr and Mrs Hughes all the happiness that could be obtained in this world, good health and long life and the guidance of the Holy Spirit throughout their careers and were very pleased to welcome Mr and Mrs Hughes into the *United States of Matrimony* (Loud Laughter).

When the Committee heard of the great event – for as such they regarded the marriage – they at once felt that should seize the opportunity of showing some token of the respect and esteem they felt for Mr and Mrs Hughes as a memento of their kind wishes on that happy occasion (Applause). The Revd T G Williams then read a copy of the address which, when completed will be of a very handsome design and framed in oak. The text will be highly embellished and at the corners are to be four pictures – the photographs of the Revd W Hughes, Mrs Hughes, the African Institute and Mrs Hughes's mission-room in Ashton-under-Lyne.

'A Partner in His Great Life Work'

The Revd T Shankland said that from the very bottom of his heart he joined in the expression of good wishes towards Mr and Mrs Hughes. As a personal friend of many years standing he had come to wish them a long and happy life. He had known Mr Hughes for many years, they having been fellow students at college … More than anything else he rejoiced that Mr Hughes had found one who would be a partner in his great life work. Everything else faded by the side of the interest and enthusiasm which Mr Hughes had always shown in the success of the African Institute. That Institute had given the Committee a great deal of trouble and consideration, and he had spent some of the hardest days of his life in considering grave questions in connection with it. People might imagine that it was an easy thing to manage a concern like that, but he could assure them that its government and general business cost the Committee generally and Mr Hughes in particular, a great deal of thought. He was very happy to learn that Mrs Hughes was deeply interested in mission work and had in a sense qualified for her position here. As a member of the Committee he cordially welcomed her, and could assure her that the Committee would gladly give her all the help that lay in their power to give. They knew that her heart was in the work and all hoped that in the near future, the African Women's Institute would receive some consideration (Hear, hear). They already had some lady students and he was sure that under the guidance of Mrs Hughes that branch of the Institute would prove a great success (Applause).

Kwesi Quainoo – the Students' Spokesman

The next incident was indeed a striking one. All the students (Ayodeji Oyejola, Alfred J Williams, A B King, Charlie Stewart, Ishmael C Pratt, James A G Lawson, James Boco, Josiah Batubo, Kwesi A Quainoo, Lawale Tubi, Ladipo Thomas, Mosanga Osata, Roul van der Most, Theo Ruhle, Theodore Klabangare and Waddy Saggo) walked towards the platform and Kwesi Quainoo who acted as their spokesman, begged their beloved Principal's acceptance of an illuminated address and an oak and silver tray, the gift of the students and staff.

Pronouncing his words with remarkable accuracy and distinctiveness and speaking with evident sincerity, his bearing being that of a born courtier, Quainoo thrilled all present when he thus addressed his Principal: 'In giving you this expression of our heartfelt congratulations, I beg to include the best wishes of our people in Africa. Every one of the negro race – a race than which none has suffered greater vicissitudes – feels glad that such work is being carried on for the evangelisation of the people in Africa. You, our dear Principal, know how all of us are grateful and thankful to you for your kindness in establishing this work for the evangelisation of our people. And you Mrs Hughes, we are very glad to welcome amongst us. No doubt you, like many

143

others who are doing good work for God, will find those people who will stand between you and your work, and I ask you in the name of God, to look up to the One Who for the joy that was set before Him endured the Cross, despising the shame. There is a promise in God's Word that Ethiopia will suddenly raise up her hand unto God and before that hand can be raised some people must take hold of it and help to raise it up. The whole body of Ethiopia is sick through ignorance and superstition, and it is only by means of the Gospel of Our Lord Jesus Christ, through you and others, that she can be cured and then she can raise her hand unto God. We all pray that God may bless you abundantly, and give you great joy in working for Him in this place'.

When Kwesi had finished there was scarcely a dry eye in the whole company. His simple earnestness appealed to the hearts of all present, and in particular to the Principal, who was evidently affected by deep emotion as he accepted the gifts.

'A Mother to His Children'

Finally it was time for William's response:

Revd W Hughes, who in rising received quite an ovation, said he was very pleased to be back once more and to receive the splendid welcome accorded him and Mrs Hughes. He could only thank them for their good wishes and for what they had done and were doing on behalf of the Institute. Much as Mrs Hughes and himself had enjoyed their tour through Germany, Belgium and Holland, they both now felt that there was no place like home and especially a home of that kind (Hear, hear). He enjoyed plenty of *life* and travel in various lands, but he was never so happy as doing his work in connection with the Institute. Alluding to the preparations made for the reception of Mrs Hughes and himself on their return, he warmly thanked all – old friends and new – for their great kindness, which, he assured them, he appreciated to the full. It was a grand sight, that gathering of sincere friends, and to see the Institute on its way to prosperity, at last, after all its trials and troubles. He had put his hand to the plough and had not looked back, and that, he knew, was the reason he had so many near and dear friends. He had no other friends and hoped his wife would have no other friends, except the friends of the Institute, whom he hoped would continue to increase in number. He valued their presents and good wishes and he would not be misunderstood when he said that the presents he valued most of all were those he had just received from the children of Africa (Hear, hear). The address was made of the same material as what he hoped would be on his grave. He did not believe in flowers, or monuments on show. He would rather spend money on the living poor than on the graves of the dead. He did not want anyone to spend a penny on his grave. He did not want it from the place of his birth, nor from Welshmen who were his countrymen, but he hoped there would be some expression from those people to whom he had given the best of his life (Applause). He was not going yet (Laughter). He had a lot of work to do. He wanted to see the Girls' Institute flourishing, and to replace that small room by a large hall with plenty of light and fresh air. Yes, he wanted to do many things before he went (Hear, hear). Coming to the subject of his marriage, he said that he had taken that step in the cause of Africa. He felt that in the present Mrs Hughes he had a friend of Africa – one who would be a mother to his children. He meant in the first place, a mother to those three little white children in his own house, and also to those two little girls, Ernestina and Lulu, between whom and his own children he had never made the slightest distinction as regards dress or anything else, and lastly her motherhood was not to stop there, but was to extend into that very Lecture Hall as well (Applause).

The Revd T G Williams, in proposing a vote of thanks to all who had contributed towards the success of the gathering, expressed his own good wishes towards Mr and Mrs Hughes... After an interval for more refreshments, a capital musical programme was given, the artistes including Madame

Williamson, Miss Cissy Harries, Mr Evans Hughes, Mr Llewelyn Jones and Mr Llewelyn Davies. This concluded the very happy and interesting proceedings.

Ashton's Mums Bid Farewell to Bessie

A week after Mr and Mrs Hughes shared the lively, entertaining and emotional wedding celebrations at Congo House, Bessie returned, alone, to bid farewell to her old associates at the Ashton-under-Lyne Mission Hall. A rather sombre event was depicted by the *Ashton Reporter*:

On Tuesday evening last (26 September), the mothers' class in connection with the Mission Room, York Street, Charleston, Ashton, met for a social cup of tea, and to say farewell and God speed to their much esteemed and devoted teacher, Miss Clarke, who is leaving in a very short time for Colwyn Bay. Miss Clarke in her untiring efforts endeared herself to a great many friends in Ashton and neighbourhood and her genial smile and ever willing hand will be missed by many. She has been recently joined in the bonds of matrimony with the Revd W Hughes, the Principal of the African Training Home, where she will in future reside. Tea over, the rest of the evening was spent in a very pleasant way, many of her friends taking part, and many were the good wishes expressed for her future happiness in her new home. Mrs Fielding, police court missionary, a dear friend of the above class, was also present, and gave a very stirring address, also accompanying the singing at the piano. Miss Clarke was also the recipient of a very neat trinket set as a small token of respect from the mothers. A very pleasant evening was brought to a close about nine o'clock by singing, *God be with you till we meet again.*

Chapter Eight

End of the Honeymoon
(1900–1907)

Eighteen ninety-nine ended in disaster. A week after the Institute's 'welcome-home' celebrations William's new wife, Bessie, travelled back to 'bid farewell to friends in Ashton-under-Lyne' and never returned to Colwyn Bay. Her relationship with William ended as abruptly and mysteriously as it had begun. No explanation was offered and no public acknowledgement of this curious turn of events was ever made.

War in Africa: 1900
Before William had time to recover from Bessie's shock departure he had to fight for the very survival of the Institute. The 1899 outbreak of the second Boer War had caused a haemorrhaging of both students and funds. Contributions that might otherwise have come to the Institute went instead to relieving the immediate distress of combatants. The physical and emotional injuries of returning British casualties appealed more directly to the sympathies of potential donors. As William reported to the Institute's Annual Meeting in June 1900, 'The funds had suffered greatly owing to the war in South Africa, so much money being contributed towards the sufferers in connection with it.' With a truce only finally reached in May 1902, financial difficulties continued throughout 1901 when William once more observed, 'Owing to the war and other causes, the funds of the mission were much affected.' 'Other causes' doubtless included the negative publicity generated by the criminality of ex-Colwyn Bay student, Anmore Ashaker.

Curious Case of the Clerical Con Man
Ashaker had arrived at the Institute in May 1898, aged twenty-one, from Buguma, capital of New Calabar, accompanied by ten-

Students and Staff at the African
Institute, 1903

A 1902 advertisement
for the African
Institute's Tailoring
Department

The African Training Institute,
COLWYN BAY.

*The Director has much pleasure in informing Subscribers
and the Public generally that a*

TAILORING . .
. DEPARTMENT

HAS RECENTLY BEEN OPENED

Under the superintendence of a thoroughly practical Tailor who has had long experience
as Cutter in the West End of London, and with a well-known Manchester Firm.

Gents', Ladies' and Clerical Garments, Liveries.

The idea of this new venture is to provide the African Students with a trade by which
they will be able to maintain themselves on returning to their native land to preach the
Gospel, while all profits received from the business will be used for the benefit of the Institute.

. . A Splendid and Varied . .
Assortment of High=class Goods.

Patterns in Suitings, Trouserings, Frock Coatings,
Dress Suitings, etc., in all the Latest Designs and Colours will
be submitted with quotations on receipt of your enquiries, which
will command our careful and prompt attention.

We will endeavour to build up the same reputation in this department that we have
gained in our Printing Department, by executing orders with care and despatch.

Fit and Style Guaranteed.   A Trial Order Solicited.

The African Institute's Tailoring Department

year-old Josiah Batubo, the little son of a local native chief. Calling himself Revd Claude Bevington Wilson (sometimes A. B. Wilson), Ashaker, who originated from Sierra Leone, came to Britain on behalf of the 'king and chiefs to secure for them a galvanised-iron church which is to hold about 1200 persons'. He had gained the trust of the local chiefs after serving them for eight months before his departure as a carpenter and preacher. He left his wife in Buguma, where she continued to teach classes of children. Although young Josiah Batubo received training at the Institute the nature of Ashaker's involvement is less clear, his name appears on the official roll of students (as A. B. Wilson) and he played alongside other students for the Congo House cricket team but he didn't attend academic classes. He preached at and on behalf of the Institute and his fund-raising was enthusiastically endorsed by William Hughes but Ashaker's exact role was left undefined and in this respect, it transpires, his case wasn't unique.

Although he subsequently tried to distance himself and the Institute from the Reverend Claude Wilson, Hughes had, embarrassingly, provided him with a glowing and lengthy open-testimonial:

Dear Christian Friends,

As one who has been to New Calabar, and knows all about the foundation, and the prosperity of the native work in Buguma and district, I have the greatest pleasure in recommending the appeal of Mr C B Wilson, who is now in this country on behalf of the native church.

I am delighted with the success of the native Christians of Buguma, which has certainly the tendency to develop their own resources, independency, and self reliance.

The hope of Africa is not in Europeans, Americans, or any other foreigners, but in the natives of the country themselves.

When I visited the place five years ago, Buguma was a perfectly heathen town. The people were exceedingly superstitious and averse to missionaries. For twenty years missionaries had sought an entrance into it, but owing to the power of darkness, and the Juju people, their efforts were in

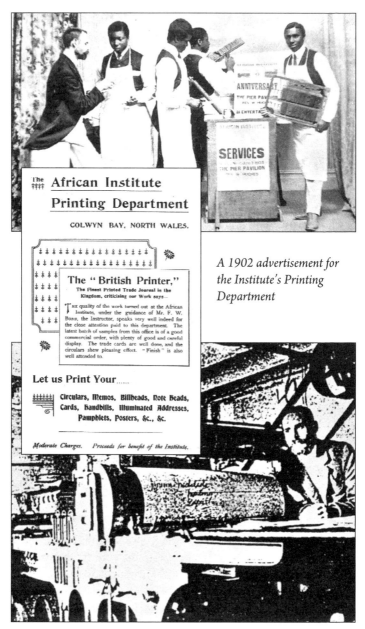

The "African Institute" Printing Department

COLWYN BAY, NORTH WALES.

The "British Printer,"
The Finest Printed Trade Journal in the
Kingdom, criticising our Work says—

THE quality of the work turned out at the African
Institute, under the guidance of Mr. F. W.
BOND, the Instructor, speaks very well indeed for
the close attention paid to this department. The
latest batch of samples from this office is of a good
commercial order, with plenty of good and careful
display. The trade cards are well done, and the
circulars shew pleasing effect. "Finish" is also
well attended to.

Let us Print Your......

Circulars, Memos, Billheads, Note Heads,
Cards, Handbills, Illuminated Addresses,
Pamphlets, Posters, &c., &c.

Moderate Charges. *Proceeds for benefit of the Institute.*

A 1902 advertisement for the Institute's Printing Department

Frederick Bond and students in the Institute's Printing Department

150

vain. However, through the industrial feature of our work, and the Divine blessing I found favour with some of the young chiefs. These canvassed the town, and ultimately succeed in bringing great pressure to bear upon the king and older chiefs, who were very much prejudiced against the Gospel.

I well remember my final meeting with them in the town, when all the chiefs were present with the king and decided to receive the doubtful messenger in, saying, in broken English, *We like them trade too much, for we sons, but we no want them God palaver,* meaning, we like the handicrafts which you teach very much, for our sons, but we do not want the Gospel. I was very much in favour of Industrial missions to Africa before but this confirmed me more than ever in my belief, and reminded me of the way the Saviour entered the hearts of men, by healing their bodies, and affording them temporal help. Thus the people of Buguma have found the Gospel of Jesus Christ an all round one, uplifting them temporally and spiritually. I never witnessed people so eager to listen to the words of life, though the prejudice amongst some of the people was then very great, and especially that of some of the old chiefs. The thirst for the water of life increased, and the congregation every Sabbath multiplied: the children and adults were most eager to learn in school.

They rendered assistance beyond all expectations in cutting down the forest and erecting buildings for the purpose of the mission. The work has since met with many difficulties, but the native converts held on, and when Mr C B Wilson went there from Sierra Leone, about twelve months ago, a great revival took place. He found in them the same thirst for the Gospel. Their earnestness in seeking for the Truth inspired him in preaching it, and the result is worthy of the Holy Ghost.

They have erected there a large native building. The congregation numbers about 1,000 every Sunday. There are 400 children in school, and Mr and Mrs Wilson are quite unable to cope with the demands of the place. There are hundreds of converts waiting to be grounded in the faith and are much in need of a greater number of spiritual teachers. The Juju Priests have laid their weapons at the feet of Jesus. The earnestness of these simple-minded Christian converts, who visit from house to house with their Bible in their hands, has succeeded in breaking down already the heathen power in the town, and I am informed now, that the whole town is on the side of Christianity. The kings, chiefs and people are determined themselves to contribute about Eight Hundred Pounds, to secure a large Iron Church, which Mr Wilson hopes to take back with him next October, but as this sum will not be sufficient for such an immense building we are appealing to Christian friends in this country for their assistance to those who have been so laudably and energetically helping themselves. Moreover, assistance is required to encourage these people in their extraordinary efforts to establish branch churches in populous districts within their reach, and to carry the Gospel to the plantations and markets, which are in touch with them.

Mr Wilson solicits help in the name of this Institute, and will give an official receipt for all monies collected for this object, a list of which, will appear in our next report. The above facts speak for themselves.

Again heartily recommending him and the work at Buguma, to the kind Christian friends in this country, and with earnest wishes for the salvation of Africa.

Yours faithfully,

W. HUGHES,

Director.

Ashaker left Colwyn Bay at the end of 1898 but instead of returning to Africa with the money he'd collected he moved down to London to spend it! As he continued to raise funds, officially for a tin-church but actually for personal consumption, Ashaker made extravagant use of Hughes' extremely helpful testimonial! Towards the end of 1899, uncomfortable rumours of the *Reverend Claude Wilson's* activities began to filter back to Colwyn Bay and just as he was beginning to come to terms with his money worries and the disastrous result of his remarriage William was dealt another potentially devastating blow by the *Daily Mail* of Saturday 18 November 1899:

CLAUDE WILSON, CLERGYMAN – Curious Story about a Negro Preacher
An African Negro, who calls himself Claude Wilson, has had a singular career in this country if a story told in the Bedford Police Court yesterday be true.

Wilson, who was attired in black clothes and a clerical hat, was accused of having obtained a bicycle without the intention of paying for it, and there were also three other charges against him..

A solicitor who prosecuted on behalf of the Treasury, stated that Wilson had been staying in this country under the guise of a clergyman ordained in the Church of England, and had taken advantage of the fact to obtain goods and money.

He was a carpenter by trade, and went from Sierra Leone, to a place called Buguma, in the Congo [*sic*] district, and being a person of superior education, he took a lead among the natives and had a religious following.

He came to England ostensibly with a view to obtaining an iron church to set up at Buguma, and he got an introduction to the Training Home for African Students at Colwyn Bay, North Wales. The principal there took an interest in him, and published an account of his work at

Mr Claude Bevington Wilson

Buguma, together with his portrait. Wilson had taken this publication about with him and represented himself as a clergyman.

Tangled Webs

Any lingering doubts of Ashaker's innocence were dispelled by evidence of his continuing life of crime. On 6 February 1902 he appeared at Clerkenwell Assize facing a charge of threatening to kill a London hotel keeper. He was still peddling the line of collecting money for Africa and had embellished the appeal of Hughes' testimonial by availing himself of a set of gilt-edged business cards proclaiming him to be Reverend Claude Bevington Wilson, MA Balliol College, Oxford. The Revd Wilson had also expanded his criminal ambitions to include, 'blackmailing relatives of white women he had induced to live with him'. When apprehended he was living with a woman from Yorkshire in Claremont Street, not far from King's Cross railway station. Previously he had stayed, at Finsbury, at a Chiswell Street lodging house run by William Child who 'had at times helped him with money and in other ways'. When the woman's distressed brother arrived in London he sought Child's help in persuading his sister to return to Yorkshire. Child obliged and accompanied the brother to Claremont Street where the pair induced the woman to leave. On his return home, Wilson was outraged and, suspecting his old associate's involvement, immediately fired off an anonymous, incendiary note to Child, informing him that he would be shot! Child took the note to the police who matched it to Ashaker's handwriting. The Court concluded that the Revd Claude Bevington Wilson, MA, had indeed been, 'living in London by fraud and by blackmailing white women' and sentenced him to twelve months in prison, with hard labour.

Obliged by journalists to once again defend the Institute from its association with the clerical-conman, William Hughes was most economical with the truth, claiming; 'Ashaker had been received kindly by the staff and African students but had been too old to study there. After Ashaker had been there about a month I received warnings about the man's past. When told what had been said against him, Ashaker left town in a hurry.' In fact, Ashaker had remained at Congo House for four months – not one, as Hughes claimed to the press – and had departed in October 1898, at the time Hughes had anticipated. Having naively supplied the testimonial that provided Wilson's spurious credibility, if Hughes had come to suspect Wilson's honesty before he left then it was incumbent upon him to publicly withdraw the reference. Instead, when rumours began to circulate in Colwyn Bay, in January 1899, Hughes wrote assuring readers of the *Weekly News*, 'I have made a full investigation ... concerning one of our students and a person who has just left for London ... and found that the whole thing is a fabrication'. Over the following decade, denying uncomfortable truths was to become a habit at Congo House, and the form of words employed in Hughes' January 1899 denial was to have a horribly familiar echo in the similarly false refutation that failed to protect the Institute from its ultimate scandal.

Insidious Influence
Ashaker's stay at Colwyn Bay was short, but his pernicious influence had already infected his erstwhile companion, little Josiah Batubo. Despite his youth and numerous warnings from Hughes, after a couple of years at the African Institute Josiah Batubo proved an impossible pupil and was finally expelled in 1900. No publicity was given to the expulsion at the time and characteristically, when news of the event eventually leaked out William at first attempted to deny it had occurred before claiming it was a typical example of the high standards of behaviour and discipline in operation at the Institute! Despite his tender years Josiah was reluctant to return to Africa and he would return to the Institute to wreak a terrible revenge.

Pillar of the Community: 1901
Deserted by his wife, embarrassed by disreputable students and financially undermined by the effects of the Boer war the twentieth century presented William Hughes with almost insurmountable problems – but he prevailed. At the Institute's

Annual Meeting in May 1901:

> The treasurer, Councillor Sharp of Leeds, was able to show that the very heavy adverse balance of last year had been practically wiped away'. After a drastic decline in student numbers, now reassured about the financial position, 'the Committee had decided to receive about 15 new students in the Institute during the next six months. Six of these would come from Lagos and six from the Gold Coast, while the Sierra Leone and the Gambia committees were prepared to contribute a further six.

William Hughes had proved his mettle and held himself and his Institute together through a very difficult period. Following the 1901 death of Queen Victoria, Colwyn Bay recognised Hughes' public standing with his appointment as Chairman of the Coronation Day Festivities Committee, responsible for organising the celebration of the anticipated crowning of Edward VII.

Delayed Gratification: 1902

In 1902 William was also appointed Chairman of Colwyn Bay's 'Free Library Committee'. Having survived the storms of previous years Hughes and his Institute had secured a well-established and widely-liked position in the town. Opposition from the BMS seemed to have subsided and in a move to consolidate and regularise the framework of Congo House in 1902 formal ownership was transferred from Hughes to The British & African Incorporated Association Company.

Combining two of his roles, Hughes issued commemorative medals marking Edward VII's coronation. Now extremely rare, the medal was struck by H B Sale of Birmingham and featured the King and Queen on one side, with an eight-line legend on the reverse, the first three of these being; *PRESENTED BY THE / AFRICAN INSTITUTE / COLWYN BAY*

Unfortunately even Edward VII created problems for Hughes when acute appendicitis caused the cancellation of his June 1902

Coronation. All over the UK there were incidents of public unrest when celebratory crowds reacted unfavourably to the cancellation of long awaited festivities. There was minor trouble at Old Colwyn but at Newtown the Chairman of the Council was imprisoned by a hostile crowd and at Watford a mob of 300 rioted, looting shops owned by members of the local Coronation Committee and setting fire to the Coronation bonfire after chasing away the watchman and then throwing his hut onto the blaze!

Fortunately there was no riot in Colwyn Bay and Hughes' most serious problem was the schoolchildren's tea-party. The postponement of the party passed off without difficulty but the committee couldn't decide what to do with the children's presentation mugs. They were marked with the original coronation date and it was feared that as any amendment would have to be painted on over the glaze the new lettering would simply wash off!

Celebration of the postponed coronation eventually took place in September 1902 and the students of the African Institute formed part of the long procession of Sunday schools (sandwiched between the Greenfield Road Wesleyans and Bethlehem Calvinistic Methodists) that marched through the town:

The route of the march was lined by thousands of spectators, who evidently enjoyed the sight. Headed by the Old Colwyn Silver Band (conducted by Bandmaster Hezekiah Jones) playing a patriotic march, the procession marched off, guided by the marshals, who carried wands topped by flags and patriotic favours, the procession marched in excellent order. The sun rose splendidly as they advanced along Greenfield Road, Abergele Road, Marine Road, Princes Road and Victoria Avenue to the Promenade, the march being made easy and safe by the excellent manner in which the vehicular traffic was arranged by Sergeant Tippett and the constables under his charge. The thousands of onlookers who lined the streets and assembled at various places were delighted with the spectacle afforded by the procession and the utmost enthusiasm prevailed ... Everything passed off most pleasantly throughout the day, no untoward incident occurring to mar the festivities or to reflect the slightest disgrace upon the town. The loyal people of this district will in years to come look back with unalloyed satisfaction and pleasure upon Coronation day.

Anyone for Cricket?: 1903

With a return to pre-war student numbers the Institute was again able to field a cricket team against local challengers:

> On Wednesday last (17 June), the African students played a cricket match at Llandudno with the County School. The bowling of the Africans was too good for the Welshmen, who only mustered 13 runs between them, and the match resulted in a victory for the Africans by 21 runs. They continued their victorious career at Abergele on Thursday, when they beat the County School by 33 runs, the scores being: Abergele, 41; African Institute, 74.

Over the next five years the Institute won more often than not, including notable victories over; Rhos College, Mr Underhill's XI, Colwyn Bay, Mr Dare's English XI before student numbers once again declined below the number needed to form a team. Congo House's best ever performance was probably in their 1905 defeat of Rhos College by 124 runs to 30 although their funniest victory was probably their win against Plas-y-coed when the African Institute only hit a total of 9 runs, fortunately they managed to bowl out the opposition for 8! The Institute's best ever batsman was Henry Poswayo who, in 1907, hit 50 runs off a Colwyn Bay team and the premier bowler was Ladipo Oluwole who, in 1904, skittled out seven Rhos College batsmen at the cost of only 14 runs.

Uncle Tom's Visit

In May 1903 William conducted a lecture tour around

Birmingham and district accompanied by a couple of students, whilst Ayodeji Oyejola toured Yorkshire before finishing his lecture series in London. Besides raising public awareness of the African Institute these trips also brought in badly-needed cash. In November the process was reversed when a touring performer paid the first of what would turn out to be fateful visits. Twenty-eight year old black Bermudan actor John Lionel Franklin was appearing in a production at Colwyn Bay when curiosity led him to visit the Institute. Franklin's show was advertised in the local press:

> On Monday and Tuesday next, Mr J Tulley's American Company will appear at the Public Hall in the well-known play, *Uncle Tom's Cabin*. As this is absolutely the finest company now travelling with this popular piece, our readers should not miss the chance of seeing it.

Uncle Tom received a better reception in Colwyn Bay than he had in London. A few months earlier, when Tulley's company were engaged at Hammersmith, three ex-soldiers had waylaid the leading actor outside the theatre, smashed a stick over his head and shouted, 'Look at that black bastard!' In an effort to defend himself the actor had injured one of his attackers before fetching a constable to record the incident. As a result the attackers escaped and *Uncle Tom* was sentenced to three months in prison!

In contrast, when *Uncle Tom* played Colwyn Bay he was not only spared actual violence but the newspaper reported that when the drama reached its emotional height in the final scene, where *Uncle Tom* is dying and his master enters and begins to kick and horse-whip the old slave, a 'well-known person in Colwyn Bay' left his seat and mounted the stage in a determined effort to defend him!

Franklin turned up at the African Institute for the Sunday service on the day before his show opened in Colwyn Bay. As Hughes later recorded, 'At that meeting he became a Christian convert and gave his heart to Jesus Christ, but did not leave the stage for some time after, although his mind was made up that he would ultimately go out as a missionary in Africa.'

John Lionel Franklin's enthusiastic response was very encouraging, he was a great performer who would return to Colwyn Bay but like little Josiah Batubo, Hughes would come to rue the day he ever set eyes on John Lionel Franklin.

Expansion into Central Africa?

In 1903 the Institute's work attracted the attention of the radical missionary, Joseph Booth. Like Hughes, Booth's independence and egalitarianism had alienated him from the established missionary authorities. Booth similarly shared William's commitment to 'Africa for the Africans' and recognised the essential role of independent industrial education in effecting this liberation. Having founded the Zambesi Industrial Mission in Malawi, Booth exhorted Hughes to cooperate with him in expanding Congo House's influence across Central Africa. Although Peter Nyambo, one of Booth's associates did subsequently attend the African Institute the Colonial authorities considered Booth's influence inimical to imperial rule and contrived to close down their joint enterprise. Early in 1904, the Commissioner of Nyasaland, Sir Alfred Sharpe contacted one of the Institute's more powerful patrons, Lord Mostyn, who prevailed upon Hughes to immediately end his association with Booth. Although one of Booth's close associates, Peter Chilembwe, did lead a violent revolt against the Nyasaland (Malawi) authorities, Hughes, Nyambo and even Booth himself confined their efforts to supporting independent African enterprise rather than attacking colonialism. By the end of 1903 it was increasingly difficult to achieve the former without also engaging in the latter.

Friend or Foe?

Since the earliest days of the Institute its annual reports proudly proclaimed as most prominent Patron: HIS MOST EXCELLENT MAJESTY LEOPOLD II, THE KING OF THE BELGIANS, yet by 1903 Leopold's Congo regime was denounced in newspapers, Parliament and in official reports as a huge forced labour camp where Africans were worked to death for the single-minded pursuit of profits for King Leopold of Belgium.

As early as 1890, black journalist George Washington Williams had identified Leopold's 'crimes against humanity' and a decade later Edmund Morel, a shipping clerk employed at Liverpool by Elder Dempster, uncovered the reality behind Leopold's highly profitable exports from Africa, publishing damning details and organising protest meetings. From the start Leopold's regime had been founded on forced labour. Hundreds of thousands of Africans were abused, hit, whipped and forced to work unpaid to produce profits for Leopold. At first the main commodity was ivory but with the invention of the inflatable bicycle tyre in the 1890s the demand for rubber was insatiable and in the Congo it grew wild. Africans were given vast quotas of rubber to collect and anyone failing to reach their quota risked ruthless punishment. Hands were routinely hacked off by Leopold's agents to spur others on to ever more exhaustive efforts.

Come to Colwyn Bay!

Hughes naively assumed the King wasn't aware of, or responsible for the crimes of his lieutenants in Africa. As late as the summer of 1903 Hughes was still grovelling to the arch-tyrant of Africa. When it appeared Leopold was about to embark on a visit to England, Hughes sent a fawning invitation to the Institute. In a letter dated 18 May 1903 William wrote:

> Our Association has noticed with pleasure that Your Majesty intends to proceed to Liverpool in Your Majesty's Yacht in July next and to visit our great friend, Sir Alfred Jones, KCMG, Colwyn Bay being only about three hours sail from Liverpool it occurred to us that Your Majesty might graciously grant us the honour of a visit at this beautiful seaside resort, where your majesty would see about twenty-five African students, in whose race your majesty has taken such deep and practical interest in the past. I can assure Your Majesty that the friends of our Institution, like Sir H M Stanley and Sir Alfred Jones,

are too well acquainted with Your Majesty's philanthropic spirit and interest in Africa, to believe that the atrocities reported from the region of the Congo river, if true, have in any way Your Majesty's approval.

Colwyn Bay, in July and August, is visited by thousands of persons from all parts of the United Kingdom, and with Your Majesty's gracious permission, our association propose, on the occasion of that visit, to present Your Majesty with an address in commemoration of the benefits conferred by Your Majesty upon the continent of Africa, and of the honour bestowed by Your Majesty in acting as the patron of this Institution from its commencement.

I am also quite sure that the municipal authorities would be only too glad to join us in paying a similar tribute to Your Majesty in our Pavilion, if honoured by such a visit.

I remain Your Majesty's most humble servant, W Hughes.

Exactly a week later, Leopold's secretary sent a brief, non-committal reply from Brussels, merely informing Hughes that if Leopold did visit Liverpool he would indeed be delighted to come to the Institute. It was enough to prompt another gushing epistle from Hughes, dated 4 June 1903, detailing the finer points of the intended arrangements:

If coming from Liverpool in Your Majesty's yacht, it would be needful to land at the pier at Rhos-on-Sea, which is about a mile from Colwyn Bay. With Your Majesty's permission we would have a band and procession with a carriage to drive Your Majesty to the Pavilion where we would arrange a short musical programme in which some of the Welsh choirs and the African students would take part, afterwards driving up to the Institute for a short visit and concluding with luncheon at one of the hotels ...

Secret Agent meets 'Pushy Capitalist'

As reports and photographs of victims of Leopold's Congo Free State regime began to circulate the King of the Belgians cancelled his visit and sent instead a secret agent to undermine Morel's campaign. As his African terror state was being openly criticised in the British Parliament, Leopold responded with two specific initiatives, and another of Hughes' Official Patrons, Sir Alfred Jones was his willing instrument in both instances. Jones acted as Leopold's Honorary Consul and in this capacity he intervened with the Foreign Office to forestall publication of Roger Casement's damning report on the Congo Free State regime. Secondly, Jones arranged a meeting in London at which a secret agent sent by King Leopold attempted to bribe Morel to keep quiet about the evidence he had collected of appalling atrocities committed in the Congo. Fortunately neither initiative succeeded but this only increased Hughes' discomfiture.

Described as a 'pushy capitalist' by Thomas Packenham, Alfred Jones' motivation in defending Leopold was purely financial for as Packenham points out, 'Elder Dempster enjoyed the lucrative monopoly of the shipping service between Antwerp and the Congo'.

'Friends of Africa'?: 1904

William had always pursued celebrity 'friends of Africa', such as H. M. Stanley, King Leopold and Sir Alfred Jones, to endorse his work and serve as official Patrons of the Institute. By 1904 this strategy began to backfire as the motives and methods of such self-proclaimed 'friends' were revealed to the public. Hughes' old hero, Henry Morton Stanley seemed less saintly once the public read that his selfless exploratory expeditions across Africa were in reality ruthless, self-serving adventures that disrupted and destroyed the lives of thousands of native inhabitants. Whilst a Foreign Office report of 1878 recorded that 'if the story of this expedition were known it would stand in the annals of African discovery unequalled for the reckless use of power that modern weapons placed in his hands over natives who never before heard a gun fired', the report was kept secret.

The *Pall Mall Gazette* had no such reticence; 'Exploration under these conditions is, in fact, exploration plus buccaneering, and though the map may be improved and enlarged by the process, the cause of civilisation is not a gainer thereby, but a loser'.

The *Saturday Review* assured its readers that Stanley 'has no concern with justice, no right to administer it; he comes with no sanction, no authority, no jurisdiction – nothing but explosive bullets and a copy of the *Daily Telegraph*'.

Stanley's Last Journey

Having suffered a paralysing stroke the previous year, on 10 May 1904 Sir Henry Morton Stanley passed away at his London home. As the newspapers reported:

> Amongst those present at the funeral ceremony in Westminster Abbey in memory of this distinguished Welshman on Tuesday last was the Revd W Hughes, Congo Institute, who has for a number of years enjoyed the personal friendship of the famous explorer. Stanley was one of the patrons of the Congo Institute. Mr T H Davies, FRSS, tutor of the African Institute, was also present. A magnificent wreath was also sent by the students, bearing the following inscription; – *From the students of the African Institute, Colwyn Bay, North Wales, and their friends. With the deepest sympathy and as a token of their appreciation of the great and noble work of Sir H M Stanley, GCB, DCL, LLD, on behalf of the dark continent of Africa.* Mr Hughes was also one of those who, as a personal friend, petitioned the authorities to allow the body to rest in the Abbey.

Details of a sequel to Stanley's death appeared in the press in July 1904:

> SIR H M STANLEY'S BIRTHPLACE – The Principal and Council of the African Training Institute desire to record their sincere thanks to Mr T J Williams, JP, of Coed Derw, Colwyn Bay, for his kindness in presenting to the Institute a model of the birthplace of the late Sir H M Stanley, GCB etc. The old house which originally stood on Castle Hill, Denbigh, has been demolished and the ground which it occupied has been

added to the castle Ground. Prior to its demolition, however, Mr Williams had this model constructed. He has been advised to present it to the National Welsh Museum; but, remembering the connection of the great African explorer with the African Training Institute at Colwyn Bay, Mr Williams has generously given the interesting work to the Institute.

Despite Hughes' undoubted feelings of sadness and loss, Stanley's death was also a timely relief for, by 1904, Stanley's association with the Institute was no longer the great asset it had once been, his reputation tarnished by reports of the cruel realities of the conquest of Africa. Despite petitions from Hughes, and others, Stanley's dearest wish to be buried in Westminster Abbey, alongside Livingstone was refused by the Dean and after the service his body was taken for burial to Pirbright in Surrey.

The Light of Civilisation
In *Dark Africa*, in 1892, Hughes had eulogised Stanley and Leopold:

> Henry M Stanley went to Africa to prepare the way and open up that vast and wealthy country that the light of civilisation and the Gospel might enter therein

and

> The King of the Belgians, a prince in his philanthropic ideas, has expended millions on the banks of the Congo, in order to give the light of civilisation to his forty million dusky subjects.

In reality in 1878 Stanley had committed himself to serving King Leopold II in Africa for a term of five years. After returning to the Congo as Leopold's agent in August 1879 he built outposts and a road around the river's rapids and, using steamboats, he travelled up and down the great Congo River and its tributaries. Employing a mixture of gift-giving and military force, he had duped hundreds of illiterate African chiefs to sign away all rights to their land. Having 'opened up that vast and wealthy country' (as Hughes had put it) along with 'civilisation and the Gospel' came King Leopold's 19,000-man private army, equipped with repeating rifles, cannons and machine guns to impose the terms of Stanley's 'treaties' upon Africans armed with only spears and antique muskets.

Sometime around 1904 it dawned on Hughes that Africans weren't so keen to be 'civilised'. John Atkinson Hobson had published *Imperialism; A Study* – which undermined the Victorian depiction of empire as a sacrificial act of shouldering the *White-Man's Burden* to better the lives of childlike Africans. Hobson exposed imperialism as naked economic exploitation driven by the demands of domestic capitalism rather than the needs and interests of Africa. The behaviour of Stanley, Leopold, Alfred Jones and others could be understood as not merely the excesses of a few greedy individuals but part of a systematic exploitation of black Africa by white Europe. Before he died in 1903, even the Empire-loyalist, and long-standing Institute Patron, Sir Samuel Lewis CMG, KCMG, the first black African to be knighted by Queen Victoria, had grown disillusioned and was reportedly 'disappointed by the evident retreat from those legal and political principles on which he had believed the British Empire to be based.'

Having long enjoyed top-billing as HIS MOST EXCELLENT MAJESTY LEOPOLD II, THE KING OF THE BELGIANS, Leopold was simply dropped from the Institute's 1904 Annual Report. Stanley had conveniently died and Leopold's Honorary Consul, Sir Alfred Jones appeared incognito, listed in the guise of 'Elder, Dempster & Co'. Hughes would never publicly denounce his old friends but realised it was time to look more to Africa for allies.

An Invitation to Africa
In 1904 Hughes had the brainwave of replacing Leopold with a black African celebrity. He desperately tried to persuade Oba

Gbadebo, the sixth Alake of Abeokuta, a Nigerian ruler, to include Colwyn Bay in his extensive 1904 tour of Britain. The Alake visited Liverpool, stayed at the *Adelphi Hotel* and met Alfred Jones, so William pressed him to make a short detour to Congo House, as the press reported:

> THE ALAKE AND COLWYN BAY – An effort has been made by the Revd W Hughes, Principal of the African Institute to induce the Alake to visit Colwyn Bay and the Institute during his stay in England. The following is a letter which has been received from Sir W Macgregor, Governor of Lagos, who has been showing the Alake around the country: Kenilworth Hotel, Great Russell Street, London.
> Dear Sir, – I regret very much that the Alake finds he cannot visit the Institute. He sails from Liverpool on the 9th of July and cannot go again to the country before leaving England. This is very much to be regretted. – Sincerely yours, W MACGREGOR.

All was not lost, for although Hughes didn't manage to meet the Alake one of his students did! When Gbadebo visited Edinburgh during his tour, Ayodeji Oyejola, an Institute student then training at the university to become a doctor, was there to greet him. When Dr. Oyejola graduated two years later, he was able to return to Nigeria and work at a hospital specially provided for him by the Alake! Even Hughes' own efforts bore some fruit for although Alake Gbadebo didn't come to Colwyn Bay, Hughes did manage to secure his formal consent to becoming the headline Patron of the Institute.

Black Consciousness and Pan-Africanism
Hughes' reluctance to publicly acknowledge ruthless aspects of Stanley's African adventures and Leopold's Congo was less due to ignorance or indifference to the negative effects of colonialism than an example of his loyalty to old friends. Two black supporters of Hughes, Frederick Loudin and Thomas Lewis Johnson played leading roles in the 1900 Pan-African Conference

King Leopold's Atrocities   *Alake Gbadebo of Abeokuta*

*William Hughes and the Colwyn Bay
Coronation Committee, 1902*

in London and in November 1904 at least four of Hughes' students were instrumental in founding in Liverpool, the Ethiopian Progressive Association (EPA) organised to raise, 'matters of vital importance concerning Africa in particular and the Negro race in general.' Colwyn Bay-educated members included, Kwesi Ewusi, Joseph A Abraham and Andrew W Neizer of the Gold Coast and Sierra Leonian, James P. Richards. Another leading member of the Association, the South African, Dr H. B. Gabashane may well have been the brother of another Colwyn Bay student, Mabel Gabashane who enrolled at the African Institute around this time. The EPA published *The Ethiopian Review*, and maintained a correspondence with well-known black American activists, W. E. B. Du Bois and Booker T. Washington.

Goodbye Charlie

Despite the ideological upheavals for the most part 1904 was taken up with the usual round of Institute activities; every Sunday morning there was a Sunday school session, open to the general public, with religious services given at 3 and 7pm. *The Weekly News* continued to carry regular updates on the comings and goings of Congo House students. February's brief story was typical:

> RETURNING HOME – The following account of the return of a promising African student to his native land will doubtless prove very interesting to our readers: – Charlie Stewart, who has been a student at the African Institute, Colwyn Bay, for the past five years, sailed for his native land, Liberia, by the *SS Coomassie* from Liverpool, last Thursday morning. Through his amiable disposition and Christian character, Charlie gained the respect and liking of all who knew him.

The ordinary, workaday tone of the story indicates the town's acceptance of the Institute and its highly visible students as part of the everyday, working life of Colwyn Bay. Whilst doubtless still interesting and unusual the African Institute had grown to become such a familiar part of town life that most residents had developed a real affection for the place and its students.

Fun to Play at the YMCA: 1905

The middle years of the Edwardian era were generally a time of consolidation at the Institute. Having laboured for three years on the 'Free Library Committee', William Hughes was delighted to at last attend the formal opening ceremony on 24 April 1905 and have his name proudly displayed on the brass commemorative plaque that still adorns the entrance today. After the disruption of the war years, donation income had settled down and a few new students had arrived from South Africa. Hughes continued to correspond with old friends in Africa, such as Ricketts and Agbebi but there seemed no new, inspiring and influential converts to the cause. In an increasingly radical age the African Institute was beginning to appear almost respectable.

As well as organising the usual round of Institute concerts, cricket matches and garden parties in 1905 the students were active in assisting the Colwyn Bay branch of the Young Men's Christian Association (YMCA). At a YMCA social, held in the Sea View Crescent Lecture Hall, in July, Sierra Leonian student, Aaron George, performed a couple of recitations; *Our Folks* and *Betty and the Bear* whilst George Dixon Montsioa of Mafeking, South Africa 'was vociferously cheered for his rendering of *The Veteran's Song.*' Later in the year the students helped organise a fund-raising YMCA jumble sale at the Public Hall. On that occasion Dixon Montsoia manned an African Curio Show with the assistance of Sierra Leonian, Edenslight Brown.

Vote! Vote! Vote! for Reverend Hughes!: 1906

In 1906 Hughes decided to put himself up for election as a Councillor to the Northern Ward of Colwyn Bay and Colwyn Urban District Council. His manifesto was hardly distinctive although it was one of the few endorsed, post-publication, by the Colwyn Bay Workingmen's Association after Hughes responded satisfactorily to a series of written questions it supplied. Reporting of the election in the local press was characteristically laconic:

> Colwyn Bay, like the stout lady in *Christmas Carols* was on Monday, one vast substantial smile. For it was the day on

which the people of Colwyn bay were called forth to speak into that powerful gramophone, the ballot-box, which was expected to magnify their united voice and to boom it forth in thunderous tones so that all the world might hear.

In other words, the fateful day had arrived when the free and enlightened electorate were expected to select out of two-score excellent candidates twenty good men and true to represent them on the District Council. Public interest in the election had been growing since the day of nominations, until it reached a degree of intensity quite unusual in the town's eventful municipal history and on Monday there was quite a buzz of excitement in the town's main streets …

The Magistrates Room in Station Road was the polling station for the Northern ward and this being the most populous division, with a list of 905 voters … Great interest was manifested in this contest, there being as many as twelve candidates for the five seats. Speculation was rife as to who would head the poll, and long before eight o'clock it was confidently predicted that Mr Edward Allen would occupy that coveted position, Councillors John Williams and Joseph Dicken came second and third respectively with only two votes separating them.

Twenty-nine votes behind Dicken came Revd William Hughes. John Jones, thirty-six votes behind Hughes, was the fifth and final of the twelve candidates elected for Northern ward.

Woking's Loss is Freetown's Gain

In November 1906 student William Lukobi-Johnson returned to Sierra Leone after training as a printer at Colwyn Bay. Besides his initial Institute tuition under Frederick Bond, William had gained valuable experience as an apprentice with Unwin Brothers at Woking, Surrey under supervisor Arthur E Collins. In Surrey, William benefited from assisting Collins with the regular printing of the *Woking News and Mail*. After arriving in Sierra Leone on 18 December, aboard *SS Tarquah*, William travelled 25 miles further West to greet his family at York, where he was born and to visit the grave of his father who had died whilst he was in Colwyn Bay. After signing up to run the Sunday school in Freetown he was taken on to run a small print department by Mr C. May, the editor of the *Freetown Weekly News*.

An Old School Friend Returns to Colwyn Bay

At the end of 1906 John Lionel Franklin was enrolled at the African Institute as a student. In 1903 he had visited Colwyn Bay as an actor in *Uncle Tom's Cabin* and sworn to dedicate, 'his heart to Jesus Christ' and 'ultimately go out as a missionary to Africa'. Recalling Franklin's route back to Colwyn Bay following that initial visit, Hughes later recorded that John Lionel:

> experienced a great struggle to extract himself from the stage and to start a new life as a missionary. His manager and fellow actors did all within their power to persuade him to remain with them, and often mocked him because of his new intention. He often refers to his struggles and trials at this time. However he was able to overcome this difficulty whilst visiting Cardiff during the time of the Welsh revival (1904-5) and he decided that he would not continue on the stage any longer. He remained in Cardiff and threw his whole heart into the work of the Revivalists and started his work as a missionary forthwith. He continued for some months speaking at Young Men's Christian Association Meetings and various other meetings in connection with the churches in South Wales. Being a coloured man, repeated applications were made on his behalf by Christian friends in South Wales, to be accepted as a student at this Institute. Ultimately the Young Men's Christian Association friends at Newport and others prevailed upon us.

Leopold's Ghost: 1907

By 1907 King Leopold had become so generally reviled that even the London-based Baptist Missionary Society were prepared to publicly denounce him. In December a BMS lecturer, returned Congo missionary, Mr J. Lawson Forfeitt, turned up in Colwyn

Bay to inform the public assembled at the town's English Baptist Chapel (established twenty years previously by William Hughes) were invited to witness Leopold's excesses. As the local press reported: 'The address was illustrated by 100 lime-light views and revealed to the large audience present, the terrible nature of the atrocities perpetrated under the rule of the King of the Belgians.' But it had taken the BMS an inordinate amount of time to speak out against Leopold despite having received critical reports of Leopold's regime for years from missionaries in the field and it appeared, as Holman Bentley indicated in a speech to the Baptist's World Congress in 1905, the final break with Leopold was provoked less by concern for African welfare than by annoyance at restrictions placed on protestant missionaries in contrast to the King's support for Catholic missions, 'For several years, with various excuses, the Congo Free State has refused to grant us fresh sites while it has allotted sites freely to the missions of the Church of Rome'. It was 1909 before the BMS was finally prepared to publish a booklet publicly denouncing Leopold and admitting:

> The painful revelations of the past few years show that the unhappy tribes are in danger of being exterminated not only in the Eastern portion of the territory but also in some of those vast districts not far from the navigable channels of trade between the Atlantic and Stanley falls and this is as a result of the cruel system of misrule by the Congo Government.

The Third Degree

Institute income in 1907 was only around the level it had been a decade earlier, stable but, never rising above £2,000 per annum. A renewed missionary onslaught on African 'heathenism' no longer seemed a viable option nor, perhaps, a desirable one. The Institute was beginning to focus its efforts on educating fewer students to a higher level. Formal examination successes featured more prominently in Annual Reports and apprenticeships diminished. For the first time, Congo House students qualified to read medicine at the highest levels. Press accounts of the

Institute's 1907 Annual Conference illustrate the academic emphasis:

> Encouraging reports were read from the tutors, examiners, treasurer and director. Three of the students had passed their London matriculation examination during the year, two of whom were now studying for their BA degree in the London University with the view of returning as schoolmasters and preachers of the Gospel in British territories. A third is preparing for his final examination as a medical student in Edinburgh with the object of qualifying as a medical missionary and returning home as such. Another student entered Liverpool University last September in order to qualify as a medical officer of health with the view of improving the sanitary conditions of the West Coast of Africa so as to safeguard the health of both natives and white men ...

'Negro Charged with Assault at Llandudno'

Hughes appreciated that graduate alumni lent the Institute academic respectability but he continued to offer apprenticeships to his diminishing number of less academic entrants. Unfortunately, in April 1907, one of these apprenticeships exploded into an extremely damaging accusation of assault. The *Llandudno Advertiser* published a comprehensive account of events:

> A dramatic story was told at a special Police Court on Wednesday, before Dr Dalton and Mr William Bevan. Some two years ago Philip Waribo, a West African lad, came over to the Congo Institute at Colwyn Bay and six months ago was on the point of returning to his native country when Mrs Prior of Barbery Hall, Colwyn Bay, became interested in his welfare and arranged for him to learn the trade of shoemaking in its entirety at the shop of Mr William Martin, Moon Street, Llandudno. The lady paid a premium of £30 and the arrangement was that Waribo was to pay 12s a week to them for his board and lodging out of the money he earned at the

shop. In this way Waribo hoped to return to his country the master of a most useful trade.

The assault complained of took place on Tuesday afternoon, in the shop of Mr Martin who told the tale. After having asked the magistrates if it was necessary to go into the incidents which led to the affair and being requested to be as brief as possible complainant said the matter arose over a very trifling affair and when the defendant mentioned it to him and said it was not worth discussing he suddenly turned the key in the shop door and rushed at him. The next moment he found himself in the corner with the defendant on top of him, holding him down. While in that position he cried to the defendant, *You don't want to fight do you?* Defendant said No and let him get up and unlock the door to let Mr Winch in. When Mr Winch came in defendant made another rush and struck at witness again and eventually floored him again and fell on him. It took three men to pull him off.

Questioned by defendant, Mr Martin denied striking the first blow. Defendant had nothing further to ask but announced that he had something to say.

Dr Dalton: *You can say what you like when the witnesses have been heard.*

Mr Winch, proprietor of Moon's Hotel described how his attention was attracted by hearing a voice cry, *Let me out, let me out* and looking through the shop window saw a struggle going on, which he took at first to be larking and went on with his occupation. A minute or two later Mr Martin tapped the window and he went to the shop but found the door locked. After going in search of another key he returned and found the door open. Both complainant and defendant were then equal with one another in passion and he tried to pacify them. The argument however went on and both went for each other again. In the struggle they were separated and witness advised Waribo to put on his coat and go for a walk to cool down. That was the end of the fracas as far as he was concerned.

Councillor Pierce Jones gave similar evidence but thought

that Waribo had tried to kick Martin while on the floor. The evidence of Mr Pierce Jones concluded the case for the complainant and Philip Waribo gave evidence on oath.

Speaking in broken English he told the Court how he could not get his washing and to seeing Mr Martin wearing his pants and using his handkerchief and that a few days later he saw his socks on Mr Martin's feet. A friend at Colwyn Bay advised him not to say anything about it until he was quite sure. That was on Sunday last, and continuing his story, witness said, "Yesterday I watch Mr Martin and when he button his boot I see my socks on his feet. Here was an opportunity. So I tell him I don't like to quarrel, but you got my socks on your feet. My pants I cannot find. I don't know what to do. He say 'You tell Mrs Brown'. I say 'You the man that I have got to do with' but he say 'Nonsense'. After dinner he say 'You make Mrs Brown give me notice to leave the house', and then point at my nose. Then he try to hit me. I not hit him or I would kill him but I take hold of him and throw him down and say, 'Are you going to knock me again?' He say 'No'. I then say I leave you alone. Mr Winch then come and we quarrel again. Mr Martin hit me on my lip and it bleed. I then say 'As long as you pull blood in me I must pull blood in you' and take hold of him again and throw him down. He then say better send for a policeman. The sergeant came but he say, 'I don't see anything in the matter'. I say, 'I am here, take me to the prison and let the public know what's come to my things."

Sergeant Williams said that was quite correct and in reply to Dr Dalton, that Waribo walked up very quietly with him. Miss Prior said Waribo was a native of Boni, West Africa, who had been in the Congo Institute. Her mother took an interest in him and he was apprenticed for two years to Mr Martin, so that he could learn the bootmaking trade in every detail and then return to West Africa. A premium of £30 was paid and Waribo was to pay 12s a week for his board and lodging and washing to them. Mr Martin on his part was to pay Waribo for the work he did and he believed even now owed him money. Waribo was a very quiet lad, with a perfect record in this country. The Revd J H Hope senior curate of Colwyn Bay also gave evidence and said the defendant was a youth of irreproachable character.

Mrs Martin, wife of the complainant, then asked to be allowed to give evidence, and on being sworn indignantly denied that Mr Martin had worn defendant's pants which she described as being so old that she refused to mend them. Waribo left his washing about and when Mr Martin asked for a pair of socks one day, she told him to take a pair that were lying about, as she did not know whose they were. The defendant behaved like a perfect madman in the house and threatened to murder her and her father and husband. *He must be taken back to the Institute!* She would not have him in the house again.

In dismissing the case and ordering the complainant, Mr Martin, to pay the costs, the Chairman said that the defendant should not have been locked up, but he had insisted upon that course being taken. Later on in the day Waribo left Llandudno in company with his benefactress, Mrs Prior, and the Revd J H Hope and returned to Colwyn Bay.

Philip Waribo was cleared and William Martin left embittered and resentful. Officially the Institute's reputation escaped unsullied but the incident discouraged tradesman from offering apprenticeships and put-off potential sponsors. Within a year Philip Beccles Waribo returned to Africa without either academic qualifications or a certified trade.

Profitable Speculation?
Ever entrepreneurial, Hughes attempted to supplement the Institute's finances with a bit of property speculation. With Colwyn Bay farmland rapidly being turned into a flourishing holiday and retirement resort, land values had recently leapt from around 3 shillings a square yard to 20 shillings or more. Hughes had made money from land he purchased at Nantyglyn, immediately selling half of his plot for what he had paid for the whole, but in 1907 it appeared that William had struck property

gold! He'd bought half an acre of land at Greenfield Road, Colwyn Bay, for £1,100, or about 10 shillings a square yard, and so was reasonably confident of making a profit. Then local newspapers announced that developers seeking a site for the erection of a new Colwyn Bay theatre had settled on acquiring his Greenfield plot! A subsequent report announced that the developers had indeed purchased the land from Hughes before it all started to unravel. Without ever identifying who was responsible for the exaggeration local newspapers began to reveal that theatre plans had never advanced beyond speculation and after interviewing Hughes they discovered that although his land had been measured by developers no contracts had been signed nor sale agreed. The projected theatre was never built and Hughes never managed to sell his Greenfield site.

A Princely Visitor

Whatever financial difficulties faced the African Institute, Hughes never failed to welcome visitors who showed the least interest in his work. When black South African 'Prince Peter Lobengula' appeared at Congo House in the summer of 1907 he was invited to stay for a while and even represented the Institute at cricket against *Colwyn Bay*.

Peter Lobengula had originally come to Britain, in 1899, to re-enact the role of a rebellious native in an African version of Buffalo Bill's *Wild West Show*. The entrepreneurial showman, Frank E Fillis, had engaged Lobengula along with wild animals and over 200 other inhabitants of the 'Dark Continent' to entertain Britain with touring performances of *Savage South Africa* – an exciting, farrago of everyday life and dramatic events in Africa designed to appeal to the vicarious prejudices of a white, English audience.

Described as the son of the late King of the Matabele, following the opening of the show in London, pen-portraits of the star of *Savage South Africa* appeared in the national press:

Prince Lobengula in his feathers and war paint is a remarkably handsome man. He must be fully six feet in his height, he is broad and muscular, and splendidly proportioned. He has a fine countenance, magnificent eyes and teeth, and altogether – in striking contrast to the other natives – he makes a pleasing picture to look upon. He is also a pleasant conversationalist, talks English intelligently and his manners are courteous and refined. He struck me, moreover, as a perfectly straightforward and simple man. His age is about twenty-four, but he looks much older.

In an interview published in the *Church Family Newspaper* Lobengula explained; 'My father sent me away from his kraal in Bulawayo about fourteen years ago to Bloemfontein to be educated as a civilised man. He wanted me taught English so that I could interpret for him when the English concession-hunters came about him.' He became a Christian, Peter said:

the first time I went to Bloemfontein. The Wesleyan missionaries took me in hand ... I have learned to know that Christianity makes people less cruel than the native tribes of Africa, and better in every way. I go to church every Sunday and do not consider that my knowledge of Christianity is yet complete, so I continue learning about the Christian religion.

By the time the 'courteous and refined' Christian Peter Lobengula visited Colwyn Bay a lot of water had flowed under the bridge. His two-year marriage to Kitty Jewell, the attractive daughter of a Cornish mining engineer, had been conducted throughout in a blaze of newspaper notoriety involving prosecutions for theft and violence, a faked suicide and endless press racism. The *Sun* newspaper marked the pair's final parting by gleefully recalling, 'When this young woman's infatuation for the dusky leader of the Earl's Court niggers first became known it was predicted that nothing but misery for her could result'!

Peter seemed to have survived the highly-charged years of his marriage to Kitty without ill-effect and in 1902 he married Lily Magowan, a Belfast girl living in Salford, where the couple settled in Pendleton. When Lobengula turned up at Colwyn Bay he had abandoned the glamorous but uncertain world of show business and with three children and a wife to support was employed as a labourer in a Lancashire coal mine. For both Peter Lobengula and William Hughes, that summer of 1907, crowned with a glorious 121 runs to 66 cricket win over Colwyn Bay, was fondly remembered. Tragedy for both lay not far ahead.

Chapter Nine

Young, Gifted and Black
(1882–1912)

Congo House embodied the personality, philosophy and fortunes of William Hughes and whilst his life and his Institute constitute the body of this book it is impossible to incorporate the biographies of his students within the narrative without reducing them to mere ciphers. This chapter therefore interrupts the continuing narrative to introduce some of the students who attended the African Institute, to add names and personalities to faces, and to trace their lives back before they arrived at Colwyn Bay and forward to their lives after they returned to Africa.

A comprehensive, chronological listing of Congo House students is included as an appendix; this chapter illustrates the lives of almost a third of those alumni. The biographies are grouped according to, and are representative of, the students' various geographical origins (modern place names used with colonial-era names included, where relevant).

Congo

Kinkasa
When William first set foot in Africa in September 1882 he was first sent to Underhill mission station where he soon came across a little native boy named Kinkasa, who was then only about seven years of age. When Hughes was posted upriver to take charge of Bayneston mission station he took Kinkasa with him and the boy accompanied William whenever he visited the villages surrounding Bayneston, acting as a native envoy. Ever loyal to Hughes, it was Kinkasa who eventually won over William's next recruit, Nkanza. After travelling back to Wales with William and Nkanza in 1885 the trio toured the chapels together raising funds for their Congo House project. Sadly Kinkasa was never to see the

The First Four Students: Nkanza, Daniel, Frank, Kinkasa

scheme reach fruition. In March 1887, when Hughes and his little 'family' were living in Bay View Road, Colwyn Bay, Kinkasa's health began to deteriorate. Aged only twelve, he died the following year on 3rd May 1888. The cause of death was certified as, 'Congo Sleeping Sickness', a long slow killer caused by the parasite, *Trypanosoma brucei gambiense*.

Nkanza Ross

According to Hughes, 'Nkanza was bright and lively, he would smile at any time, he had no fear of anything'. Sometime in early 1883, after Kinkasa and William had visited a nearby village called Vunda, the village chief brought Nkanza to Hughes at Baynestown to see if he could do anything for Nkanza's painful feet. When William examined Nkanza he found he was so severely afflicted with 'jiggers' that he could hardly stand. After digging out the parasites that had bored into the soles of Nkanza's feet, William bathed and treated them and so made another friend for life. Unfortunately, as William soon discovered, Nkanza and his mother, were both owned by the Chief as slaves. Whilst Nkanza's mother pleaded with the Chief to release Nkanza into Hughes' care, the Chief refused to do so without payment. After satisfying the Chief with a bale of cloth Nkanza, sadly said goodbye to his mother and like Kinkasa, became William's constant companion.

In 1886, when William and the boys were still touring the chapels of Wales, Nkanza learnt that his mother had died in the Congo, still in servitude. Despite his obvious sadness the boy continued to prove an irrepressible handful to Hughes, who later recalled, 'For about three years after we came to this country, Nkanza gave me a little anxiety, for he retained the lively humour which I discovered in him the first day we met; and he took readily to the tricks and ways of his little white friends and companions'. Fortunately, Kinkasa acted as an elder brother and remained a steadying influence on Nkanza who eventually buckled down to some serious studying. He received a prize for, 'improvement in English grammar' from his Colwyn Bay teacher E Owen and he impressed Mr H W Powlson, who operated the town's commercial printers in Rhiw Road, where he was sent for practical training. Eventually Nkanza, 'committed to memory every word of the new Testament in English. At first he could only memorise six or eight verses a day but as his English and his memory improved by practice he gradually got to learn a chapter in a very short time. He committed the whole book of Revelation to memory in nine days.'

Nkanza learnt both English and Welsh and people in Colwyn Bay noted that he spoke English with a pronounced Welsh accent! After Kinkasa's death, Hughes referred, affectionately, to Nkanza as 'my eldest son' but in vain. Although Nkanza was, 'converted, baptised and received in fellowship at Colwyn Bay in September 1889' he grew increasingly lonely and yearned to return to the Congo. As Hughes recorded in *Dark Africa*, 'The idea of going home grew in him as he grew and now it is the ardent wish of his heart and burns within him...though there is no home where there is no mother; still it is the country where he was born and there he will go.'

It was not to be, after a short illness, Nkanza died from acute heart failure caused by congestion of the liver, on Sunday morning 3 April 1892. He was buried at Old Colwyn the following Tuesday 5 April. 'At a service held at the Congo House Institute the Revd Thomas Roberts, Abergele, read a portion of Scripture from Revelations.' Following further readings and speeches, 'the assembled friends sang *Bydd myrdd o rhyfeddodau* ('There Will be a Myriad Wonders'). The cortege then wended its way towards the place of interment. The coffin, which was covered with beautiful wreaths, was placed in Mr Edwin Jones' modern hearse, following which were six mourning-coaches and then the pedestrian mourners...Much sympathy was shown on all hands, Nkanza, who was sixteen years of age, was much liked by all who knew him.'

Frank Teva

Frank was born in 1875 at Palaba, a place on the south bank of the river Congo, and about 112 miles from its mouth. In 1880, his father enrolled him at a new school begun by a Scottish missionary, Revd Henry Craven, one of the first missionaries sent to the Congo by the Livingstone Inland Mission. Frank proved an excellent scholar and one Sunday afternoon in about 1885 he attended a talk at the school given by a Scottish lady called Miss Kakle that really 'touched his heart'. As he later confided to William Hughes, 'From that moment I determined I would follow Christ and be God's child and I have followed him ever since.'

Frank was baptised by another Scottish missionary, Revd Joseph Clark, and received into fellowship. Clark was so impressed by Frank's potential that he arranged for his further training at Colwyn Bay where he enrolled in February 1888. He quickly established himself a popular character in both the Institute and the town. During his time at Congo House Frank trained as a wheelwright with Thomas Davies of Colwyn Bay and studied first-aid and simple surgery with Dr G Herbert Rutter, also of the town, who presented him with two medical books, a medicine chest and twenty-two shillings and sixpence on his return to the Congo.

Frank sailed for Africa on the *SS Gaboon* in November 1892 accompanied by his old mentor, Revd Joseph Clark, who was returning to the Congo under the auspices of the American Baptist Mission Union (ABMU). Clark had been visiting Congo House with his wife and had engaged Frank to assist him in his Congo mission. Frank returned with a considerable number of gifts from his friends in Colwyn Bay, including a pocket knife, a hand saw, chisels, planes and other assorted tools, a writing desk, two inkstands, a songbook, soap, six handkerchiefs, a collar and tie and a pair of slippers.

Once back in Africa Joseph Clark continued their mission at Irebu whilst Frank, with the help of eight labourers, began constructing a new mission station at a town called Ikoko. Joseph visited him every couple of weeks to ensure all was going well. Meanwhile, Frank dispensed the men's wages every day and bandaged their wounds when necessary. Writing to Hughes in 1894, Frank emphasised how useful his basic medical training had proved and advising William, 'I think it would not be a bad idea for every student in your Institute to know a little about medicine before he goes out to the work, for it is a very useful thing.'

Frank kept in touch with Colwyn Bay over the years and he

continued to work with Joseph Clark and the American Baptists but in 1898 the ABMU transferred some of its outposts to Leopold's Free State. Frank's station was one of the first to be given up and he was posted to take charge of a mission station in Upper Congo on the shores of Lake Tumba half a day's steamer ride from Ikoko. When that mission was given up he was posted to the main station at Ikoko, which ran a school for 250 pupils. Hughes also wrote to Frank from Colwyn Bay, enclosing photographs of his family.

Whilst at Ikoko, Frank would regularly paddle his canoe to preach to the villages around the shores of the lake and to attract a good audience he learnt a new skill, playing the piano accordion. As he confided to Hughes, 'When I played it almost the whole town would come out to see what the noise was and then we would preach to them. It is very helpful indeed.'
Frank is believed to have spent the rest of his life building up the Ikoko Mission Station until he passed away in 1927.

Daniel Harvey

Coming to Colwyn Bay in 1888, Daniel was the last of the four Congo students trained by Hughes before the Institute occupied Myrtle Villa in 1890. In 1889 Daniel contributed recitations to evening entertainments that Hughes organised at Colwyn Bay's Tabernacl Chapel. During his time at the Institute, then based at Bay View Road, Daniel was trained by craftsman Isaac Hughes at a local carpentry workshop, as well as being thoroughly schooled in scripture. After a couple of years, Hughes felt Daniel had already become the most accomplished carpenter likely to be found along the coast of West Africa and he arranged for him to travel back to the Congo. The Elder Dempster Shipping Company agreed, in lieu of payment, to let him work his passage, and a farewell meeting, to be held at Tabernacl Chapel, arranged for the evening of Monday 14 July 1890.

As the first of Hughes' students to be sent back as a missionary to Africa, it was made clear to Daniel that he bore a heavy weight of responsibility upon his shoulders. At the farewell meeting Simon Jones of Wrexham reminded the assembled friends and supporters, 'The Institute's success depended largely upon Daniel's future course for if he, the pioneer, let his earthly calling monopolise his thoughts to the exclusion of his missionary labours, then the success, and possibly the life, of the Institute would be seriously jeopardised.'

In Africa Daniel received several offers of employment, some of which would have proved materially very rewarding, such as one from Heydes, a trader, who wanted him to act as his transport agent at Matadi. Daniel declined, preferring to pursue missionary work with the ABMU at Lukunga, a settlement on the south bank of the river Congo. Daniel's carpentry skills proved both practically useful and attractive in drawing admirers to whom he would then explain his religious ideas. The inhabitants of the villages surrounding Lukunga were fascinated to hear of his experiences in Britain and these tales caused him to become affectionately known as, 'The Black-whiteman'. Unfortunately for Daniel the natives were less keen to learn about Jesus!

In 1891 Daniel was looking forward to being given sole charge of his own mission station at a place called Kinkamba but there was a snag, as he revealed in a letter he sent back to Colwyn Bay, 'I am anxious to get a native hut there until I will put up my own house. Some are anxious to be taught by me carpentry and some are asking me to teach them English and they say, We are willing to let you have one of our houses to live in until you build your own, but you must not go about preaching; and then I told them, If I live with you and teach you only what you think best I should be doing a wrong thing against God and against you.'

Sadly, Daniel's mission was cut short as he fell victim to Congo Sleeping Sickness and died in 1895.

William Lufwilu

When William arrived from the Congo on 22 May 1891 the Institute had already moved into its permanent Myrtle Villa accommodation. Willie came from the Congo on board *SS Benguela* with three other Congo boys, Thomas, George and Samba who were fortunate in arriving in time to be able to accompany William Hughes in meeting H. M. Stanley in

William Lufwilu

Thomas Wamba

George Fraser

Samba

Caernarfon the following month. After a year and a half's training at the Institute Willie was scheduled to return to Africa. At the 15 November 1892 farewell meeting he offered up to his audience a prayer delivered in his own native language. The following morning he sailed for Africa aboard *SS Gaboon*. Although Willie, like Frank, had been sent to Colwyn Bay by Joseph Clark he hadn't particularly distinguished himself at the Institute or made himself as popular as Frank and possibly as a consequence he wasn't as laden down with presents and had to make do with; two books, a pencil, a pen and an inkstand, some soap, a necktie and a silk handkerchief. According to Frank the voyage home didn't go too well; 'We had very bad weather when coming through the Bay of Biscay, all of us were sick…Again when we came near Boma the ship stuck on sand and we had to stay there about two days, and then they sent a boat from Boma to fetch us, which took some of the things and brought us to Matadi. In about a week afterwards we heard that she had got off …', and there the trail disappears. Although Willie, like Frank, was supposed to be engaged to work with Revd Joseph Clark of the ABMU, unlike Frank he didn't keep in touch with the Institute and nothing further is known of his subsequent career.

Thomas Wamba
Thomas arrived from the Congo with Willie in May 1891 and proved a little more accomplished. In January 1892 his teacher, Rhys Morgan noted that, 'He reads with considerable freedom and spells very fairly. He composed a letter in which he showed a very commendable grasp of simple English and he has also acquired a reliable knowledge of the elementary facts of the geography of Europe … he can work sums in simple addition and simple subtractions with accuracy but because his knowledge of the multiplication tables is imperfect he cannot be trusted for accuracy in multiplication'. Tested, in 1892 by W. B. Jones on his knowledge of the life of Christ as described in the Gospel of St John, the examiner, W. B. Jones of Pontypridd, noted that Thomas, 'seemed to know the chief events recorded in the said Gospel by heart'. Tom also, 'served for some time as an

apprentice with Messrs Lewis Bros, Drapers, Conway Road'. Clearly he, 'was a most promising youth.'

Despite this promise Thomas Wamba was prematurely returned to the Congo to assist the American missionary, Revd Clarence B. Antisdel, on 22 April 1893 on 'medical advice, on account of ill-health, having suffered for some months from rheumatism and debility.' Tom took with him the following presents; a bible, an album, a book, stationery and an inkstand, a work-box and some medicines, three shirts, a looking glass and an easy chair. Antisdel eventually returned to America to become the first white President of Benedict College, South Carolina, but the fate of Thomas Wamba is unrecorded.

George Fraser
George was the child of a Scottish father and black African mother. When George's father died his only legacy to the young boy was a copy of *Pilgrim's Progress* that neither George nor his mother could read. The Scottish missionary, Joseph Clark, offered to educate George at his mission station and as he grew, Clark began to believe he would benefit from training at the Institute and so George arrived at Colwyn Bay in May 1891. Examined by Mr O. Waldo James in 1892 George appeared, 'well grounded in secular and religious knowledge.' In 1894, his new teacher, E. J. Davies, was similarly pleased with his school work. George also developed his social skills at Congo House and for the 1895 Grand Bazaar at the Public Hall (now Theatr Colwyn), George, along with Alfred Dibundu and Mojola Agbebi manned the African Curiosities Room, where they eloquently introduced crowds of fascinated local residents and holidaymakers to the Institute's unique collection of artefacts. It seems George might actually have advanced his social skills a little too far and there were rumours that he had acted improperly with local girls in Colwyn Bay and been thrashed and expelled as a result; although Hughes later refused to formally acknowledge this, Fraser didn't return to the Congo and although he was reported to have sailed to Ghana no further reference to him appeared in Institute publications.

Samba

Samba was born into slavery in the Congo about 1877 and never knew his father or mother. Revd Joseph Clark bought him out of slavery and sent him to Colwyn Bay in May 1891. Samba soon proved both popular and keen to learn. His teacher, Revd E. J. Davies spoke very highly of him and having been at the Institute for only eight months, on 29 February 1892, 'Samba together with other the other students, after school hours went out to play in the adjoining field, where he accidentally fell, receiving internal injury, and although he ate pretty well during his illness, about four days previous to his death neither food nor medicine would remain in the system and on March 9th he somewhat suddenly expired, the sad news causing great gloom throughout Colwyn Bay'. It seems that Samba's fall had ruptured his liver. He was the second student to die and within a month his death was to be followed by that of Nkanza.

> The coffin was covered with beautiful wreaths sent by loving friends poor Samba had made since his arrival in our midst ... He will be mourned for and greatly missed by Mr Clark and by his fellow-students, who *en-masse* followed his remains to the grave.

Ernestina Francis

Ernestina was the first female student enrolled at Colwyn Bay. She was the child of the unmarried union of the young Dutch trader Frederikus de la Fontaine Verweij, and his black African consort, that William met when he first set foot in the Congo as a missionary in 1882. Born the following year at Banana, Ernestina's father preferred not to take his black, illegitimate daughter back with him on his return home to Hilversum and was only too pleased to pack her off to Wales as soon as Hughes was able to accept her, in August 1891. Her father also supplied Hughes with a generous endowment to cover her living expenses and education.

Aged eight, Ernestina was enrolled as a student at the Institute and Hughes anticipated she would be the first female of many,

Ernestina Francis

Lulu Coote

Roul van der Most

Charlie Stewart

with frequent appeals for funds to create a dedicated girls' department at Colwyn Bay. Despite being formally registered as a student, William treated Ernestina as his own daughter. Ernestina was baptised by Hughes at the Institute in July 1898 along with Katie his birth daughter. In August 1899 she served as a bridesmaid at Hughes' second wedding along with his own identically dressed daughters.

Whilst at the Institute Ernestina gained a Teaching Certificate and also fell in love with fellow student Joseph Morford (see below) who departed for Nigeria in October 1904. Having been parted for two years, on 2 December 1906 Ernestina sailed for Africa aboard the *SS Fantee*. Arriving in Lagos on 16 December, she was overwhelmed when Morford turned up to greet her. Less than a fortnight later, at 4 pm on 28 December Ernestina and Joseph were married in Lagos by Mojola Agebei with Ayodeji Oyejola (see below) standing in for Ernestina's absent father.

Together, the pair first taught at Buguma but after Ernestina developed health problems due to the damp climate they transferred to Onitsha in southern Nigeria where Joseph ran the boys' school whilst Ernestina was headmistress of the girls' school. In 1909 Ernestina and Joseph took a six months holiday, visiting both America and Britain, with a short time spent at the Institute. They paid an extended visit to Colwyn Bay in the summer of 1913 when the pregnant Ernestina decided to stay on and have her baby born in Wales although in September Joseph was obliged to return to Africa to resume his teaching duties. Sadly it was not to be, 'after a very short illness' Ernestina died on 11 January 1914 of acute double lobar pneumonia. As the local newspaper observed in its report of her burial at Old Colwyn, 'The deceased lady was well-known in Colwyn Bay and all who knew her had the highest esteem for her.'

Lulu Coote

Lulu Coote was born in 1890 and came to Colwyn Bay in 1897 from Banana, Congo River. She was the second female student at the Institute and like Ernestina was the offspring of a white Dutch trader and black African mother and also like Ernestina she was informally adopted as a daughter by William Hughes. Both Lulu and Ernestina attended William's 1899 wedding as bridesmaids. During her training she was always determined to become a nurse and her tutor Mr T Herber Davies noted, 'for which profession she has a special aptitude' and so he arranged her curriculum with this goal in mind. Once she was old enough Hughes arranged her transfer to Ashton-under-Lyne District Infirmary for completion of formal medical qualifications. In 1911 she was employed as a nurse at Ashton-under-Lyne but her later career is unknown.

Angola

Roul van der Most

Roul arrived at the Institute in 1891 from St. Paul de Loanda, 150 km south of the river Congo, in modern-day Angola. Throughout his time at Colwyn Bay he applied himself to all aspects of his training with skill and determination. In 1897, for example, he scored 100 per cent in 'English Grammar', 100 per cent in 'Arithmetic' and 96 per cent in 'Geography' and proved the most academic of the thirteen students then at Colwyn Bay. A popular performer at the Institute's regular public concerts in February 1897 his 'turn' received patronising praise in the pages of the 'Weekly News'; 'Another attractive little man from the *Dark* Continent, Master Roul, recited remarkably well, *The Walrus and the Carpenter*'.

In 1900 Roul returned to Africa but took up mission work in Sierra Leone, rather than Angola. He was reported to be doing sterling work a decade later but thereafter nothing further is known.

Liberia

Charles Stewart

Of all the Africans to come to Colwyn Bay, Charles Stewart had the most traumatic childhood. His life story appeared in several Institute reports. As a boy, 'he saw his mother and father beheaded by another tribe, who fell upon them suddenly in the dawn. He was made to carry the very sword that beheaded his parents. He was sold many times, when a boy of twelve or thirteen, from one master to another. At last a good-hearted negro missionary from America, who had been a slave himself, took a journey to the interior of Liberia. Providence directed his attention to Charlie, and he resolved, there and then, to redeem him from slavery; this he did with ten kegs of gunpowder – value 30 shillings in English money:

> He brought him to the coast and taught him in school where he made gradual progress in English and other elementary subjects. Whilst in this school, when the gospel truths were revealed to him, Charlie found Jesus Christ ... After two years he accompanied the missionary to England and then America. Together they visited negro churches and institutions in America, and roused the educated negroes of the United States to practical sympathy with the educational work commenced and projected in the Dark Continent. After more than a year in America, (in 1899) the missionary brought Charlie to the African Training Institute (Colwyn Bay), and left him there to be trained; he himself returning to his field of labour in Liberia.

Charlie Stewart proved a reliable student with good marks in all subjects and a particularly impressive 96 per cent score in Latin. After five years at the Institute, on Thursday, 28 January 1904, he sailed from Liverpool, on board *SS Coomassie*, bound for Liberia. 'The following lines were found pinned on the Tutor's door on the morning of Charlie's departure:

> The day, oh what a day is this,
> My heart with sorrows swell,
> I now must leave my comrades all,
> And say to them 'farewell.'
>
> Oh, such a happy time I spent
> While roving in this dell;

Joseph Burnley

George Steane

Alf Dibundu

Kofele

But ah! The clock of time strikes twelve,
And I must say 'farewell'

My comrades here, be peaceful still,
While I away must dwell,
My eyes with tears, ah yes, do fill,
'Farewell' my boys, farewell.

Once he reached Liberia Charlie, accompanied by other converts from the coast, journeyed 200 miles into the interior to the very place he himself had formerly been enslaved. There, 'by the help of my brother, who is now King of the Pessy tribe, I am freeing many boys and girl from slavery to the influences of Christianity by buying them from the warriors and chiefs of the tribes.'

Cameroon

Kofele M'besa

Kofele was the first student Hughes accepted from outside the Congo River region but his arrival at Colwyn Bay came via a rather tortuous route. Kofele was born in 1875 in Cameroon and received some initial training with Revd Wright Hay of the BMS who brought Kofele with him when he travelled to Edinburgh in 1885. The pair remained there from February 1885 until March 1886 when Revd Hay was posted to India by the BMS. Kofele was then returned to Cameroon by a party of Baptist missionaries on their way to the Congo. He stayed in Cameroon, in the care of local Baptist missionaries, from April 1886 until they sold their properties to German missionaries and left the locality in August 1887. Kofele was very upset by the departure of the Baptists but some friends managed to arrange a new home for him, hundreds of miles away, with a Mrs Wilson in Old Calabar. This lady was the widow of a Church of England clergyman who had gone out to Africa, at her own expense, to conduct her own independent mission work. In June 1890 Mrs Wilson travelled to England with Kofele, having provisionally arranged a place for him at a prominent, non-denominational training school in London, run by a Mrs Grattan Guinness. When they arrived at Liverpool they found the anticipated vacancy wasn't available, but fortunately by August 1890 there was a place available at Colwyn Bay.

At the Institute Kofele was schooled by Revd E. J. Davies but as his main interest was in receiving some basic medical training he was also apprenticed to Mr W. H. Roberts, Chemist of Colwyn Bay and latterly to Dr Rutter who presented him with a medical book and a medicine chest on his return to Cameroon in November 1892. Kofele's other gifts on departure included two writing desks, an inkstand and a clock, assorted books and albums, two lots of 'useful clothes', a quantity of collars, three handkerchiefs, a brush and comb and a ring.

Back in Africa, Kofele kept in touch with his friends in Colwyn Bay. Initially he worked at Buguma, New Calabar (Nigeria) before moving back to Cameroon where he worked for a short period with Joshua Dibundu. Having demonstrated his worth from December 1894 he was given sole charge of a mission station at Bimbia which he ran in connection with the German Mission. In 1895 Kofele married the daughter of a deceased native minister who was being brought up by her mother. She supported his mission work but after a few years Kofele became much troubled by illness and convinced that the climate of his homeland was to blame he began taking holidays in Ghana to recuperate. In 1911, during his third trip to Ghana he wrote to Hughes from Accra keeping him up to date with his news. Kofele is thought to have continued his mission in Cameroon throughout the First World War period but nothing later is recorded.

Joseph Ebakise Burnley

Joseph Burnley was born in Victoria, Cameroon. His father, Stephen Burnley, was a pioneering member of Alfred Saker's congregation who, on 12 August 1858, transferred to Ambas Bay on the mainland from Fernando Po in response to Spanish demands that islanders abandon their protestant faith. The Baptists renamed their new home 'Victoria' after the reigning British monarch and Joseph Burnley was born in this new settlement in 1872. He enrolled at the Colwyn Bay Institute in 1892 and proved an excellent student, achieving a 'first class honours' in an externally set Latin exam. Joseph was equally accomplished in practical skills. He learnt tailoring with Lewis Bros, Bradford House and photography with J. W. Thomas, Kensington House. Returning to Africa in October 1895 he laboured, voluntarily, at his hometown of Victoria until July 1896 when he was nominated for mission work at Soppo, one of the larger inland towns, about 45 miles from Ambas Bay.

After moving to Soppo, situated at the foot of the Cameroon mountains, in August 1896, Joseph stayed with Chief Sako, who unlike his predecessor was very supportive of the missionaries. In fact, Joseph was told by Mokako, the Chief's brother, that the previous Chief, Woloa, had on one occasion actually ordered him to fire upon Revd Thomas Lewis Johnson and his brother-in-law and only Sako had prevented him complying with Chief Woloa's command and killing them both. Joseph Burnley was clearly very pleased that the inhabitants of Soppo had been 'civilised' having not long before been 'very wild and bloodthirsty' and he was grateful to be able to play his part in further civilising the natives. His training seems to have produced a disdain for the beliefs and practices of Burnley's fellow-countrymen. Writing in November 1897 Joseph confided to Hughes:

> As I told you, when at Colwyn Bay, the people believe very much in witchcraft; the Ju Ju men have got a very great influence over them. My aim is to try and get hold of the children, and, by the aid of the Holy Spirit, plant the mustard seeds in their hearts while they are young.

Even the use of an African drum to summon the faithful seemed inappropriate to him, 'I would be thankful to anyone ... who would supply us with a church bell, for we are in need of one very much. At present we have been obliged to use the African elimbi (drum).' In May 1898 Hughes noted, 'A bell has already been presented by a Birmingham friend and is on its way to Africa'.

In March 1898 Joseph was married in Soppo where his

wedding was enthusiastically celebrated by crowds of local people. An extensive list of wedding presents included a goat from Chief Sako and a cow from Chief E. E. Metombe. Joseph's mission work prospered and he continued to correspond with William Hughes until about 1916.

Joseph Ebakise Burnley is still fondly remembered in Cameroon as 'the first African pastor of the Native Baptist Church in Victoria' where he served until his death in 1936.

George Steane

Kofele endured the most extended route to Colwyn Bay but George Steane suffered the most terrifying! Born in Victoria, Cameroon, in his youth George spent three years assisting missionaries in the Congo and by saving his modest wages accrued the grand total of eight pounds sterling. With his heart set on training at Colwyn Bay, in 1891, he first returned to see his mother and brother Robert in Cameroon, and gave them six pounds of his savings. Then after packing a tin trunk with his clothes and a bible he boarded the 2,625 ton Elder-Dempster Liverpool-bound steamer, *Soudan*. As Elder-Dempster allowed Hughes' students free passage, George had two pounds left in his pocket to enjoy himself. All was going well until about five-hundred miles into the voyage, off the Ivory Coast, the *Soudan* hit a rock:

> Everybody made their way to the boats as quickly as possible. Many of the sailors had shown themselves to be ungodly men but when the ship stuck they fell on their knees and prayed … George's first thought was to rescue his precious bible. He forgot his tin-trunk and his clothes … The captain who was kind, told him to get into a boat but as he was about to do so, a selfish man, who feared the boat might be overloaded, pulled out his revolver and said: *This boat is not made for niggers!* … George got into another boat and he and his bible were rescued. The steamer sank. The boat was tossed about for three days and three nights; there was no food, the waves broke over the boat, and at night they suffered from the cold.

After three days a ship picked them up and took them to Sierra Leone.

Once ashore he was spotted by the good-natured captain who bought George a new suit of clothes and arranged his onward travel in another Elder-Dempster steamer. Once at Liverpool he was looked after by a local supporter of the Institute who arranged for the final leg of his journey to Colwyn Bay. He arrived at the Institute in July 1891.

Early in 1894 George contracted a very heavy cold which just seemed to get worse. Eventually it developed into pleurisy and on Thursday 17 May 1894 he passed away. On Saturday 19 May George Steane was buried in an unmarked grave in Old Colwyn cemetery (the grave can be located between the marked graves of William Hughes and that of Ernestina Morford. It is shared with Alfred Johnstone, who died just three weeks later).

Alfred R Tongo Dibundu

In February 1893 Revd Joshua Dibundu of Akwa town, Cameroons wrote to Hughes arranging the training at Colwyn Bay of his son Alfred Tongo, born 1875. In August 1895 Alfred ran the curiosities stall with Agbebi and George Fraser. On returning to Africa in October 1895 he continued his father's mission work at Akwa, Cameroon. In January 1897 he wrote to William thanking him for the gift of a camera and informing him of his order for more chemicals from Liverpool. Throughout the years Alfred continued as one of William's most loyal correspondents. On 10 July 1916 he wrote from Duala informing Hughes:

> We have suffered greatly by this terrible war out here. The Germans who ought to have been our supporters and protectors proved to be our deadly enemies; hundreds of natives were massacred, many villages burnt down, properties were looted and many starved to death ... As most of my books and properties were stolen and looted my certificate as late student of your Institution and minister of the Gospel is also

Koffee Twintoh

Kwesi Quainoo

Joe Morford

Paul Daniels

looted and I do beg of you to kindly send another, because it is much better at this time to have a certificate of one's profession ... Your former student, devoted and loving, ALFRED DIBUNDU.

Dibundu continued to write to Hughes until August 1917 when he began to collaborate with newly arrived French missionary, Elijah Allegret, but Allegret soon tired of Dibundu's resurgent nationalism, just as the Germans had previously tried to suppress his father's spirit of independence.

Ghana

Koffee Twintoh

Often refered to in Institute documents by the European name of 'Albert Darlington', Koffee arrived from Chama, Ghana in 1901, aged twenty. His father was called Kwesi Dapatame, his mother Abbah Poprodo. Koffee trained in blacksmithing with David Jones & Co. of Colwyn Bay. His blacksmithing skills proved superior to his religious knowledge, in which he came last in the class of 1901–2. Koffee did achieve a third class pass in his College of Preceptors Examinations in 1904 just before he returned to Ghana in 1905. At first he found it difficult to secure missionary work in Africa and so accepted a post with the Seccondee Lighterage Company. Eventually he was recommended to the Revd Mark Hayford, who asked him to help with his mission at Cape Coast. Koffee proved an effective night school teacher and in 1910 recommended three of his pupils to William Hughes for further training, advising Hughes, 'they have got well-to-do relations, but are heathens'! His last letter to Hughes, from 'Seccondee' (Sekondi) was dated 29 April 1911 and thereafter nothing more is known.

Kwesi Quainoo

Born in Saltpond, Gold Coast in1877, as a small boy Kwesi was sent by his Christian parents to a mission school where he determined to take up missionary work himself but his father was too impoverished to continue his education. Kwesi then persuaded his father to send him to stay with his brother on the coast at Accra. His brother, a telegraph clerk didn't have sufficient funds to finance his schooling but he did secure employment for Kwesi, cleaning and running errands at the Customs office where he worked. Whilst Kwesi saved his meagre wages to pay for school fees he learned that there were good men and women in England who sometimes financed the education of poor children. When he raised the topic with his brother he just laughed at the idea, pointing out the fare alone to England cost £25 and then he would also need warm clothes and thick boots to survive in such a cold place.

Kwesi wasn't too discouraged because he believed, ultimately, 'God would provide'. One day in the office he spotted on an old notice on the wall bearing the names of prominent Englishmen and decided to try his luck and write to a couple of them. After selecting the names of Gladstone and Coleridge, the Lord Chief Justice he begged the clerks to let him have some writing paper for his letters. Refusing to hand over government property, they handed him a few sheets of scrap paper.

After work that night he cut off the spoiled bits of paper leaving sufficient to write pitiful accounts of his plight to Coleridge and Gladstone. The next day one of the clerks gave him enough change to buy one stamp and he stuck it on the letter to Coleridge. It was two months before a reply came, and it wasn't what he wished for. Coleridge's secretary claimed his Lordship felt sympathetic but was overwhelmed with appeals for assistance and was unable to help him. Undaunted, Kwesi wrote again and two months later he received a provisional offer of assistance and a series of questions. Kwesi's third letter was forwarded by Coleridge to William Hughes who agreed to accept him at the Institute. When Kwesi finally received his acceptance letter he realised there was only twelve days before the steamer departed for England and as a Government employee he was required to give thirty days notice. At first indignant, the Comptroller of Customs only relented when he realised the social status of Kwesi's English sponsor.

Stepping onto the appointed steamer in March 1893 without a penny in his pocket Kwesi worked his passage by washing dishes and scrubbing floors. Docking at Liverpool he left the ship with six shillings donated by new-found admirers. Taken to the shipping office Alfred Jones slipped him a pound pocket-money, telegraphed ahead to Hughes and Coleridge and arranged Kwesi's onward train transport to Colwyn Bay.

Arriving at Congo house in April 1893 Kwesi continued to correspond with the Lord Chief Justice who duly invited him to spend his nine day Christmas vacation with him and Lady Coleridge at their home, Heath's Court, at Ottery St Mary in Devon. Coleridge subsequently wrote to Hughes expressing the regret he and his wife felt at parting with Kwesi who, 'as to conduct and manners seems to us quite perfect'. If Coleridge hadn't died in June 1894 it was planned for Kwesi to return to Devon for his summer vacation.

At Colwyn Bay Kwesi received daily gardening lessons from Mr Edwards. His teacher of academic subjects, Stanley Wood, noted that, 'His style in English composition and in translation from Latin and Greek is both simple and clear'. After receiving some initial medical training from Mr Brindley BA, tutor of Dinglewood College, Colwyn Bay, Quainoo proved so adept that in 1898 it was agreed to send him to Edinburgh to pursue his medical studies.

During his years at Colwyn Bay Kwesi played an active role in all the Institute's garden parties, cricket matches and concerts. In one particularly successful 'entertainment' in July 1898, Kwesi 'in native costume' sang to 'a very large and appreciative audience', *Ayey* ('Praises') in his native *Fante* tongue. The audience 'were highly delighted with the evening's performance'. Kwesi was clearly exceptionally talented and on the return of Hughes and his bride after their 1899 honeymoon it was Quainoo that was chosen to be the voice of all the assembled African students.

Tragically, on his planned return to Africa in 1900 Kwesi Quainoo died on the voyage and was buried in Sierra Leone.

America

Paul Gbese Daniels

Daniels was born on 9 June 1872 at Charleston, South Carolina, USA. As a young man and an accomplished musician with little prospect of gaining a decent education in his own deeply racist homeland, in 1895 he crossed the Atlantic with the Jenkins Orphanage Band. Sailing on the SS Paris, Paul landed with the band at Southampton in September 1895. In England the band received support from Sir George Williams, founder of the YMCA movement and sponsor of the Colwyn Bay Institute. Following their successful tour of England the band returned to New York on the *SS Teutonic* in October 1895, leaving Daniels behind at Colwyn Bay.

A valedictory meeting was held at the Institute on Sunday 25 October 1899 to bid farewell to Daniels. The collection raised £6 and he departed with glowing testimonials and many gifts. Paul sailed on Wednesday 28 October intent on assisting the Jenkins Orphanage that was responsible for arranging his Colwyn Bay education.

Joseph Morford

Joseph's life was extraordinary. Born in America at Chattanooga, Tennessee of African-American parents, after a basic schooling he expressed a wish to serve in Africa as a missionary but unable to find any American organisation prepared to sponsor him he decided to try his luck in England. Landing at Liverpool he met with no better luck in finding a missionary sponsor. Even supporting himself was difficult so he travelled to London to seek an improvement in his prospects. Eventually he came across the Young Men's Christian Association (YMCA) and was befriended by a Mr James, who was the Secretary of the Welsh division of the Association. Although James testified to Morford's good character he wasn't able to get him missionary work but helped him, at least, gain secure employment in the pits of South Wales. Initially engaged as a labourer at Treherbert colliery in Glamorgan he later moved to Maesteg where he improved his position and worked as a miner earning a good wage but he never lost sight of his goal, the African mission field. Over the next three years underground he continued to apply to foreign missionary societies begging for a position but, as was later reported, 'no-one expected to find a diamond in a coal mine' so he was repeatedly rejected.

After hearing of Congo House he decided it offered an ideal opportunity to improve his prospects of securing a missionary post and so in 1900 he sent off his well-supported application. As Hughes recorded in 1905, 'to satisfy ourselves further, we told Morford if he paid his fare we would give him a week's trial. He agreed heartily. After the week's trial we were completely convinced that he was a suitable candidate. We soon found he had a gift for preaching and speaking and the qualifications to become a missionary in Africa.'

During his time at the Institute Morford gained a Second Class teaching Certificate, with Honours. In October 1904 he sailed from Liverpool for New Calabar with Mojola Agbebi. In November 1904 he began work at Buguma, where he informed Hughes, 'most of the people here are pagans. We have 175 members in our church and over 100 applicants for baptism. A small school has been set up which is growing every day. This is the only Christian church in Buguma, a very large town with 70–80 Chiefs, 6 of whom are members with us, the others being pagans and with unusual powers and influence.'

In 1906 Morford was joined by Ernestina Francis (above) and the pair subsequently moved to Onitsha where he was appointed headmaster of the boys' High School.

Sierra Leone

Dr Ishmael Charles Pratt

Born in Freetown, Sierra Leone, in 1879, Ishmael arrived at Colwyn Bay in 1899 and remained to become one of the Institute's longest-serving and most accomplished students. Ishmael gained initial success in 1903 with a pass in the Medical Preliminary Examination. In the summer of 1910 Ishmael finally

Ishmael Pratt

Aaron George

Davidson Don Jabavu

Mabel Gabashane

qualified as a fully fledged medical doctor after passing a final medical degree at Edinburgh University, even then his studies continued. At Christmas 1910 he passed a Diploma course at Liverpool Tropical Disease Hospital and in 1911 Pratt gained a midwifery diploma at Dublin University. As a model student, whenever he had free time, Ishmael was included in 'deputation work', in which Institute students toured venues around Britain explaining and advertising the Colwyn Bay scheme. In March 1910, for example, accompanied by Ladipo Oluwole, he addressed the famous Stockport Sunday School, including in his performance two solo songs, *The Holy City and I heard the Voice of Jesus Say*. In the autumn of 1911 Dr Ishmael Pratt returned to Practice medicine in Sierra Leone where he was reportedly still working in 1917.

Aaron James George

Arriving at Colwyn Bay from Freetown, Sierra Leone in 1904 Aaron was a musical youth whose favourite party piece was singing Ira Sankey's hymn *One by One*. Deeply religious, at the Institute Aaron's preferred trade was photography. More accomplished with the camera than the cricket bat, Aaron made his sporting debut for the 'AFRICANS' against 'COLWYN BAY' in August 1895 when he was bowled out for a duck by A. J. Fleet. Whilst at Congo House, Aaron was an active member of the local branch of the Young Men's Christian Association (YMCA), whose founder, Sir George Williams, was a long-time patron of the Institute. After a couple of years at Colwyn Bay Aaron returned to Africa, and settled in Liberia. In Africa Aaron found it difficult to make much money from photography, informing Hughes that printing would probably have proved more lucrative, still he made a living from the trade and also found time for mission work. That proved equally challenging as he observed, 'Mahomet is gaining much of the ground where Christ's religion should be flourishing.' From his base in the capital, Monrovia, Aaron ventured inland to places such as 'Brewerville, which is five days walk' to preach to people he referred to as 'heathens'.

Keeping in touch with Hughes long after he left the Institute,

Aaron George remained eternally grateful for his time in Colwyn Bay and on 24 November 1910 informed William:

> Since I left you I have been fairly successful in all my undertakings. I have built a house here in Monrovia, finished and painted in the European style ... I am now married and have a daughter. My wife was trained in a mission school; she can teach both vocal and instrumental music. I talk so much of the white man's country and what he has done for me that she is anxious to come over and see England and the white folks also ... Remember me to all the students in the College as one that never forgets your untiring work for Africa ... Dear Principal, Yours for Africa, Aaron J George.

South Africa

Davidson Don Tengo Jabavu

Jabavu was, possibly, the most influential student ever educated at the African Institute, going on to become an outstanding South African educator and political leader. Born in King William's town, Cape Colony on 20 October 1885, Davidson was the eldest child of John Tengo Jabavu, a newspaper editor, and his wife Elda Sakuba. Davidson's father was a great advocate of the Colwyn Bay scheme which he publicised in the columns of his newspaper. After Davidson completed his primary level education in the Cape, he was refused a place at the local whites-only government secondary school. Refusing to be beaten by the system, Davidson's parents then arranged for him to continue his education at Colwyn Bay.

Whilst studying at the African Institute from 1903-1906, Davidson passed several formal examinations, including; 1903, Preliminary Medical Examination; 1905 Mathematics – first class (South Kensington External) and College of Preceptors' Examinations – first class, 1906: London Matriculation. William Hughes observed that, 'He is passionately fond of music and has always a book in his hand ... Jabavu will prove a bright star in South Africa'.

Continuing his higher education at University College, London, in 1912 Davidson graduated with a BA in English. He then went on to receive a teacher's diploma from the University of Birmingham in 1914. During his time in Birmingham he also managed to fit in a three-month visit to the famous Tuskegee Institute in Alabama, USA.

Returning to the recently formed Union of South Africa in 1914 Davidson helped found the hugely influential South African Native College at Fort Hare, Cape Province, where he was also one of the initial two academic staff. Throughout the following decades it was the principal provider of university education for African students from throughout southern Africa.

In the 1920s, in response to the government's assault on the African franchise, Davidson became increasingly politically active. After publishing *The Segregation Fallacy*, in 1928 he went on to help organize groups defending African rights, culminating in a 1935 conference of more than 400 delegates. The All-African Convention emerged from the conference with Jabavu as its president, a position he held until 1948.

Continuing his interest and engagement with black rights, education and culture until the end, after publishing his last book in 1954, Davidson Don Tengo Jabavu died on 3 August 1959 in hospital in East London, Cape Province, South Africa.

Mabel Gabashane

Mabel Gabashane was enrolled at the African Institute in 1904 from Potchefstroom, then in Orange River County (now Lesotho). It appears she was brought to Colwyn Bay by Dr Henry Barton Gabashane (1882–1929), who came to Liverpool from South Africa in 1904 to found The Ethiopian Progressive Association with the help of, amongst others, Kwesi Ewusi of Congo House. The Association planned to discuss, 'matters of vital importance concerning Africa in particular and the Negro race in general'.

At Colwyn Bay Mabel followed a largely academic curriculum, passing her College of Preceptors Examinations in 1907. After completing her education, in September 1909 Mabel Gabashane returned to Orange River County to work as a school teacher.

Dr Ladipo Oluwole   *Dr Adeji Oyejola*

Nigeria

Dr Ayodeji Oyejola

Born 1876 in Yorubaland, Ayodeji came to Colwyn Bay in 1897. An excellent academic career began with Ayodeji achieving the top aggregate score of all candidates enrolled at the Institute in 1898. Transferring to Edinburgh to complete his degree level studies he was amongst a small group of African students who welcomed Alake Gbadebo during his two day visit to the city in 1904. Determined to qualify as a medical doctor, Ayodeji attended the lectures of Alexander Bruce and Harvey Littlejohn at the Surgeon's Hall, Edinburgh and both lecturers wrote to Hughes praising both his conduct and academic attainment.

Oyejola gained practical medical experience serving under Doctor Byron Bramwell on the wards of the Edinburgh Royal Infirmary and Dr Bramwell's reports on Ayodeji were as positive as those as his colleagues. Oyejola passed all his final medical examinations with honours.

Having been away from home for nine years Ayodeji sailed for Africa with Ernestina (above) in December 1906 but he didn't enjoy the voyage. He was initially overcome with emotion as he waved goodbye to Hughes and his old friends from the Institute as their tender disappeared into the distance at Liverpool:

> I had great difficulty in keeping my face dry ... I felt the departing very deeply... Tea time came but I took no notice of it, I was not feeling well ... seasickness had taken hold of me ... I went to the table but I could not sit for long because looking at the food made me feel worse. I rose soon and went to my resting place where I was very sick. We went to the Bay of Biscay on Sunday afternoon and it was very rough, in my opinion, although the sailors said it was nothing to speak about. I spent almost the whole of Saturday, Sunday and Monday in bed eating almost nothing. You can imagine me in my coffin-like bed ... I stayed in bed until Tuesday morning, when I got up with some difficulty, and for the first time I went to the table to have breakfast. After breakfast I was glad to see Ernestina and she told me she had not been sick at all.

On his return to Yorubaland as a fully qualified medical doctor he received an emotional welcome from relatives he hadn't seen for almost a decade. Patron of the Colwyn Bay Institute, Alake Gbadebo had a hospital specially built for him at Abeokuta. As William Hughes observed in 1908, 'He will be able to attend to the bodily infirmities of his people and preach the Gospel'. In 1910 Dr Ayodeji Oyejola had six assistants working under his supervision in a constant battle against the ravages of smallpox.

Dr Ladipo Oluwole
Doctor Oluwole was another of Congo House's outstanding successes. Arriving from Abeokuta, Nigeria in 1903 Ladipo was always very focused on academic study but also proved the best cricketer ever to represent the Institute. Where few of the Institute's batsmen ever reached double figures in 1905 he not only made 17 runs in one match and 23 in another but also

skittled out most of the opposition too. After passing London Matriculation in 1906 Oluwole went on to study medicine at degree level at Liverpool University, where he gained distinctions in almost all his examinations. Passing out in 1911 with degrees in general medicine (M.B.) and surgery (Ch.B) he was recognised as the first African to gain those particular qualifications. Of the 21 candidates who sat the final qualifying examinations, ten failed, eleven passed and eight achieved honours, including Oluwole! He was thrilled to have his degree conferred upon him before a packed, admiring audience assembled at Liverpool's prestigious St George's Hall.

Returning to Nigeria in 1911, Oluwole went to work in Yorubaland as a doctor at the same hospital as returned Institute student, Ayodeji Oyejola.

Complete Listing of Institute Students
(in order of enrolment)

Kinkasa (Years at Institute 1882–88) born Congo 1875 – (Post Institute) died Colwyn Bay, 5 May 1888 of 'Congo Sleeping Sickness'

Nkanza (1882–92) born Congo 1877 – died Colwyn Bay, 3 April 1892 of 'heart failure caused by congestion of the liver'

Frank Teva (1888–92), born Palabala, Congo 1875 – Missionary Upper Congo

Daniel Harvey (1888–90) born Congo – died 1895 on *SS Nubia*

Kofele M'Besa (1890–92) born Cameroon 1875 – returned to Cameroon to undertake mission work

Thomas Wamba (1891–93) born Congo – prematurely returned to Upper Congo 1893 with 'rheumatism'

William Lufwilu (1891–92) born Congo River

Samba (1891–92) born Congo 1877 – died Colwyn Bay 9 March 1892 from ruptured liver caused by a fall whilst playing at the Institute

George Fraser (1891–96) born Congo River

Roul van der Most (1891–1900) born St. Paul de Loanda, Angola – went to Sierra Leone

Ernestina Francis (1891–1906) born 1883 Banana, Congo; Headmistress in Nigeria – died Colwyn Bay 11 Jan 1914

George Steane (1891–94) born in Cameroon – died of pleurisy at Colwyn Bay 17 May 1894

Joseph Ebakise Burnley (1892–95) born Cameroon – preacher in Cameroon

Alfred Dibundu (1892–95) born Cameroon – preacher in Cameroon

Samuel Dibundu (1892–98) born Cameroon – died soon after return to Cameroon

Henry Cobham (1893–99) born 1878 in Old Calabar – returned to Old Calabar

George Etim Duke (1893–98) born Old Calabar – returned to Old Calabar

Kwesi Quainoo (1893–1901) born 1875 at Saltpond, Gold Coast – died on voyage home and buried in Sierra Leone

Mimpowkwa (1893–5) born Congo – returned to Upper Congo

N'Kanza Leger (1893–5) born Congo – returned to Upper Congo

Eyo Ekpenyon Eyo (October–December 1893) born Old Calabar – returned to Old Calabar

Alfred W. Johnson (1894–94) born Freetown, Sierra Leone – died Colwyn Bay 9 June 1894

Alexander Mars (1894–6) born Liberia – elected Member of Liberian House of Representatives

Waddy Saggo (1895–1900) born Monrovia – returned to Sierra Leone

James Ekanem (1895–98) born Old Calabar – returned to Old Calabar

Bobby Smith (1895–6) born Liberia – returned to Kru Coast, Liberia

Seahfa Washington (1895–6) born Liberia – returned to Monrovia, Liberia

Paul Gbese Daniels (1896–99) born 1872 Charleston, South Carolina, USA – Baptist Pastor and Assistant Supervisor (later President) of Jenkins Orphanage, Charleston USA, died 1961

Daniel Cheeseman (1896–96) born Liberia, adopted son of President J. J. Cheeseman – returned to Grand Bassa following the President's sudden death

Lawale Tubi (1896–1904) born Lagos 1881 – returned to Nigeria

James Glyn Agamazong Lawson (1896–1900) born Freetown – initially returned to Preach in Sierra Leone, but subsequently settled in England, joined the Birkenhead *Bohemian Lodge* of the Freemasons and was appointed a Methodist Pastor in Liverpool

James P. B. Richards (1896–99) born Freetown 1877 – pastor in Sierra Leone

John Kitano (1896–8) born Zambesi, East Africa – returned to Zambesi

Andrew Neizer (1896–8) born Elmina 1879 – returned to Gold Coast, later settled in Liverpool

J. B. Annan (1896–7) born Gold Coast – returned to Gold Coast

J. H. Annan (1896–7) born Gold Coast – returned to Gold Coast

Lulu Coote (1897–1908) born Banana 1890 – nurse in South Africa

Mosanya Osata (1897–1900) born Lagos – returned to Nigeria

Sujah Dowlah (1897–1900) born Lagos – returned to Nigeria

Thomas Ladipo (1897–1900) born Lagos – returned to Nigeria

Dr Ayodeji Oyejola (1897–1905) born Yorubaland 1876 – doctor in Nigeria

William Ballantyne (1897–99) born Old Calabar 1878 – returned to Old Calabar

Henry Barleycorn (1897–99) born on the island of Fernando Po – returned to Fernando Po

Okon Boco (1897–99) born Old Calabar – returned to Old Calabar

Fatuse Jimsana (1898–1900) born South Africa – returned to South Africa

Anmore Ashaker (1898–98) born Sierra Leone 1877 – exploited credentials provided by William Hughes to pursue a career of criminal deceit in England

Josiah (Karibi) Batubo (1898–1900) born Buguma 1888, New Calabar – expelled but settled in Bangor, north Wales

Alfred Williams (1898–1900) born Gloucester, Sierra Leone – returned to Sierra Leone

Dr Ishmael Charles Pratt (1899–1911) born Freetown 1879 – doctor in Sierra Leone

Theophilus Ruhle (1899–1901) born Gold Coast – returned to Gold Coast

Charles Stewart (1899–1904) born in Liberia – returned to Liberia

William Quarde (1899–1900) born Gold Coast – returned to Gold Coast

Edenslight A. Brown (1899–1905) born Sierra Leone 1882 – returned to Sierra Leone

Cecil Barger Conton (1899–1904) born St Albans, Bermuda – missionary in Gold Coast but transferred to Sierra Leone

Joseph A. Abraham (1899–1901) born Cape Coast, Ghana – founder member of The Ethiopian Progressive Association in 1904

Kwesi Ewusi (1899–1900) born Cape Coast, Ghana 1881 – founder member of The Ethiopian Progressive Association in 1904, after further studies on return to Africa founded a successful trading company in Nigeria, where in 1924 he died

A. B. King (1899–1901) born Lagos – returned to Nigeria

Robert Anyancor (1899–1901) born Gold Coast – returned to Gold Coast

Joseph Morford (1900–1904) born Chattanooga, USA – headmaster in Onitsha, Nigeria

Moses Etroo (1901–1903) born Chama, Gold Coast 1880 – returned to Gold Coast

Koffee Twintoh (1901–1905) born Chama – returned to Gold Coast

James Kwesi Mensah (1901–1905) born Elmina, Gold Coast – returned to Gold Coast

Asaph Leslie Kanyane (1903–07) born Pretoria, South Africa – returned to South Africa

Dr Ladipo Oluwole (1903–11) born Abeokuta, Nigeria – first Nigerian Medical Officer of Health

Amos Olusanya Delo-Dosumu (1903–11) born Jebu Remo, Lagos – teacher in Nigeria

William Lukobi-Johnson (1903–06), Sierra Leone – on return to Freetown taught Sunday school and employed managing a department of the *Sierra Leone Weekly News*

Philip Beccles Waribo (1903–07) born Sierra Leone – returned to Nigeria

Arthur Ernest Ajibode Nicolls (1903–12) born Sierra Leone 1883 – returned to Sierra Leone

Carter Ajagbe Konibagbe (1903–12) born Sierra Leone, 1883

Aaron James George (1903–06) born Sierra Leone – returned to Sierra Leone

George Dixon Montsioa (1903–07) born Mafeking, South Africa 1885 – third African barrister in South Africa, joint founder of South African Native Convention (later ANC) in 1912, served as SANNC Secretary under Presidency of Revd John Dube

Davidson Don Tengo Jabavu (1903–06) born King William's Town, Cape Colony 1885 – on return to South Africa became lecturer and anti-apartheid activist

Thomas Granville Sutton (1903–06) born Sierra Leone; returned to Freetown, Sierra Leone

Henry Njcubu Poswayo (1904–12) born Engcobo, Tembuland 1874, South Africa – returned to South Africa

Peter Nyambo (1904–06) born Zambesi, East Africa – missionary and political activist, East Africa

Mabel Gabashane (1904–09) born Potchefstroom, Lesotho – teacher in South Africa

Wilson Mongoli Sebeta (1904–12) born Basutoland – returned to South Africa

Francis Lambert Barkie-Johnson (1905–07) born St Lucia 1884 – transferred to St Paul's Industrial School, Laurenceville, USA in 1908, eventually returned to Africa to teach agriculture at Wilberforce Farm, Sierra Leone

John Lionel Franklin (1906–08) born Grenada 1875 – missionary employed by the Church Missionary Society in Nigeria he pursued a criminal career until convicted. Engaged on his return to Britain by William Hughes on deputation work in 1911 he precipitated the downfall of the Institute

Kobina Boodoo (1906–09) born Gold Coast 1887 – died Colwyn Bay 11 April 1909 from tuberculous meningitis

J. G. Pratt (1907–09) born Freetown, Sierra Leone – returned to Sierra Leone

Akinlawon Olumuyiwa (1908–12) born Yorubaland 1882 – returned to Nigeria

Willie Prest (1909–09) born New Calabar 1898 – after brief stay returned to Nigeria

Oladipo Lahanmi (1909–12) born Abeokuta, Nigeria 1889 – founder and Secretary of West African Students' Association in 1916, established in response to London University Club's refusal to admit black students, subsequently returned to Nigeria

Jamieson Pearce (1909–11) born Lagos – returned as doctor to Nigeria

Daniel Essoun Gwira (1910–12) born Gold Coast 1891 – barrister in Nigeria and officer of Sierra Leone Judicial Service

Augustus Merriman Labor (1910–11) born Freetown, Sierra Leone (1878) – writer, barrister, and political activist in England. Bankrupted and disbarred, he died in London in 1919 in poverty and obscurity

Chapter Ten

'Black Baptist's Brown Baby'
(1908–1911)

By 1908 Hughes' finances were severely stretched. His property speculation had hit the buffers and he was borrowing heavily from family and friends to keep the Institute afloat. Outwardly he remained upbeat, enthusiastically involving himself and his students in all aspects of the life of Colwyn Bay. Nonetheless, a mere handful of students enrolled at the African Institute after 1908 and so this was to prove the final season that Congo House could field a full cricket team but they went out on a high note. Local press coverage of their matches was extensive and evocative, as exemplified by the *Colwyn Bay and West Coast Pioneer* report of their exciting August match: AFRICAN INSTITUTE v. MR DARE'S ENGLISH XI:

Africa's Last Stand: 1908

Much interest is always centred in an encounter in which the students of the African Institute, Colwyn Bay, take part for the coloured men can always turn out a remarkably strong eleven and very seldom meet with defeat. So far this season their record is untarnished. On Saturday Mr James Dare got together a strong eleven, including several leading local players and visitors to the town to meet them. The game was played on the Rhos College school pitch, one of the finest pitches in the district and what with the good weather the conditions were perfect.

Oluwole, for the Institute, won the toss, and elected to bat first, sending in Dosumu and Poswayo to open the innings in the presence of a fair number of spectators. By the way it should be mentioned that the Africans had their strongest possible eleven, all the students being home from the various universities and colleges for the summer vacation.

The batting was opened to the bowling of Hammersley and Ashworth, the latter taking the first over. Runs came pretty freely, twenty being soon telegraphed. At 21 a separation was effected, Illsley catching Poswayo off Hammersley when he had scored two. This was hard luck for the Africans as Poswayo is their best bat. Montsioa took his place, but only a couple had been scored when he was smartly caught by Dare off Kay. Pratt was the next man in and aided in adding ten before Dosumu was clean bowled by Hammersley after scoring a useful 18. From this stage onwards the score mounted steadily until it reached 78 at which the side was dismissed. Pratt scored 13 but had several 'lives' through skying. Nicolls was next top scorer with 12. Dare behind the wickets was fairly keen and in all caught three opponents. The fielding, taken all round, was loose. Five bowlers were tried, all proving fairly sound. Hammersley and Tonkin, considering that this was their first appearance, this year, doing great service.

The opening of the Englishmen was disastrous, for with his second ball Sebeta dismissed Philips before any score appeared on the board. Three runs later, he took Dicken, and with the total standing at six dismissed Clarke. At seven Oluwole bowled Hammersley so that the outlook was very bad. Illsley and Dare took the score to 12 when the former was taken behind the wicket by Olumuyiwa. Tonkin and Dare made a short stand, the former scoring 11 being eventually bowled by Oluwole. This with three from Dare, brought the total to 26. The arrival of Kay was responsible for another stand, the score reaching 39 before Oluwole claimed Dare's wicket. Two runs later S Hughes was dismissed, Ashworth was the next man in and he assisted in adding a further 13 when Kay unfortunately skied a ball, which M'bella held. The last man in was J P Hughes, but before the score could be supplemented Sebeta disturbed Ashworth's wicket. The total amounted to 54, leaving the Africans winners by 24 runs!

Oxygen of Publicity

The Institute's cricket team prompted positive local publicity but after two decades, Congo House was frankly old news. It was no longer easy to secure coverage in national newspapers or magazines, but in 1908 Hughes did attract the attention of two publications, the magazine *Good Works*, and the London *Evening Standard* newspaper. Both mainly rehashed old accounts of the Institute, but each also included some fresh observations.

Good Works described:

> SUPPORT FROM AFRICAN POTENTATES – The work of this unique missionary enterprise receives warm support from many influential African natives. Prince Ademuyiwa, a converted native potentate, who wears on State occasions a gorgeous crimson velvet crown embroidered with gold, and a blue velvet cloak covered with fanciful designs in gold lace, is greatly impressed with both the spiritual and material good work the Institute is doing. A well-known native barrister at Accra, Mr Assam, considers that a most important part in the development of heathen Africa will be played by this institute. In the near future, he says, this country will have to recognise Mr Hughes and his work in a way yet unknown.
>
> Think of the wonderful work for Christ that is being done at this beautiful Welsh seaside resort! There are boys there destined to carry the Word, who, perchance, in their own country, would have been sacrificed to some petty despot's anger and sold into slavery. Others in the depths of some Congo forest, would be the victims of white men's avarice for rubber, well named 'red' by the missionaries who have witnessed the awful crimes perpetrated on the unfortunate natives in the Congo Free State'!

The *Evening Standard* reflected:

> Perhaps the last place in the world where one would expect to discover a colony of negroes would be North Wales. But at Colwyn Bay, under the shadow of the Great Orme, of the glorious Pwllycrochan Woods you may find a number of

young men from tropical Africa, apprentices to a work which bids fair to revolutionise the Dark Continent...

In answer to the question; Will they preach and work on their return? Mr Hughes roundly declares that there is no risk incurred, no failure possible. They will do for Christian English ideals just what the disciples of Mahomed are doing for their ideals. There is a college in Cairo where hundreds of young Mahommedans are grounded in their faith, each student on leaving is provided with a simple outfit, a camel and a Koran, and sets off to evangelise. Some have been on the Gold Coast, 3,000 miles from their institution. As coloured men, they are received with friendliness; each sets free his camel to eat the sweet grass, and receives such gifts as a mat to sleep on, fruit, sweet potatoes and yams. Mr Hughes' students will do what these Mahommedans are doing – they will leaven the very heart of Africa, but with a purer yeast ... Search the history of the world, says Mr Hughes, and you will not find the record of any people evangelised by foreigners.

Bringing the National Eisteddfod to Colwyn Bay

Hughes' objection to foreigners imposing alien cultures sprang from his own experiences as a Welshman in a country dominated by England. His response was subtle rather than confrontational, preferring to promote Welsh rather than attack English. In 1908, Hughes was a prime mover in a campaign to bring Wales' annual festival of national language and culture, the National Eisteddfod, to Colwyn Bay. To faint-hearted sceptics concerned whether there existed sufficient local support, Hughes, revealingly, replied, 'It is my experience that enthusiasm has to be created, it never came of itself at the outset. (Hear! Hear!)'

William Hughes was duly appointed Honorary Secretary of Colwyn Bay's Eisteddfod Committee but it soon emerged that Liverpool, with its large resident Welsh population, was the town's chief rival in being selected as the venue for the 1910 Royal National Eisteddfod of Wales. True to his word, Hughes generated enormous enthusiasm for the Eisteddfod in the town and Colwyn Bay awaited the final decision with bated breath.

A Man and a Brother

African Institute students also played their part in the community and some were members of the local 'Brotherhood', a national Christian fellowship movement. At the October 1908 meeting in the English Congregational Church, after a 'charming and helpful address' on the subject of 'Books' delivered by 'Miss Hovey, BA, the esteemed Lady President of Penrhos College, Colwyn Bay' it was time for prize-giving. Four Institute students were amongst the recipients, who were handed 'appropriate volumes' by Miss Hovey: Kobina Boodoo received *How Can I Help England*; Mongoli Sebeta, *On God's Lines*; Akinlawon Olumuyiwa was given *John Halifax, Gentleman,* and Ajibode Nicolls, strangely, *French Revolution*!

Inspiration from Africa

The Revd S. A. Coker of Lagos visited the Institute in June 1908 and speaking at the regular Sunday service he informed his audience of recent achievements of returned Congo House students in Africa. He went on to explain his personal commitment to the Independent African Church movement. In association with Mojola Agbebi's Native Baptist Churches, he laboured alongside Jacob Kehinde Coker in seeking to persuade independent African churches to combine in defence against the persecution and threats of the government and European missionary churches. J. K. Coker claimed, 'Many Africans had been spiritually lost because of the evils of the hypocritical life of the mission churches. They led African Christians to feel Christianity was not their own religion, indigenous to the soil and that it was therefore a foreign religion.' William Hughes could not have put it better himself.

Not the Gospel Truth: 1909

It is now some time [says the *Christian Age*] since mention was made in these columns of the British and African Incorporated Association otherwise known as the African Training Institute, Colwyn Bay. The Institute certainly deserves to be better known. The founder and director, Revd

AFRICAN TRAINING INSTITUTE,

Colwyn Bay,

NORTH WALES.

Mai 3ydd, 1911.

Anwyl Frawd,

Yr wyf yn amgau i chwi Bamphledyn, gan hyderu y cewch amser i'w ddarllen, ac i roddi i'r pwnc pwysig, yr ymdrinia ag ef, ystyriaeth ddifrifol.

Os dewisiwch gael ychwaneg o copiau, mae digon wedi eu hargaphu genym, ac anfonir hwy i chwi gyda phleser, yn y gobaith o symud yr enwad Bedyddiedig yn Nghymru, i fod yn gyson ag ef ei hun trwy roddi yr un egwyddorion i'r Paganiaid, a pyny ar linellau naturiol ac ysgrythyrol, ag a bregethir genym cartref.

Cofion caredig,

Yr eiddoch yn frawdol.

W. Hughes

William's Welsh Epistle from the Institute, May 1911

W Hughes, has now laboured twenty-six years for Africa. The Institute has been in existence for nineteen years and so far has been honoured by God and used wonderfully to spread the light of the Gospel in the different parts of the Dark Continent. About eighty students have returned to labour in their native land ...

Readers were informed that 'The number of students has gradually increased' and finally 'an attempt is now being made to raise a special fund of £50,000 for the maintenance and extension of the work'. If all was going as well as the article suggested it seemed rather odd to be seeking a sum equal to twenty-five times the Institute's annual operating costs. A charitable interpretation might consider the appeal over-ambitious, a cynic might sense desperation for despite the article's claiming the opposite, students numbers had, by 1909, drastically reduced to a mere handful and annual income was continuing to decline.

A Triumph – of Sorts!

William's March 1909 re-election to Colwyn Bay Council was one of the few positive events in that year's calendar. Just as three years earlier, Hughes was returned in fourth place out of five elected, with a further six unsuccessful candidates. It was claimed that his policies on electric-tramcars and the lighting of Abergele Road was particularly popular with the voters.

Though Councillor Revd William Hughes could not have known it at the time, fate would intervene to prevent his completion of this second term of office.

Tragedy

The pleasure of victory proved fleeting for within a week William faced the death of one of his best-loved students. News of the funeral appeared in the press:

> We regret to announce the death of a very interesting young African, Kobina Boodoo, which sad event took place on Sunday, at the African Institute, aged 21 years. Kobina was a well-known young man in the Bay, and was popular in many circles. He was a Good Templar of the genuine stamp, and was transferred to Colwyn Bay. 'Pioneer' Lodge, from a large Lodge in his native town on the Gold Coast, West Africa. The funeral took place on Tuesday, at the Old Colwyn Cemetery, when about twenty of his Templar brethren attended in the regalia of the Order, and the full service at the grave was given by members of the local Lodge, who had formed a complete circle around the grave. The speakers were Bro. E Jones, CT,

Bro. Hill, Secretary, and Bro. R James Jones, LD. This was the first Templar funeral that has taken place in Colwyn Bay. The whole service was very impressive, and cannot fail to make the Order and its observances more popular. The Lodge will probably go into mourning for six months.

The Good Templars were an international mutual aid organisation based on the model of the Freemasons that continues to operate in Ghana.

Kobina's death was formally recorded as due to tuberculous meningitis.

'Think of Me with Jesus'

With little opportunity to recover from the death of Kobina Boodoo, the following month William's eldest daughter, Katie, died from kidney failure. Moving testimonies to her character and last days were printed by the local press:

She peacefully passed away on Monday, 24 May, in her 22nd year, after being a great sufferer for the long period of seven years from chronic rheumatism. For nearly three years she was bedridden, but bore her severe trial with true Christian fortitude.

The Revd Abel J Parry, DD, who visited the young lady frequently and who was greatly impressed by her sweet nature and Christian resignation, says of her: She was a remarkable personality; had she lived she would have left her mark in whatever sphere of life Providence should have led her to. She was deeply religious, and this sincerely impressed all that came into personal contact with her. Notwithstanding her ailment and its constant strain upon her body and mind, she showed a remarkable power of endurance, never complained, but always spoke of it as a moral and spiritual discipline. Her influence over the household and the Institution was most wholesome, and elicited the profound appreciation and love of all. She possessed a remarkably magnanimous spirit, and great appreciation of the good qualities of all that came within

Katie Hughes, William's daughter, during her final affliction

the circle of her knowledge. She was truly a lesson to her friends in this remarkable feature of her noble character. Her illness brought her many friends, who were ever ready to do all that lay in their power to help her in any way...Her influence for good over the students during several years was very great and highly valued, and will be lasting in its effects upon their future lives. Invalid though she was, the Institute will suffer great loss by her early death.

The following is the first verse of a favourite hymn of hers, which she often loved to quote:

O Christ in Thee my soul hath found,
And found in Thee alone,
The peace, the joy, I sought so long,
The bliss till now unknown.

A few days before her death, Katie composed a personal letter to friends and family with a most touching conclusion;

I must now close. I am going out of pain and suffering into perfect joy and bliss. I am going to be with my dear Saviour, whom I love, and shall be happy when I see Him and am with Him. Do not mourn for me; think of me with Jesus. Decide for Christ without fail and do not fear to confess Him. You will be happier for it. God bless and be with you till we meet again'
With dearest love from your loving KATIE

In December 1909 the Grim Reaper claimed William's long-serving patron, Sir Alfred Lewis Jones of Elder Dempster shipping. Since the early days of the Institute, Alfred Jones had assisted William by agreeing to convey African students to England free of charge, and then return them, gratis, on completion of their training. Free passage for students was an essential ingredient of the Institute's financial viability. Without the enthusiastic support of Sir Alfred Jones, Hughes would find it difficult to persuade the Board of Elder Dempster to continue providing the African Institute with this key facility. Despite Jones' alliance with King Leopold, Hughes never broke relations with him. After his death, William paid tribute to Jones in the following Congo House report: 'Not only this Institute and its friends will mourn the loss of Sir Alfred Jones but all those who are interested in the Dark Continent and in many other parts of the British Empire'. With no hint of irony, Hughes added, 'He was one of the greatest of the Empire builders'!

Peace Makes an Unwelcome Appearance

Financially and emotionally, it had been a very difficult year for William Hughes. But in a cruel twist of fate, in December 1909 an old rival reappeared as if to taunt him. A huge touring exhibition celebrating the success of the Baptist Missionary Society (BMS) arrived in Llandudno. Despite William's pioneering work with the African Institute there was no role for Hughes and no mention of Congo House. Pushing the traditional colonial model of missionary work, the fund-raising appeal of the exhibition threatened to further undermine the already precarious financial position of the Institute. The *Weekly News* played its part in promoting the event:

VIVID DESCRIPTION OF LIFE ON THE CONGO
A very fine missionary exhibition is being held in the Llandudno Pier Pavilion during this week and promises to be a great success. The proceeds are in aid of the Baptist foreign missions and the exhibition has been arranged to arouse interest and sympathy with the work, and to assist the Society

by securing additional support for the work in foreign lands ... The basement of the Pier pavilion had been transformed into a palace of beauty and interest. Large panoramic paintings adorn the walls and various courts have been neatly arranged ... there is interest and novelty in every turn, depicting the realities through which missionaries have to go ...

If William had steeled himself to attend he might have reacquainted himself with his Congo Baptist mission of a quarter of a century earlier. He could have listened to, 'Revd S. S. Stevens' powerful and heart-stirring Congo Lecture, with Bioscope living illustrations of native life – so interesting that it was given again on Saturday evening, by request.' William's memories, and undoubtedly his emotions, would certainly have stirred at the sight of, 'One of the exhibits held in veneration by all Baptists, the battered and broken portion of the little *SS Peace*'; the very boat whose assembly he, as a young Congo missionary, had helped organise. 'In the same section were placed a Congo native hat and a large relief map of Central Africa, showing the course of the river Congo and position of the Baptist Mission Stations to the furthermost station, Yakusu.'

Bloodied but Unbowed

Despite his personal trials and tribulations Hughes never neglected his commitment to Africa. Just as he had done a decade earlier against the Government's imposition of an African 'Hut Tax', in 1909 William mounted his soap-box and denounced Britain's capitulation to South African racism. In 1909 Hughes railed against Parliament's collusion with the Boers in creating a Union of South Africa that, from its foundation, incorporated a racist constitution. Long before the world awoke to the evils of 'apartheid', William Hughes denounced South Africa's officially endorsed and enforced domination of its black population by the ruling white elite.

In the *Manchester Guardian*, in a piece headed 'THE COLOUR BAR IN SOUTH AFRICA – NATIVES EXCLUDED FROM NEW PARLIAMENT, Councillor, the Revd William

Hughes, Founder and Director of the African Training Institute, Colwyn Bay, who was for some years a missionary in South and West Africa', wrote:

> I have read the accounts of the debate in Parliament as to the South Africa Bill and it has given me much pain to think that our fellow-subjects in South Africa have allowed themselves (in what is to be feared their prejudice towards the coloured race) to be carried away from the lines of justice and fair play and to insert in their bill what is termed by Parliament the colour bar.
>
> This colour bar is an insult to 360 millions of coloured people who are to be found in the different parts of our Empire and who are about 7 to 1 of the white men ... They sided with us in the South African War and now we are deserting them by bending to the Boers' ideas of government ... I believe in every effort being made to unite South Africa but this bill, with this colour bar unites only a small section, and in my humble opinion it would have been far better for the British Parliament to strike out this part and take the consequences for the time being. It is our duty as a nation to stand to our traditions and uphold the right. The Prime Minister and Mr Balfour have expressed their regret at this portion of the bill, as well as other members of Parliament, and they hope that the same people who have inserted the colour bar will take it out. This hope, I fear, has a very poor foundation. If they have been capable of inserting it, the probability is that it will not be deleted for a very long time, and during its operation no one can predict what the consequences will be in South Africa ... There is a day coming when the British people will look back upon this colour bar with shame, as we are now looking back upon slavery.

An Ever-shrinking Income: 1910

Institute income for the financial year 1909–10 was the lowest it had been since 1894, leaving an annual operating deficit of almost £300. Although the Elder Dempster & Co. continued to be cited as 'Patrons', despite the death of Sir Alfred Jones, it is unclear whether students continued to enjoy free passage on their ships as the Institute's 1909-10 accounts include a charge of '£31 6s 8d passage money for Joseph Morford'. The accounts also include substantial 'Deputation Expenses' of £53 16s 6½d; the consequence of numerous fund-raising, promotional trips around England and Wales undertaken by Hughes and his students. One of the Institute's most popular 'deputies' was ex-actor and Congo House old boy, John Lionel Franklin, who had, by 1910 returned to Britain after a spell labouring in Africa. So taken was Hughes with Franklin that he was engaged on deputation work on unusually generous terms, permitting him to retain a portion of the funds he raised as commission.

Spreading the Word to Stockport

In March 1910 two other Institute students made a 'deputation visit' to 'what is considered the largest Sunday School in the world'. The *Stockport Brotherhood Journal* recorded the event:

> March 13 – (Open Sunday) The visit of two coloured missionary students, Mr Oluwole and Dr Ishmael Pratt from the African Training Institute, Colwyn Bay, was a great attraction and the service was of a very inspiring order. The conductor, Mr George Bennett, cordially welcomed the visitors and said the part they were taking in the service was an illustration of the way the spirit of brotherhood extends to every nation and colour. Mr Gosling, Secretary to the Institute, who accompanied Mr Oluwole and Dr Pratt briefly spoke of the work of the Institute. Mr Oluwole who gave his address very fluently and spoke in good English held the close attention of the vast congregation. He expressed warm thanks for the welcome they received and said that men of his colour did not always receive such a reception. He confessed it made him nervous to address such a great audience and humorously remarked that he could speak to them with greater facility if he used his own language. Dr Pratt, who is a fully qualified medical man, and who returns to Africa in about 12 months

added to the success of the service by two solos, *The Holy City* and *I Heard the Voice of Jesus Say*, which were greatly appreciated by the congregation.

The *Stockport Express* reported :

> Mr Oluwole had to leave Stockport for a Liverpool University examination on Monday but Dr Pratt was able to take part in an entertainment at Edgeley Park Church. A good audience assembled. Mr Gosling presided; Miss Waterhouse proved a very good solo pianist and accompanist; Miss A. Moody sang sweetly, although suffering from cold; Mr J. E. Carter gave two tenor solos in fine style, receiving an encore. Mr W. Hedgecox's fine zonophone was very good. Mr Alfred Davies, in his Lancashire sketches, five in all, caused much laughter, Dr Pratt remarking he had never laughed so much before at recitals – he should remember Mr Davies for many years. Dr Pratt was encored for each song he gave. He also addressed those present, as did the chairman, on the claims of the Institute. After singing of *God be with You* a happy evening terminated.

In terms of generating positive publicity, the Stockport event was a great success but as William later admitted, deputation work was a financial failure, consistently consuming more money than it raised.

Celebrating Native Cultures

Although William remained a popular Colwyn Bay Councillor, within the town the Institute no longer enjoyed the high public profile of previous years. Public events at the Institute, such as the August 1910 concert presented by the American Jubilee Singers – 'their vocalisations being much enjoyed', were largely a thing of the past. Without such initiatives from Hughes, Colwyn Bay would have little opportunity to experience 'black culture' untainted by racist stereotyping.

William's work in promoting Welsh culture came to fruition the following month with the long awaited arrival in Colwyn Bay of the National Eisteddfod. Beginning on 13 September, the five day festival of Welsh literature, poetry and music involved the whole town as well as thousands of visitors from all over the principality and beyond. In recognition of his role as Honorary General Secretary of the event, a photographic portrait of William Hughes prefaced the official Eisteddfod programme. It was the highpoint of a distinguished career that was about to go into tragic decline.

A Devastating Audit

William's public demeanour remained calm and confident but behind the scenes the Institute was in serious trouble. Student numbers and income had contracted to such a critical point that on 13 October 1910 the Institute's auditors, Messrs Walmsley Jones & Co of Chester delivered a most damning report:

> We are struck by the serious disparity between the total expenditure £1,557 13s 7d and the number of students, 5.5 (the average number during the year), maintained at the Institute. We can appreciate that certain establishment charges are incurred irrespective of the number of students but we think that the attention of the subscribers should be drawn to the disparity we have indicated, so that a timely consideration may be given to the matter.

The auditors went on to suggest that if this was not done the figures mentioned might be quoted to show that the continued existence of the Institute was no longer justified. Very hostile criticism must be expected unless the number of students was increased or the expenditure reduced to reasonable comparative proportions.

Hughes and his Management Committee responded by keeping the report secret. The Institute's solicitor, Mr Nunn of Colwyn Bay resigned when refused sight of the report. Congo House students, Patrons and Subscribers remained entirely in the dark.

Don't Panic! Don't Panic!: 1911

The Institute's 1911 Annual Report carried the usual lists of past exam successes supplemented by glowing accounts of the work of Congo House 'old boys' but no reference to Messrs Walmsley Jones & Co's damning conclusions. Hughes was determined to appear calm and unruffled and maintain every appearance of 'business as usual'. No new students were taken on but none of the handful remaining had their training cut short.

The 23 June 1911 edition of the *North Wales Weekly News* carried an entirely upbeat account of the African Institute's Annual Meeting at Colwyn Bay, at which:

> The Director presented the annual report, which was interesting and encouraging... The report of the work in Africa carried on by returned students of the Institute and others was encouraging. There are 2,000 members in connection with the work at the Cameroons. The mother church, apart from its branches, at Aqua Town has 608 members, 60 candidates for baptism, 200 attending the Bible class, 300 attending Sunday School, 13 Sunday School teachers, 100 in the inquiry class, 200 at the mothers' meeting, 12 evangelists assisting the pastor, and a congregation of 1,100. The work is no less encouraging under the superintendence of Dr Agbebi at New Calabar ...
>
> Dr Mark C Hayford sent a report of his work on the Gold Coast, stating that he had 129 members and over 200 inquirers; also that he is pushing on with his industrial scheme, teaching the natives different trades as well as Christianising them. Reports were also received from returned students in South Africa and from a white gentleman residing in the land who sent a subscription of £10 as a result of a visit a few years ago to this Institute. He states in his letter: – To give these native youths Christian training in a Christian home, and treat them not merely as fellow-men but as brother-Christians will, I think, if faithfully persisted in, give astonishing results in the near future.

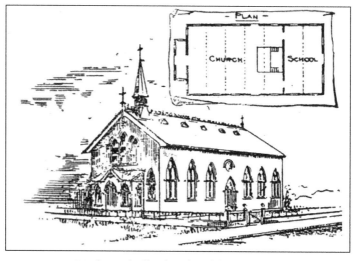

Mark Hayford's Chapel, Gold Coast, 1911

A Cunning Plan?

William Hughes was no fool. The optimistic façade was intended to provide time to effect a desperate remedy. Swallowing his pride, Hughes planned to persuade erstwhile critics in the Welsh Baptist Union to offer him salvation. At the September Congress he hoped the Baptist Union might agree to shoulder the financial burden and take control of his beloved African Institute. It would be a bitter pill to swallow but it would be better than bankruptcy and the destruction of his life's work.

Having enjoyed a rather frustrating relationship with the London-based BMS, in 1900 Welsh Baptists had created the Welsh Missionary Council to develop an independent missionary policy of their own. Little progress had been made by 1911 but William Hughes' offer of ownership and control of the African Institute would have provided Welsh Baptists with a distinctly different approach to missionary work.

At the Congress Hughes offered to transfer the entire enterprise, including the Institute buildings, grounds, printing works, teaching equipment etc for a very reasonable £5,000. Discussion took place but the legitimate concerns of some were reinforced by the personal animosity of others. Long-held resentments of Hughes' temerity in founding his Institute without the blessing of the Baptist establishment were allied to personal attacks orchestrated by Revd Evan Kenffig Jones of Cefnmawr. It was hopeless, the Welsh Baptist Union had never endorsed the Institute and had refused it recognition as a legitimate Baptist congregation.

Hughes left the Congress downhearted but not yet beaten.

Another Cunning Plan?

Having tried a top-down takeover and failed, Hughes attempted a radical bottom-up approach. An Extraordinary General Meeting held in Colwyn Bay on 19 October 1911, passed a special resolution amending the qualification criteria for Institute membership. By relaxing the requirements and allowing in more members Hughes hoped to greatly expand his network of supporters and fund raisers. The most significant amendments were as follows:

- Clause c – was changed from membership requiring an annual contribution of one guinea (21 shillings) to a payment of only 10 shillings
- Clause d – ministers previously qualified if their congregation contributed five guineas annually, after the amendment they merely needed to permit an annual collection for the African Institute to take place (with no minimum amount required)
- Two extra clauses were added allowing 2 members to qualify from each contributing Baptist Church, 2 from each Baptist association in Wales and a further 6 from the Welsh Baptist Union
- Article 23b – was amended to increase membership of the African Institute's Governing Council from 12 to 50 members

Mindful of the destructive determination of some past members and fellow Baptists to undermine the Institute, there was also an interesting amendment to Article 6:

- The required declaration that 'I am a Christian, that I hold the Protestant faith, that I am in sympathy with the main objects of the Association viz. the diffusion of Protestant Faith according to the text and doctrine of the Holy Scriptures' was swept away and replaced by, 'No person shall be a member until such person has been elected by the Council and enrolled on the register of Members. The Council may, in the exercise of their uncontrolled discretion, and without giving any reason for so doing, decline to elect any person to be a member.'

Behind this attempt to breathe a new populist energy into the Institute was a determination not to jump out of a financial frying pan into a fire of acrimony and division. This amendment to Article 6 relaxed the Council's ideological demands on prospective members but granted it the absolute power to veto anyone it didn't approve of, with no justification required.

It was a bold, imaginative scheme but could it be established quickly enough to keep the Institute out of the clutches of increasingly impatient creditors?

Nightmare before Christmas

As the end of the year approached Hughes knew he faced a race against time. The last great Welsh religious revival had collapsed and died in 1906; football, films and public houses were now all more popular than chapel. In an increasingly secular age it would be an uphill task to revive funding and support for the African Institute but William remained implacably optimistic. At least he remained optimistic until the middle of December 1911.

Then, just a few days before Christmas, rumours and gossip swirling around Colwyn Bay concerning Hughes and the Institute were dramatically fanned into flames by an incendiary newspaper headline plastered up overnight on notice boards all over the town:

BLACK BAPTIST'S BROWN BABY

Chapter Eleven

Scandal and Disgrace
(1911–1912)

'BLACK BAPTIST'S BROWN BABY', proclaimed posters heralding the arrival in Colwyn Bay of the latest instalment of *John Bull's* shocking exposé of Reverend William Hughes and his African Institute. Plastered up all over town, Hughes couldn't avoid the posters or the scandal and his blood ran cold as he realised the game was up. Two consecutive issues of national news magazine, *John Bull*, in December 1911, ran articles accusing Hughes and the Institute of financial impropriety, sexual immorality and miscegenation. The effect was devastating. William Hughes declared: 'The attacks in *John Bull* killed the Institute and the Institute killed me', but he wasn't done yet.

The Xenophobic Voice of *John Bull*
The first article in *John Bull*, 16 December 1911,was headed, 'A BAPTIST MISSION SCANDAL'. It introduced the basic aims and claims of the Institute and described details of a 'personal visit' to Congo House made by 'Special Correspondent', Vincent Watts.

> I selected Sunday for my visit. I did so because I was informed that Divine service was conducted there afternoon and evening and that the public were cordially invited to attend. The congregation consisted of the Revd Mr Hughes, two young Europeans – one a girl, the other a youth – and five negroes. Four of the latter I subsequently found to be students, and the fifth, whose name I understood to be Josiah, was simply there on a visit.

The reporter went on to allege that during Bible Classes William Hughes' interpretation of scripture was lewd and improper.

In the second article, the same reporter claimed that although Hughes denied one of his students had recently fathered an illegitimate 'brown baby' with a white girl, this was a lie. Although Edmondson's gentlemanly instincts caused him to withhold the mother's name he had no hesitation in naming the 'black scoundrel' as John Lionel Franklin. After attending Congo House Franklin had allegedly, not only been imprisoned in Africa for theft but on returning to Colwyn Bay been employed by Hughes on 'deputation work', despite Hughes having been informed of his criminal conviction! The reporter went on to claim this student was no exceptional case, that in his experience such native converts inevitably 'exhibit all the vices of the white man and none of his virtues'.

Both articles betrayed the prejudices that not only characterised *John Bull* but also typified today's popular press, with its casual diet of gossip, scandal and xenophobia. A paragraph, headed 'ENGLISH LADIES AND NEGROES', in the second article, was obviously intended to pander to readers' assumed racism:

> During the summer months at Colwyn some of the lady visitors act in an astonishing manner towards these natives. They may be seen seated with them on the sea front, in earnest, if not affectionate, conversation. Afternoon tea parties are arranged, and when the dusk of evening arrives, *black and white* may frequently be seen strolling together down the road behind the Institute. Drawing-room meetings are frequently held. At one of these, so impressed with the preacher were those present, that four ladies promised to each support a student for four years. A collection was made at another, and £75 was realised. I may say that this particular meeting was held almost within a stone's throw of where British men, women, and children were existing in a state of semi-starvation. How these black boys must laugh!

Facing Up to Prejudice
Subscriptions and support for the Institute evaporated overnight.

William decided to sue *John Bull* for libel. Bravely attempting to face down his local critics who obviously believed 'there is no smoke without fire', at 2.30pm on Thursday 4 January 1912 Councillor Reverend William Hughes attended the regular General Purposes Committee meeting of Colwyn Bay Council. Despite having sat as a Councillor for the previous six years, his colleagues made him feel sufficiently unwelcome that he thought it diplomatic to absent himself from Council meetings for the remainder of his term of office. Over succeeding months William attended a series of bankruptcy and winding-up hearings at Bangor and Caernarfon Courts. Throughout this period, both William Hughes and *John Bull* were aware that the real 'decider' of both their futures was the planned legal action for libel. Scheduled for the summer of 1912 this libel action would definitively determine whether Hughes and the African Institute would survive. If *John Bull*'s accusations were proved Hughes was sunk but if disproved, and libel established then all the Institute's financial problems were solved as the damages awarded were likely to be considerable.

Congo Institute versus John Bull

William Hughes' libel action against *John Bull* finally began at 3.45 pm on Wednesday 12 June 1912. *The Welsh Coast Pioneer* set the scene:

> Considerable interest was manifested in a libel action brought before Mr Justice Lush at the Ruthin Assize yesterday. The plaintiffs were the British and African Incorporated Association, Colwyn Bay and William Hughes, and the defendants, Horatio Bottomley, *John Bull* Ltd, and Odhams Ltd ... a large number of people attended, not only from Colwyn Bay but also from Llandudno, Abergele, Rhyl, Denbigh and Ruthin.

Odhams Ltd were the printers and publishers of *John Bull*, but remained essentially sleeping partners throughout the proceedings, as did the British and African Incorporated

John Lionel Franklin

Horatio Bottomley

Sir Charles Montague Lush

Ralph Vincent Bankes KC

Association. The courtroom drama that summer in 1912 was effectively a trial of strength between two men. Two public characters who had formerly thrived upon publicity but whose fortunes had lately fallen into decline. The case attracted enormous public interest both for its sensational subject matter – sex, race, money and religion – and its high-profile protagonists.

Who was Horatio?

Press barons are rarely run-of-the-mill individuals, but even amongst his peers Horatio Bottomley stands out as extraordinary. He not only rose from rags to riches, obscurity to fame and ignominy to acclamation, but he also reversed those dramatic transformations at intervals throughout his life. During his chequered career he played a huge variety of roles including office clerk, recruiting sergeant, Member of Parliament, shorthand writer, publisher and prisoner, but his joint outstanding and enduring areas of expertise were as a journalist and a swindler!

Unlike Hughes, Bottomley hadn't enjoyed the benefit of a stable, loving childhood but was raised in a Birmingham orphanage until, in 1874, he ran away at the age of fourteen. Employing a mixture of journalistic talent and sharp-practice, in a little over a decade he managed to acquire a stable of magazine-titles. When ambition prompted him to launch his publishing business on the stock-exchange fraud charges and bankruptcy finally caught up with him. Widely expected to be found guilty he conducted his own defence with such brilliance that he was acquitted.

Convinced of his own financial genius and personal invincibility, he launched more and more enterprises, which despite doing little for investors netted Bottomley a fortune. This wealth enabled Horatio to indulge what Frank Harris described as Bottomley's 'intense greed for all sensual pleasures' which others more prosaically identified as champagne, racehorses and 'petite, blonde working-class girls'.

Ever more ambitious, in 1906 Bottomley founded *John Bull* and was also elected Member of Parliament (MP) for Hackney South. A financial maverick and political demagogue, Bottomley was never really trusted by polite society but as an irredeemable populist he played on the prejudices of the majority.

In 1908 he was again charged with fraud and although the case was eventually dismissed he went on to lose a succession of damaging suits arising from his fraudulent schemes. Treated as a pariah by fellow MP's Horatio was dismissive, asserting political leaders, 'for the most part do nothing or seek only to serve their own ends' and 'all parties are only organised hypocrisies' [*sic*].

Characterising himself as the voice of the ordinary Englishman he was returned to Parliament twice more, in fairly rapid succession, before once again becoming entangled in accusations of underhand dealing and dishonesty. At precisely the time he was subjecting Hughes to ordeal-by-newspaper Bottomley was trying to evade creditors, led by the Prudential Assurance Company, who claimed he owed them a fortune. Admitting his liabilities exceeded his assets by £200,000 and aware that as a bankrupt he would be debarred from Parliament he applied for the Chiltern Hundreds on 24 May 1912. To the great relief of his fellow MPs, Bottomley departed the House just before he appeared at Ruthin, defending himself and *John Bull* against William Hughes' libel action.

'Widespread Interest'

'Widespread interest was taken in the case throughout the Principality' noted the *Weekly News*. Spectators came from far and wide to witness the proceedings. In a crowded courtroom there were just four main players; the judge, Sir Charles Lush; the defendant, Horatio Bottomley; the plaintiff, William Hughes and his barrister, Ralph Vincent Bankes KC. At 45 years of age, Bankes was a decade younger than the other three men. Born at Soughton Hall, Northop, Flintshire, of a leading north Wales family, Bankes enjoyed a competent if unspectacular career at the bar. His role in establishing Hughes' plaint was to be characteristically workmanlike.

Horatio Bottomley was guaranteed to play to the gallery and certain to prove a crowd-pleaser but Reverend Hughes might expect the judge, Sir Charles Montague Lush to be less easily impressed by oratory. Lush enjoyed a reputation for candour and simplicity, and coincidentally, his maternal grandfather, Revd Christopher Woollacott, was a Baptist minister. The reaction of the jury was the real wildcard. As the *Welsh Coast Pioneer* observed, 'When the special jury was called, it was noticed that a number of Colwyn Bay residents had been summoned, but the court officials passed them over and selected a jury from the Wrexham district. One juror was challenged by the defendants; he was withdrawn and another took his place.' Would a Wrexham jury empathise with Hughes and his barrister with their strong local connections or swallow the silver-tongued sophistry of the fallen ex-MP?

A Drama in Three Acts

The courtroom drama comprised three acts, the first two, substantial and lengthy, the third swift and definitive. Act One fell entirely to Hughes and his counsel, Ralph Bankes. Their task was to convince the jury of the fundamentally honest, decent and worthwhile nature of Hughes and his African Institute. In the course of so doing they intended to establish that *John Bull* had printed inaccurate, malicious untruths that had caused serious damage to the plaintiff's reputation and finances. Act Two was the fight scene, where Horatio Bottomley, supremely confident of his own abilities, dispensed with counsel and conducted his own combative cross-examination of William Hughes. A swiftly-paced Third Act delivered the Jury's damning verdict.

ACT ONE – Straight and Honourable in the Service of Christ

Much of the plaint presented by Ralph Bankes through sympathetic questioning of Hughes will be familiar to readers but to appreciate the jury's perception of events it is worthwhile studying the account of 'Act One' published in the *Llandudno Advertiser*:

> Mr Bankes said this was a singular action and a very important one, the attacks made in *John Bull* were of a very offensive character and now it was to be said they were true, and if they

were true, the plaintiff, the Rev William Hughes, the Director of the Institute and the plaintiff association were persons about whom nothing too hard could be said. They were hypocrites and humbugs of the worst character – people who in the name of religion carried on an institution where immorality was considered the proper thing. These were serious allegations to make against any people, more particularly those who had for years devoted all their money and their services to what they believed to be the best interests of the service of Christ.

Mr Hughes was a man who many years ago went out as a missionary to the Congo. There were many good people who sat at home and sneered about missionary work but who would not go to a place like that; but he went and gained a good acquaintanceship and knowledge of the mission field. He there contracted malarial fever, as many did, and he came back to England and started in Colwyn Bay an institute, out of which the African Institute arose. It had been found that there was difficulty in English missionaries doing this work in Africa largely owing to the climate and to lack of proficiency in the language. Mr Hughes thought the best plan was to bring natives here and train them in an institute like that at Colwyn Bay to get them acquainted with English life, to teach them a trade and bring them up as useful Christian citizens. There might, of course, be right-minded people who thought that was a mistake – that it was a mistake to bring black people to this country – and if *John Bull* chose to express that in proper terms none could complain. There was no doubt that the work of the Institute was carried on in a perfectly straight and honourable way. It had gained such success that there was this moment 45 mission stations in Africa which were being carried on by old pupils of the Institution, and he would not overstate the matter when he said that there were probably some four thousand converts due to the same work. Mr Hughes was a Fellow of the Royal Geographic Society and a man of some position.

About eleven years ago what till then had been a private

institute was incorporated as the British and African Association of which Mr Hughes was director and the affairs of which were managed by a committee largely consisting of Baptist ministers, but including some laymen. In the course of its history the Institute had had the patronage of some distinguished people – Mr H M Stanley, Lord Coleridge (who actually got a boy sent to the Institute), Mr Gladstone (who presented his books and other books to assist it) and Sir Alfred Jones (who used to convey the students to and fro on his steamers).

Like every other charitable institution, the Institute was probably not carried on on [*sic*] the best business lines, and there was a small deficit; but they had a very substantial subscription list of £1,300 to £1,400 a year. In 1911 they had a deficit of £108. The number of students actually in residence at the time was less than it had been before. The number ranged from sixteen to five, as some come for longer or shorter periods. At the end of last year it was in a fairly flourishing condition, and would probably have gone along in that way had not *John Bull* disturbed it.

The intervention arose in this way. There was a scandal in Colwyn Bay. A young woman had had a baby and it was stated that someone connected with the Institute was its father. Mr Hughes investigated the matter and satisfied himself that the man spoken of had nothing to do with it and he published a warning in a small newspaper which was amongst the things they carried on in connection with the Institute. *John Bull* issued the article in which they contrasted the Christmas appeal with this notice and they put on the contents bill certain words to promote the sale of their paper, without minding other people's feelings in the least. As to the article, it appeared to be the work of a gentleman named Edmondson, who came down to the Institute and introduced himself to Mr Hughes as 'Mr Vincent Watts'. He came on a Sunday and did not say what he came for, though his object was to find something to hold up to ridicule in *John Bull*. The address which Mr Hughes gave and which was criticised in the article was made before his own daughter and other women. The jury would see Mr Hughes and counsel asked, could anything be more repulsive than the way in which Mr Vincent Watts presented the subject? As a result of the publication of the article the income of the Institute shrunk at once and the result of *John Bull*'s word was that Mr William Hughes was in the bankruptcy court and the British and African Association was being wound up.'

Mr Bankes said that if he proved his case he should ask for substantial damages.

The Mysterious Mr Watts

The case presented by Bankes and Hughes was modest and workmanlike, with an absence of obviously exaggerated or unsupportable claims and an admission that, 'Like every other charitable institution, the Institute was probably not carried on on the best business lines'. The only, proven act of deceit and dishonesty apparent to the jury at this stage had been committed by *John Bull* when its Special Commissioner concealed both his purpose in attending the Institute's Sunday service and his real name. Introducing himself to Hughes as 'Vincent Watts', he was in reality, Robert Edmondson, an ex-sergeant major who had been cashiered for deserting his post in the South African War. Every bit as self-seeking, cynical and crudely populist as his boss, for his Sunday morning visit to the Institute, Bottomley's Special Commissioner had appropriated the forenames of his nineteen-year-old bank clerk son, Vincent Watts Edmondson, as his 'nom de guerre'.

Whilst the Jury and readers of *John Bull* were misled that the purpose of the Special Commissioner's visit to the Institute was straightforward, open-minded fact-finding, in reality Edmondson had conspired with, Josiah, another of the visitors present at that Sunday morning Bible study session, in Hughes' entrapment.

Josiah Batubo, originally of Buguma, New Calabar, had nursed a grudge against Hughes since William had expelled him from the Institute for 'unmanageable behaviour'. Special Commissioner Edmondson was a muck-raking journalist out to create a sensational story.

In Court and in *John Bull*, William Hughes was derided for provoking inappropriate responses to Scripture at the Bible study session but responsibility for disrespectful behaviour lay with Edmondson and co-conspirator Batubo, for it was their intention to disrupt the event. Of Josiah's response to Revd Hughes' analysis of St Mathew's gospel, Edmondson recalled, 'He laughed, and enjoyed the whole business. The other darkeys [sic] seemed annoyed.' Edmondson blamed Hughes and absolved Josiah, for 'I gave Josiah the credit of being an honest man.' Edmondson justified his supposed faith in Josiah's integrity with the claim that he 'took his degree at the Bar. He is now a solicitor'.

Edmondson's testimonial to Batubo's character was spurious as Josiah was neither honest, nor a lawyer but a humble coffee roaster employed by a Bangor (north Wales) tea merchant. Edmondson's claim that Josiah 'was simply a visitor' was equally untrue, intended to convey the impression that Batubo was previously unknown to him, yet it is incredible that a student expelled by William a decade earlier should return to attend a Bible study session at the Institute at precisely the same time as a journalist intent on destroying Hughes' reputation. The unbelievable nature of the coincidence was apparent to William Hughes, who, it was reported, told the Court, 'He was very surprised to see the expelled student Josiah at the meeting. He did not say that the Special Commissioner brought him; but he had his doubts on the matter. It was the only time he came.'

Hughes didn't say that the Special Commissioner brought Josiah, but his counsel should have suggested precisely that in the strongest possible terms at the earliest possible opportunity. It was typical of William Hughes that his submission to the Jury amounted to a plaintive appeal for them to recognise his good intentions and forgive his human weaknesses. Unfortunately, it was also typical of his lacklustre barrister, Mr Ralph Vincent Bankes KC, to rest on his non-existent laurels and refrain from energetically setting about the opposition. Horatio Bottomley had no such qualms and his questioning of William Hughes was utterly ruthless.

ACT TWO – Horatio Bottomley versus Revd William Hughes

As Horatio Bottomley stepped up to cross-examine William Hughes each man knew their performance that day would determine their future. Both men's public reputation was at a low ebb and neither could afford to be judged a liar and a charlatan by the jury. Hughes' testimony had created a favourable impression with the jury, now it fell to Bottomley to destroy that wholesome image and justify the scandalous article he'd published in *John Bull*.

Fortunately *The Welsh Coast Pioneer* published a virtual transcript of the verbal exchanges between Bottomley and Hughes enabling us to assess the comparative credibility of these two characters, as presented to the judge and jury.

Bottomley carefully structured his questions around a series of key issues, opening with a direct assault upon Hughes' denial of sexual impropriety at the Institute.

Misconduct with White Girls

The plaintiff, in reply to questions said that he knew that a placard was circulated bearing the words, *Black Baptist's Brown Baby*, and he connected that with the Institute as there had been trouble about a black student and a white girl in Colwyn Bay but he had got to the bottom of it and found that it was as untrue as *John Bull*'s article was false.

I suggest to you that you yourself expelled at least two students – black students – on the ground of misconduct with white girls. Do you remember it or do you deny it? – I don't deny it, I remember one. I do not remember the other; though it shows the discipline of the place.

I think you will remember the other case before we have finished. Your own minutes show it. You reported that you had expelled at least two students for such misconduct? – You have the advantage of me Mr Bottomley. I have not had the books for months, and you have been searching them.

Throughout Bottomley's cross-examination, William frequently claimed memory-lapse but Bottomley returned inexorably to his theme and the judge insisted on more substantive answers from Hughes.

Were complaints made to your Council of molestations by black students of white girls? – No.

In your minute book of 1907 these words appear: *These four students' offence was staying out late at night. The tutor received complaints that they were seen in the woods late at night with white girls.* – I don't remember it.

The Judge: Surely Mr Hughes you were responsible to some extent for the conduct of your students. Don't you remember some complaints made? – Yes, some, but I don't remember anybody coming to see me for that purpose.

The Judge: I press the question. Were complaints made to you with regard to the conduct of black students towards white girls? – In what way do mean conduct, my lord?

The Judge: I shall not ask you again.

Witness (WH): There are some complaints, but not of immorality.

Bottomley: Do you remember a student named George Fraser being expelled or thrashed for some scandalous conduct towards a white lady? – No.

Don't you remember him being publicly thrashed in your Institute for gross behaviour towards a white lady? – I don't remember it.

And so it continued, as Horatio threw a punch, William ducked and dived, and from time-to-time, in the interests of fair play, Mr Justice Lush, intervened.

Bottomley: You remember the log-book? – I remember it, but I have not read it. The committee got the report and it referred us to the log book, but we did not read it. I only saw the outside of the book.

The Judge asked whether the witness did not look at the log-book to see how the students were behaving themselves and he replied that neither the committee nor himself looked at the log-book.

I suggest to you that the log-book is teeming with such complaints and that it was your duty to refer to it

The Judge suggested that the witness should look at the log-book.

The book was handed to the witness, who said he would prefer not to look at it.

After further questioning, William, said that when he saw the placard and read the libel it caused him a great deal of mental anguish and material damage and discredited him as a minister with the Baptist connexion. He hoped that that he had a good reputation up to that time.

The Baptist Connexion

As soon as Hughes uttered the claim that *John Bull* was responsible for his low standing amongst fellow Baptists Bottomley asked him about events at the 1911 Baptist Congress, held three months before the alleged libel appeared.

You said that you had a good reputation up to that time? – I hope so, I say.

Did they disown you at the Congress last September? – What do you mean?

Did they pass a resolution disassociating themselves from you and your Institute? – No. They had an argument, that is all.

Do you remember Mr E K Jones? – Yes

Did he make a severe attack upon you at the Congress? – Yes

And subsequently did they pass a resolution that an independent mission should be established and so have nothing to do with your Institute? – I know nothing about it. I never heard or read that.

You never read of it? – I never read of it, and I don't think it is true.

Dishonoured Cheques

From the start of the cross-examination Bottomley appeared supremely confident and in control, Hughes seemed unsure, evasive, even shifty. Keen to press home his early advantage, Bottomley switched to financial matters, another recurrent theme.

You say amongst other things the article caused you is that your credit has gone? – Yes.

Was it pretty good up to that time? – As good as any ordinary minister's.

How many dishonoured cheques had you floating about at that time? – I have had some dishonoured.

Is that typical of the ordinary minister? (*laughter*) I think they are usually hard up. (*laughter*).

Did you cash cheques when you had no money to meet them? – Yes, I do not want to deny the truth. I did give some cheques that I could not meet at first. I was in hopes of having money to meet them.

Did you sometimes get cheques cashed in Colwyn Bay by tradesmen when you knew you had no money to meet them? – I meant to meet them and I have done so.

The Judge: That is no answer to the question.- Yes. I was in hope of meeting them. I met the cheques in the long run.

Is it a fact that when the libel appeared you had a considerable number of dishonoured cheques in circulation in Colwyn Bay and the neighbourhood? – I don't think so. I cannot answer that. I cannot say.

You cannot remember whether you had or not a lot of dishonoured cheques in circulation? – I met the cheques in the long run.

The Judge: You mean that the cheques were sent out and you had no assets to meet them? – Yes I had some cheques dishonoured before but I cannot specify any particular time.

Throughout the year 1911, prior to the publication of this libel you were constantly having dishonoured cheques in circulation? – Now and again.

I put it to you that you had 20 in 1911? – Well, I cannot tell you. You must ask my banker.

The Judge: You may have had as many as twenty? – I do not think so myself.

By this stage, even the Judge was becoming frustrated by Hughes' reluctance to give direct, definitive answers.

'Fields of Labour'

With Hughes' credibility seeming to slip, Bottomley questioned him about ex-student Josiah Batubo who had visited the Institute on the same Sunday as the 'Special Commissioner'. Hughes had claimed to have been very surprised to have seen him there as he had been expelled many years before, 'because he was unmanageable'.

Would you be surprised to know that in your last annual report you published his name as one of your representatives doing glorious work in the field of work, New Calabar? – It cannot be. It must be his father, because the boy is in this country.

Was his father a student?- No, he was not.

This is your last list of students to date (*holding up a printed report*)? – It does not say he is there (*laughter*). I knew the boy was in this country. It shows he would be in New Calabar in the future (*laughter*).

You expelled him, and, as you say, you washed your hands of him? – Yes, but still the fellow may do good. Because we expelled him that does not mean he is ruined for ever.

The Judge: I cannot follow that.

Plaintiff: Neither can I, my lord (*laughter*)…

Do you really deny my suggestion that this book is produced for the purpose of getting subscriptions for your Institute from the pious and charitable public you meant to convey that all the men are doing Christian work in these districts on behalf of your Institute or under its auspices?

Hughes refused to give a straight answer and clearly dissatisfied with William's claim that Josiah would in some indeterminate period return to labour in Africa, Justice Lush put his own supplementary question to Hughes:

> The Judge: But why did you say some time ago that the name must refer to his father? – I thought so when I produced it.
> The Judge: Did you ever know his father? – Yes.
> The Judge: Was he a student? – No
> The Judge: So it could not refer to him? – It is not so. It is not the father. It is Josiah himself.

By this point Hughes' evasiveness was apparent to all, but Horatio had more to ask about reported 'fields of labour'.

> Mr Bottomley mentioned the case of Willie Prest, described in the 22nd Annual report of the Institute as a student located now at New Calabar. Was that student at the time his name appeared in the list a boy of eight years of age, the son of an African Chief, who sent the boy over for three weeks? – He was 12 years of age and sent for three months, I believe, and then left.
> And he now appears as one of your students at this date carrying on God's work and his field of labour is New Calabar? (*laughter*) – Yes, that is an exception.
> And he appears as one of your students carrying on work in a *field of labour* in New Calabar – a boy of twelve? – I am bound to include the name in the list on the instructions of my committee.
> The Judge: Are you bound to do that? – Yes my lord, the committee ordered me.
> The Judge: Do you think it was right? – I had to obey orders, my lord.
> Do you suggest now that you have a field of labour for that little boy in New Calabar? – Have we not all our fields of labour?
> There is such a thing as hard labour you know (*laughter*). I put

it to you in plain language that the object of the list of students was to deceive charitable people to the idea that these were your missionaries working in your field of labour? Is that not your object? Is it honest to represent this 12 year old boy working in a field of labour in New Calabar when you were paid for his board and lodgings? – You can pick out one.
Was that your object? – Yes.

With the help of the Judge's refusal to allow William's convenient lapses of memory, Bottomley was punching holes in the perfect picture of life at the African Institute presented to the jury by Hughes and his counsel. He went on to accuse Hughes of even faking photographic images of the Institute.

Lady in the Photograph
Bottomley cross-examined Hughes:

> as to the photographs appearing on the cover and first page of the last annual report, and he said that the groups shown were groups of students and staff. The outside photograph was taken last year, but the other was a much older photo. All the coloured men included in the former were at the time students at the Institute. He explained that the students who were at college spent their holidays at the Institute, and the blocks for the report were made up from the photographs taken. He admitted that the photo of a lady appeared twice in the same group but the explanation was that it was pasted on the photo, and in the post the picture got displaced and the block now reproduced the lady twice by pasting her photo in the wrong position (*laughter*)!

The Notorious Franklin
Mr Bottomley: This man Franklin, the alleged father of the child, was he originally a student of your Institute? – Yes.
And then he went back to Africa, did he go to north Nigeria? – Yes.
About twelve months ago did he come back to the Institute? –

Yes.

Did you engage him as one of the Association's missionaries or deputations? – Yes, I gave him a home when he had none.

Did you pay him a commission on the subscriptions he could get? – Not then.

Later on did he preach for you? – He spoke.

Was he taken round to show what splendid work could be done by these natives? – I did not show him off. I could have shown three or four doctors. I believed he was honest, sincere and immoral – moral, I mean (*laughter*).

Are you sure you did not make a slip? – Yes.

Did you receive reports of Franklin in 1909? – Yes.

Do you know that whilst he was back in Nigeria after your training he was charged with a series of abominable offences and imprisoned for six months? – Only for four months.

Did you receive a letter from the Church Missionary Society in North Nigeria dated 19 November 1909, giving you this man's record after he left your place? – Yes, I received the letter.

There was a report to you that while this student was out there he served a term of imprisonment on two charges brought against him by the public of the place he was working in, one of which was a trial of five days for extorting money? – I don't remember it.

He was further charged with taking goods by force or by intimidation? – A tree from a native chief (*laughter*).

Did you hear that he was living a life of the grossest immorality? – No, but I have an explanation.

The Judge: There is no need to explain; just answer the question. Did the letter give a good character to this gentleman? – (*laughter*) – No.

Did it give him a bad character? – Yes.

Bankrupted by *John Bull*?

As Hughes's credibility slipped away, 'Mr Bottomley questioned the witness about an appeal that was issued in February last.' William's desperate appeal begged contributions from Institute sympathisers to stave off imminent bankruptcy and crucially placed the entire blame for Hughes' financial distress on *John Bull*. 'Mr Hughes said that he submitted it to the members of the committee but not to Mr Nunn, the Institute's solicitor. He issued a few of the appeals – about 500; he called that a few. (*laughter*)

Mr Bottomley pointed out that the appeal which was addressed to a few friends stated that the untruthful article in *John Bull* had diminished the receipts of the Institute and caused their creditors to press them unmercifully and had compelled him and the Institute to file petitions.

> Please tell me of any creditor who pressed you after the article in *John Bull* who had not pressed you before? – John Heywood, Manchester. I owed them £60 or £80 at one time but they never pressed me and now for £23 they issued a writ and put the bailiff in the place in December.
> Any others? – I can name at least four.
> Who had never pressed you before? – Stead and Simpson. I owed them £8 or £9.
> Another? – Roberts and Jones, Colwyn Bay. They issued a County Court summons.
> Was that any novel experience? – I had had a few (*laughter*).
> How many had you had in 1911? – Two, three or four.
> It might be a dozen? – No, it could not be.
> Mr Bottomley here produced an account by Messrs. John Heywood showing that they had proceeded before the libel.
> The Judge said the libel evidently had nothing to do with it.

Mr Bottomley in concluding his long cross-examination suggested that the Institute was in a hopeless state of financial embarrassment when the articles in *John Bull* appeared and that the plaintiffs seized upon the articles as an excuse for closing it up. He added: I think I have said enough to show that the man was incapable of being libelled.

ACT THREE – The Verdict

His Lordship said that they had listened to a very powerful cross-examination. Was it not possible to ask whether the case must be tried out?

Bottomley: It rests with the learned counsel for the plaintiffs.

The foreman of the jury said they were prepared to state the conclusion they had come to.

The Judge made a suggestion to counsel in writing and the plaintiff retired with those interested in the case for a consultation.

The Judge returned to court and asked if anything had been decided upon.

Mr Bottomley said they had not yet arrived at a conclusion but he noticed that Mr Bankes was tying up his papers (*laughter*). Again some of the counsel retired and after a few minutes they returned when Mr Montgomery (Bottomley's counsel) said that it had been agreed that the case should end on the terms that there should be judgement and verdict for defendants with an agreed sum for costs.

The Judge remarked that he did not think it wise that the action, should proceed any further after the admissions made in cross examination. The jury then returned a formal verdict for the defendants.

Hughes had not only lost, he had been humiliated, destroyed by an out-and-out rogue. Bottomley was an utter humbug but a consummate showman whose ruthless yet witty cross-examination had even impressed Mr Justice Lush. As the *Pioneer* observed, 'On leaving the court Mr Bottomley was cheered by the public who had assembled.'

SALE ON WEDNESDAY NEXT.

By Order of the Liquidator.

COLWYN BAY.

HIGHLY IMPORTANT SALE of the Valuable FREEHOLD PROPERTY known as MYRTLE VILLA and THE AFRICAN INSTITUTE, with the Valuable BUILDING LAND adjoining.

MR. F. A. DEW is favoured with instructions from J. H. Jones, Esq., of Llandudno, the Liquidator, to Sell by Auction at the Hotel Metropole, Colwyn Bay, on Wednesday, 31st July, 1912, at 3.30 p.m. (subject to Conditions of Sale), the beautifully situated and highly valuable

FREEHOLD PROPERTY.
known as
THE AFRICAN INSTITUTE,
MYRTLE VILLA,
and the
BUILDING LAND ADJOINING
THE SAME,

which is ripe for immediate development. The Property will first be offered in one Lot, and if not so sold, then in Lots as shewn in Particulars of Sale and Plan.

Plans, Particulars of Sale, and further information may be obtained from J. H. Jones, Esq., Accountant, Grange House Llandudno; Messrs. J. M. Porter & Elcock, Surveyors, Colwyn Bay; Mr. F. A. Dew, Auctioneer and Estate Agent, The Property Mart, Colwyn Bay; or from

Messrs. CHAMBERLAIN & JOHNSON,
Solicitors,
Llandudno.

African Institute Auction Notice, July 1912

Chapter Twelve

'Do Not Forget to Remember Me'
(1912–1924)

Just two weeks after William's disastrous libel action the entire contents of the African Institute, from 'a large cricket pavilion' to 'a number of African curios' were auctioned off. Three weeks later, on Wednesday 31 July, the 'freehold properties known as The African Institute, Myrtle Villa and the building land adjoining' went under the hammer at Colwyn Bay's Hotel Metropole. The last few students had been sent home but loyal friends collected together enough money to enable William and his two surviving children, Stanley and Claudia to stay on, as tenants, at Myrtle Villa.

Another Tragedy

Following the libel action William withdrew from public life and although a few friends rallied round most preferred to avoid him. He didn't return to the local Council but kept in touch by letter with a few ex-students, particularly Ernestina, whom he'd treated as an adopted daughter before she left Colwyn Bay in 1906 to work with and marry ex-fellow-student Joseph Morford in Africa. Having visited Hughes at Colwyn Bay in 1909 the couple returned to stay with him at Myrtle Villa throughout the summer of 1913. When Ernestina realised she was pregnant they agreed she should stay on to have the baby in Wales whilst Joseph returned to Nigeria to resume his teaching duties at the opening of the new term in September. Although Ernestina intended to rejoin Joseph as soon as the baby was born it was not to be. During the winter she caught pneumonia and, in January 1914, died.

Local press reports of Ernestina's death inadvertently illustrate William's continuing disgrace:

The death took place on the 11th inst. after a very short illness, of Mrs Joseph Morford, of Southern Nigeria, West Africa. The deceased lady was well-known in Colwyn Bay, and all who knew her had the highest esteem for her. At the end of her course of training in this country, she was married to Mr Joseph Morford, and they worked together for eight years in conducting a school under the English government in Southern Nigeria.

Both paid a visit to this country last summer on six months furlough. It was decided that Mrs Morford should remain during the winter in her old home in Colwyn Bay, when Mr Morford left in September to resume his duties in Africa. Their combined work in Africa had been a success, and there will be much sorrow among the natives when they receive the sad news of Mrs Morford's death. She was buried at the Old Colwyn cemetery on Tuesday afternoon. The Revd Peter Jones officiated. He referred in sympathetic terms to the many beautiful traits of the deceased's character. She was kind and tender-hearted, conscientious in all things, and faithful to the truth. The revd gentleman prayed for the bereaved husband in Nigeria, who would not receive the sad news until another three weeks had elapsed. Wreaths and other floral tributes were sent by the following: Her Father (who presented two wreaths, one on behalf of her husband); 'All at Myrtle Villa', Miss Batty, Mrs Sharp, Leeds: Mrs and Miss Holt, Miss Brown, Miss Ainsworth; Miss Yatwood and Toolery.

All reference to William Hughes and the African Institute has been neatly excised. Even in 1914 it was still a topic best avoided.

From Bad to Worse

On 4 August Britain declared war on Germany. Hostilities rapidly extended to Africa, effectively ending William Hughes' correspondence with Alfred Dibundu and other old friends and ex-students in Cameroon. On 5 November 1914 William's long-time friend and fiery supporter in the Welsh Baptist press, James 'Spinther' James, died unexpectedly. From the earliest days of the

Institute Spinther had been a stalwart supporter of Hughes and an invaluable ally against the BMS and Baptist Establishment who were determined to destroy these Welsh upstarts. Spinther was never afraid to advocate the independent approach of the African Institute through the columns of *Seren Cymru*. As a fellow Baptist minister, author of a four-volume history of the Welsh Baptists, a poet and a fearless social activist, Spinther's death came as a further cruel blow in a very depressed period of William Hughes' life, yet all was not gloom and doom.

'A Sportsman of the Higher Type'

William's son Stanley had been enjoying great success as a footballer, not only for Colwyn Bay but also for a variety of regional and junior international teams. In later years a sporting biography in *The North Wales Weekly News* celebrated his career:

> The subject needs no introduction to football enthusiasts on the Coast to whom he is familiarly known as *Stanley*, and he is as popular as he is well known. A sportsman of the higher type, a gentleman on the field and off, *Stanley* has not a single

Stanley Hughes 1912 team photograph (North Wales Coast F. A.)

William Hughes in 1916

enemy and the sport would be all the cleaner if we had more players of his type. No matter what provocation he receives in the shape of being fouled, he has never been known to retaliate, although perhaps he has more occasion to retaliate than any player on the Coast, as there is no one more keenly watched than he is by his opponents. He is rightly regarded as one of the most dangerous forwards on the Coast and if he shows how the game should be played it is more than can be said of many of his opponents who when he has beaten them by fair means, resort to dirty tactics. He is also a peacemaker, when trouble brews with other players and his example in this respect could profitably be copied. A native of Colwyn Bay, *Stanley* learnt his football at Abergele County School, under the tutorship of Mr W J Evans, who has done a great deal for football in this district.

The article continued but made no mention of Stanley's well-known father, and despite the passage of time Colwyn Bay continued to cold-shoulder William Hughes.

A New Leaf?
By 1916 Britain had gained control of much of the former German-occupied territories of Africa and William Hughes had regained some of his former confidence. Realising that he wasn't going to recover his reputation at home he decided to explore the idea of resuming the career that he had abandoned as a young man. On 23 March 1916 he wrote to ex-student Alfred Dibundu in Akwa Town, Cameroon with an extraordinary proposal:

My dear Alfred, – I have been thinking for some time to write to you as I have you and the work at Cameroons still at heart. I have watched the proceedings of the war there and I know that the Germans have been cleared out of the colony. I consider this a great blessing to all the natives and I do hope it will be under the control of the English or French in the future. By right it should be an English colony. You know how interested I am in your native churches and how the natives should be encouraged to develop their own work in serving their God.

Now I have a proposal to make. I should very much like to come there to assist you – not in any way to govern you, or to interfere with the native ministers, but to encourage you in the Lord's work…

I am writing a similar letter to the Revd Joseph Burnley …

Desperate, Mad or Dedicated?

As a thirty-year-old, Hughes had found it impossible to survive in Africa, so what had persuaded him to try again aged sixty? Obviously desperation was one explanation, but both his son and daughter were earning and able to support him in modest comfort so he didn't need to work, but a mixture of mission and ego compelled him to do more. Hughes was a driven man, to some an inspiration, to others an irrational obsessive who didn't know when he was beaten. He knew enough to realise that after the death of his shipping sponsor, Alfred Jones, he no longer had the means to return to Africa so he included in his letter to Dibundu an appeal for financial support. 'I cannot start from here unless you, as churches together, can send me £30 for my passage, and £20 for the freight of the books…I would also require £30 a year from your churches as contribution for maintenance …' This was certainly an ironic twist on his original scheme of African missionaries being self-financing.

Africa Beckons

After an exchange of letters Hughes received the response he was seeking from Alfred Dibundu, dated 4 November 1916:

The Native Churches have again met in a conference and have unanimously consented to your offer. Enclosed is a cheque of £30 (thirty pounds sterling) to be drawn from the firm of R & W King of Bristol ... The £30 is for your passage. The £20 for the freight of the books you asked for will be considered and sent later on ...

A further exchange of letters followed including the following from Hughes on 1 June 1917;
'My Dear Alfred, – I am now busy packing my books, which I will forward about the end of this month ...'

In response to further financial pleas from Hughes, on 21 July 1917, Dibundu wrote to him from Akwa Town, clearly frustrated and asking, 'Can't you get the £50 there from anybody, so that we can send same after your arrival here? That will prevent any further delay on our part.'

Unable to cadge £50 from personal acquaintances, Hughes produced a slim booklet outlining the aims and objectives of his 'third return to Africa' and appealing for financial support to be sent either to, 'Treasurer – Azariah Jones, Gwylfa, Erskine Road, Colwyn Bay or Revd W Hughes, Native Mission House, Duala, Cameroons.'

Goodwill or Good Riddance?

Hughes despatched copies of his Cameroon booklet, accompanied by a copy of a testimonial he secured from local worthies on the strength of a mixture of sympathy and past friendship. Doubtless, some wished as much to speed his departure from Colwyn Bay, as facilitate his arrival in Africa. When his initial appeal proved unsuccessful he re-dated his covering letter from 12 November 1917 to 9 May 1918 and tried again, but he had by then exhausted all the goodwill that survived his libel trial. He had also lost the possibility of help from one of his closest and most faithful African collaborators, for Mojola Agbebi passed away in Nigeria in 1917.

No Peace at Myrtle Villa

On 11 November 1918 peace was declared, but William had little heart to celebrate following the failure of his second, and final, attempt to raise funds for a return to Africa. He also had little time to emotionally regroup before he was dealt another body-blow, as reported in the *Weekly News* of 12 December 1918:

In Affectionate Remembrance

of

Claudia Hughes,

The only daughter of the Rev. W. Hughes,
Myrtle Villa, Colwyn Bay,

Who entered (through Pneumonia) into rest
in Jesus, on December 9th 1918,

In her 30th Year,

And was interred at Old Colwyn Cemetery,
on December 11th

"My days are past, my purposes are broken off, even
the thoughts of my heart."—JOB xvii. 11.

"Thy will be done.'—MATT. xxvi. 42.

MYRTLE VILLA,
NANT-Y-GLYN ROAD,
COLWYN BAY.

Claudia Hughes' death notice,
December 1918

Much sympathy is felt for the Revd William Hughes of Myrtle Villa, on the death of his only daughter, Miss Claudia Hughes, which took place early on Monday morning from pneumonia, consequent upon an attack of influenza. Miss Hughes, who was in her 30th year, was of a frail constitution and of a reserved disposition, but highly esteemed by all who had the pleasure of her acquaintanceship. She was a gifted musician and a good teacher. The funeral, which was private, took place yesterday at the Colwyn cemetery. The Revd Arthur Jones officiated, assisted by the Revs Thos. Frimston, J J Morgan (curate), Thos. Parry, Wm. Edwards (Llandudno), and the Revd Azariah Jones …

Farewell to Colwyn Bay

Claudia had played the piano accompaniment to 'silent' films at the cinema in Penmaenmawr and had kept William in touch with the lighter side of life. After her death he grew increasingly depressed and detached from everyday reality. As old friends died off he was ever-more isolated and developed a taste for alcohol.

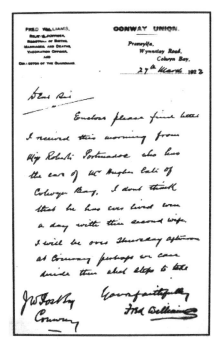

Letter from the Workhouse authorities re. William Hughes, 1923

When Stanley returned from war service with the Royal Welsh Fusiliers in 1919 he wanted nothing to do with his father and by then a rather pathetic figure with no income he was taken in by a relative, Margaret Roberts, of 25 New Street, Portmadoc. Initially granted ten shillings a week out-relief, or financial support by the local Festiniog Poor Law Union, William was technically the responsibility of the Conway Poor Law Union, as Colwyn Bay was William's last official 'place of settlement'. On 17 November 1923 David Jones, Clerk to the Festiniog Union therefore contacted J. W. Post, Clerk to the Conway Union, assuming that Conwy would 'grant non-settled poor relief, as the old gentleman is so well known your Board will no doubt be ready to accept his chargeability.'

Unfortunately Margaret Roberts found the maintenance allowance inadequate and so, on 26 March 1923, she wrote to Conway Union complaining that the ten shilling maintenance payment wasn't sufficient, especially as William's son, Stanley, wasn't paying the additional monies he had promised her. Margaret also suggested the authorities might pursue William's estranged wife, Bessie Hutton Hughes, for a contribution.

Unsurprisingly, after cursory enquiries officials of the Conway Union soon concluded that this would prove an unrewarding enterprise. With matters unresolved Hughes' health continued to decline until just before Christmas 1923, almost twelve years to the day after *John Bull*'s placards had appeared in Colwyn Bay, he was admitted as a pauper to Conwy Workhouse. Once a well-known and well-respected townsman, welcome in any home in Colwyn Bay, as he lay dying in the poorhouse not even his own son would offer him houseroom. On Monday 28 January 1924 William Hughes passed away in poverty and disgrace. The death certificate gave the cause of death as heart disease and recorded the address as 12 Waen Terrace, Conway. Perhaps the arterial condition identified forty years earlier by Dr Roberts caused Hughes' demise and certainly his heart was broken, but the drink didn't help. Waen Terrace was a complete fiction, created to disguise the shame of dying in the Workhouse.

In the Company of Good Friends

Hughes was spared the ignominy of a pauper's funeral and was buried with due ceremony in Old Colwyn cemetery. Lying beneath the shadow of an impressive white marble memorial stone, William shares his grave with infant daughter Edith Mary, who died in 1893, his first wife, Katie, who passed away in 1894, and Katie, the bedridden daughter who died in 1909, aged twenty-two. Hughes' grave is surrounded by those of two further family members, Claudia Hughes and sister-in-law, Edith Jones and seven students, Ernestina Morford, Kobina Boodoo (Joseph Emmanuel Abraham), Alfred Johnson, George Steane, Nkanza, Samba and Kinkasa.

William's funeral even merited a mention in the *North Wales Weekly News* that reported 'an impressive service was conducted at the Tabernacl Welsh Baptist Chapel'. Several ministers from the old days of the Institute took part as well as a youthful Lewis Valentine, Pastor of Tabernacl, Llandudno and Plaid Cymru's first parliamentary candidate. As a boy Valentine had attended classes at Colwyn Bay Higher Grade School (now Eirias High School) alongside Institute student Oladipo Lahanmi, who he admired and befriended. Valentine acknowledged his personal debt to William Hughes as an inspiration and encouragement in pursuing his own ordination. Like Hughes, Lewis Valentine would suffer for challenging the Establishment.

'*Bydd myrdd o ryfeddodau*' was feelingly sung at the graveside.

The grave of William Hughes

The chief mourners were Mr Stanley Hughes, son; Mrs Stanley Hughes, daughter-in-law; Revd T. Idwal Jones, Mrs Roberts, Mrs Wilson and Mr R. W. Williams (Llanelian). Members of Tabernacl Church (Colwyn Bay) acted as bearers.

An Insignificant Failure?
Stanley Hughes would never again speak about his father, even to members of his own family and as memories of William Hughes and his Institute gradually faded the significance of this pioneering venture was ignored. The graves of Hughes, his family and African students remain, along with the plaque recording William's role in founding Colwyn Bay Library, there is the Tabernacl chapel he founded and the Congo House building in Nant-y-glyn Road; even some of his 'African curios' have been retained. Colwyn Bay is full of reminders of the glory days of the African Institute for those who care to look, but in the end was the whole enterprise anything more than a curious historical bye-road leading nowhere or, does Congo House represent a significant episode linking the history of Wales to the liberation of black Africa? Before embarking on further analysis let's complete the narrative, tie up the loose ends and record the fate of the supporting actors in our drama.

Mark Hayford's Story
Baptist minister Dr Mark Christian Hayford of the Gold Coast, had attended Hughes' Ashton-under-Lyne wedding to Bessie Hutton in 1899 as 'the representative of the black race'. Over the years Mark had kept in touch with William and an up-to-date account of his mission and sketch of his new Cape Coast church appeared in the African Institute's final annual report, published in 1911. After starting the first independent African Church in Ghana he had forged effective links with other separatist movements across West Africa in an effort to consolidate churches seceding from western missions. In cooperation with Agbebi and others he organised a fellowship of independent Baptist Churches that eventually stretched from Sierra Leone to Cameroon. With the support of Elder Dempster shipping,

Hayford travelled extensively in both Britain and America. In 1910 Hayford attended the World Missionary Conference in Edinburgh and in 1912 he was at a conference in Alabama organised by the renowned black activist, Booker T. Washington.

In 1911 the African Institute's final report announced that Hayford sought a further £3,750 to erect a school for his Cape Coast congregation. He had, apparently, already received a donation of £1,000 from Sir Thomas Glen-Coats, the Paisley-based, cotton-thread manufacturer and was continuing with fund-raising yet, like Hughes, he never seemed able to collect enough to fund his ambitious educational mission. By the 1920s his widely published intention was to raise £50,000, an amount identical to William Hughes' ultimate target for the Institute and then, in an uncanny parallel, he was accused of impropriety, sued to protect his reputation and lost. Disgraced and impoverished, in 1935 Revd Mark Christian Hayford died in Bath Workhouse.

Rise and Fall of Horatio Bottomley
Despite being forced out of Parliament in disgrace in 1912, immediately before Hughes' libel action, Horatio Bottomley remained ever-ebullient. Celebrating his libel victory Bottomley rubbed Hughes' nose in his abject defeat through the columns of *John Bull*. Revealing the depths of his own racist depravity on 22 June 1912 Bottomley wrote, 'Colwyn Bay is delighted to be rid of the pest Hughes and his niggers … a sensuous, barbarous and cunning lot of niggers, some of them of the lowest order of intelligence and morals … an ever present menace to the safety of white women.'

With the beating of the war-drums in 1914 Bottomley was in his element, as A. J. Morris observed, 'War afforded a national stage for his huckstering demagoguery. *John Bull* spewed out venomous chauvinism, demanding that all 'Germ-Huns' in Britain, whether naturalized or no, be exterminated'. Within a few months of the outbreak of war, on Thursday 19 November 1914 Bottomley was back in north Wales where he brought his self-promoting, tub-thumping recruitment road-show to the Pier Pavilion Colwyn Bay. One can only wonder at the traumatic effect Bottomley's visit had on William Hughes. Perhaps it even prompted him to consider emigration to Africa?

In 1918 Horatio Bottomley was, for the fourth time, elected to Parliament! In 1921 he brought a criminal libel action against a former associate but it rebounded upon him, revealing that his Victory Bond Club, launched in 1919 in *John Bull* and raising almost a million pounds, was an utter swindle.

In 1922 he was charged with fraud and sentenced to seven years' penal servitude. His legal appeal was rejected and he was expelled from the Commons. Despite the privations of prison Horatio's sense of humour never entirely deserted him and, recognised whilst repairing a mail-bag, by a prison-visitor who called out, 'Sewing, Bottomley?' he famously replied, 'No, reaping'.

He was released after five years in gaol, but his former friends had deserted him and he drifted into obscurity before dying in hospital, in poverty and alone, on 26 May 1933.

Mysterious Mrs Hughes

Bessie Hutton Clarke (1848–1924) married William Hughes in August 1899, yet when Fred Williams, Relieving Officer for the Colwyn Bay District, was asked, in 1923, if he might be able to persuade her to contribute towards Hughes' welfare he pointedly observed, 'I don't think he has ever lived even a day with this second wife.' Bessie disappeared immediately after her enthusiastic reception at Congo House and never returned to Colwyn Bay. Despite her recent wedding vows Bessie went straight back to her previous life at Ashton-under-Lyne. Living alone at 38 Wellington Street, she signed herself 'Bessie Hughes' and on official forms, described herself as 'married' but in no other way acknowledged her marriage to William.

Latterly she moved to a two-up, two-down terraced house at 27 Uxbridge Street, Ashton-under-Lyne and, perhaps as an unconscious reflection of her further estrangement from William, added her maiden to her married name, officially signing as Bessie Hutton Hughes. She generally introduced herself as 'Miss Clarke'. Still living alone, she continued to work to Christianise the heathens she lived amongst on the eastern fringes of Manchester. Neighbours recalled how she would lure their children, with promises of cough sweets, to pray with her at her 'Home Mission' housed in a room above some shops in Warrington Street.

Despite her modest way of life Bessie Hughes was really quite a wealthy woman, having inherited money from her stepfather, gas works manager David Clarke who had died just before she married William.

In a curious twist of fate, when William Hughes died on 28 January 1924 Bessie survived him by barely a month, dying on 3 March 1924. When William was declared bankrupt in 1912 his gross liabilities were stated in court to be £4,932; when Bessie died in 1924 the value of her estate was declared to be £5,045 12s 3d. She could have cleared his debts at a stroke.

The Black Baptist's Brown Baby

Before Mr Justice Lush, William repeatedly denied the existence of the 'Black Baptist's Brown Baby', but the liar and swindler Horatio Bottomley was, for once, telling the truth. Whilst employed by Hughes as a professional fund-raiser, ex-African Institute student John Lionel Franklin, had illegitimately fathered a child with Edith Dale, a white girl working in Colwyn Bay. Hughes knew all about it but thought he might get away with a denial because of two inaccuracies in *John Bull's* account of events. Bottomley had incorrectly identified the baby's date of birth, it was actually born in September not February, as the article had claimed, and also the baby wasn't really 'brown'. The *John Bull* article actually described the baby as 'half-caste' but the promotions department couldn't resist the alliterative allure of the more 'colourful' description.

Born 1875, in Charlotte Town, now Gouyave, Grenada, John Lionel Franklin was a charismatic rogue who alternatively exploited the stage and the pulpit to take advantage of credulous victims. Besides the 1911 bastardy and the 1909 imprisonment in Nigeria he might well have been the 'darkey named John Frankling' imprisoned for a month in London in 1906 for stealing a leather apron. 'Frankling's' reportedly cocksure, flippant demeanour in court certainly sounds like John Lionel Franklin.

Edith Dale, on the other hand, was an unsophisticated seamstress, living on the Great Orme in Llandudno, but employed at the drapery store of Pugh & Sons at Colwyn Bay's West End. Ten years younger than her Grenadian paramour, like many others, she succumbed to his good looks and stage-polished charms. Their son, Stanley, named after William's Hughes original inspiration and later patron, was born at the home of a friend of Edith's in Lawson Road, Colwyn Bay. After the birth Edith returned home to 7 Belle Vue Terrace, Llandudno where she lived with Stanley for the rest of her life. Predictably, Franklin disappeared, not long after the baby was born.

Like Stanley Hughes, William's son, Edith Dale refused to ever speak of the 'Scandal at Congo House' and took her secrets to the grave. Her son, Stanley Dale, the 'Brown Baby' only discovered the identity of his father after his mother's death, when in 1980, at the age of sixty-nine, he was traced by Llandudno reporter and local historian, Ivor Wynne Jones, who showed him a photograph of John Lionel Franklin, which matched one he had lost during service with the Welsh Guards in World War II.

During the course of their unpublished interview Stanley Dale confided to Jones, 'My mother did not tell me much. She never named him, but told me he was from Grenada, and had worked in Nigeria. They had spent a holiday together in Scotland. I remember very well an incident in 1922, which remained a mystery to me until today, when my mother took an extraordinary interest in the gaoling of Horatio Bottomley, telling me he had got what he deserved. She never married, telling me she had never found anyone to match my father. She looked after me, and then I looked after her until she died in 1955.' Stanley Dale died in Llandudno in 2001.

An Unmitigated Disaster?

A century has elapsed since scandal brought down William Hughes and his African Institute allowing ample opportunity to evaluate his legacy with the benefit of hindsight. Superficially

Hughes' life appears an unmitigated disaster. Having failed to survive as a Congo missionary, Hughes attempted to run a missionary training college at home but this failed too. His first wife and most of his children died prematurely and the only two members of his immediate family to flourish, Stanley and Bessie, abandoned him. Seven of the students he brought over to the supposedly healthy environment of Colwyn Bay ended up in the local cemetery, another died on the ship on the way home, at least three spent time in jail and one even conspired to destroy him. He alienated many of his fellow Welsh Baptist ministers as well as the hierarchy of the Baptist Missionary Society. He was cavalier with other people's money and economical with the truth.

Radical or Ridiculous?

During his dramatic trial William appeared a weak, evasive and inconsistent individual, but this wasn't the whole man. As a young man, in his determined preparations to serve as an African missionary, he demonstrated an impressive, consistent strength of character. He simply wouldn't take no for an answer and duly succeeded in getting out to the Congo. It is true that he couldn't tolerate the conditions but he didn't just limp back with his tail between his legs, he devised a daring and imaginative 'Plan B': his home training scheme. He could have just opted for a comfortable life as a pastor at any of the north Wales chapels that were so keen to have him, but he took on the much greater challenge of serving Africa. In founding Congo House he consciously challenged the Baptist Establishment, who judged his scheme a threat to their own 'missionary business'. The incipient racism of the Great British popular press was always another potential enemy, ready to pounce on the slightest scrap of raw meat. Once Hughes introduced a group of adolescent African boys, freed from the bounds and expectations of their own traditional societies, into the polite, white bosom of Edwardian society he was sitting on a potential powder keg.

It was an extremely brave and ambitious idea to open the African Institute. Hughes had correctly identified many of the inherently objectionable aspects of the traditional model of missionary work and imaginatively attempted to create an alternative.

He appeared pathetic in court because he tried to maintain the fiction that his alternative, his beloved African Institute, was flourishing until the day it was attacked by *John Bull*. In truth, the Institute was already on the verge of collapse and *John Bull* supplied the last straw.

When Hughes realised he couldn't survive the Congo environment he was decisive and devised a radical alternative. Once he realised the financial model of Congo House wasn't sustainable he should have been similarly decisive but instead he deluded himself, and others, with ever more unrealistic and ambitious plans for expansion. As late as 1911 he pleaded for funds, 'To develop the Girls' Institute at Colwyn Bay', although there wasn't then a single girl in residence at the Institute. I suspect his proposal and marriage to wealthy spinster Bessie Clarke, who was eight years his senior, was motivated more by economics than Eros, and that Bessie's bizarre departure was precipitated by a sudden realisation that William's worldly wealth amounted to less than nothing.

An Unsustainable Pipe-dream?

Hughes knew at the outset that his two potential sources of finance were the Baptist movement and the commercial interests trading with Africa. As the Welsh Baptists were at odds with the London dominated BMS he hoped they might give his scheme their official support but influential ministers, like Benjamin Evans (Gadlys), not only pre-empted that option but waged a continuing war against him. Individuals and congregations provided money but that stream of funding was unreliable and difficult to sustain. Hughes received enduring moral support and encouragement from some influential Baptist ministers, including Thomas Shankland and 'Spinther' James. Secular 'celebrities' such as H. M. Stanley, Sir Alfred Jones and King Leopold II were Patrons, but none supplied adequate finance.

Desperate for donations, William felt obliged to keep up appearances, exaggerate the Institute's accomplishments, and conceal serious acts of student misconduct. When sufficient donations weren't forthcoming he first helped himself to Ernestina's £295 trust fund, then began borrowing money from friends and family, including a debt of £300 he owed to his sister and her husband. Hughes then turned to commercial money lenders who supplied short-term finance at crippling interest rates. When he couldn't keep up the repayments he obtained essential supplies from local tradesmen with dud cheques, in the Micawberish belief that 'something would turn up'. Unfortunately that something was *John Bull*.

An Instrument of Imperialism?

John Bull complained of the 'futility of the mission' and implicitly preferred the traditional model of sending out white men to civilise natives, but a century later we are more sceptical about the whole enterprise and inclined to regard Victorian missionaries as an integral part of Imperial expansion and *Rule Britannia*. If *John Bull*'s Special Commissioner had granted the Colwyn Bay Institute a five-star rating of missionary efficiency we would hardly be reassured of Hughes progressive credentials.

In 1910, a member of the British Parliament, Mr Spencer Leigh Hughes (no relation), wrote approvingly to William Hughes, 'You have my complete sympathy in the admirable work you are doing in the African Training College at Colwyn Bay. Such work, apart from its religious aspect, really represents **the noblest kind of Imperialism** (my emphasis)' A century of bloody anti-colonial struggles has left few black Africans with a good word to say about imperialism, yet even in the heyday of Empire critical voices were raised against the Imperial project.

Hughes didn't believe Africans were less intelligent or occupied a lower evolutionary plane but he did believe in the ultimate superiority of European 'civilisation'. He didn't think African beliefs should be mocked or sacred objects smashed but was convinced that 'natives' would benefit from accepting the 'truth' of the Gospels. He promoted craft skills and economically independent African churches and missionaries but believed Africa would gain from the introduction of European-style capitalism.

Imperialism undermined the inherent strengths of African society. Wangari Maathai traces the causes of Africa's current poverty and unrest back to 'the destruction of Africans' cultural and spiritual heritage through the encounter with colonialism', claiming that:

> however well-meaning the missionaries may have been in spreading what they perceived to be the Good News of Jesus Christ, the result of their evangelism was the beginning of a deep cultural inferiority among their African converts ... Within a few decades, everything foreign – that which the colonial administrators and missionaries brought forth – became synonymous in the local peoples' minds with what was more advanced, closer to God's wishes, and in all ways preferable to their previous way of life and values.

The eminent British historian of Africa, Lonsdale, considered that 'the most distinctively African contribution to human history could be said to have been precisely the civilised art of living fairly peaceably together not in states', a civilised art extinguished in Europe by exploitative elites bent on enshrining, extending and legitimising their dominance through the creation, initially of Nation-States and later, overseas Empires.

Nigerian historian Kenneth Onwuka Dike claims: 'Little of permanent value came to West Africa from the 400 years of trade with Europe. In return for the superior labour force, the palm oil, ivory, timber, gold and other commodities which fed and buttressed the rising industrialization they received the worst type of trade, gin and meretricious articles.' Christians would reject any suggestion that the Bible be lumped in with other 'meretricious articles' but ultimately it served the Imperial project for missionaries to disrupt African communities, alienating traditional loyalties and opening up Africa to European goods as well as European gods.

Hughes criticised only exceptional aspects of the Imperial project and is tainted by his association with some of its more vigorous practitioners, but his options were limited. He was attempting to do something radical within a conservative framework, to appeal to the powerful for money and support to enable the powerless and impoverished to become more economically and intellectually self-sufficient. His advocacy of Christianity ultimately reminded black Africans that there was a higher authority than Imperial power. He was no revolutionary and endeavoured to appeal to the better part of human nature, rather than attack or undermine opponents but his support for independent African churches was a radical policy that implicitly challenged the Imperial model of colonial domination.

Ripples from Colwyn Bay

William Hughes achieved a tremendous amount with limited resources, both financial and intellectual. He was brave, imaginative and enlightened but he just wasn't up to the enormous task he set himself. He allied himself to men far less altruistic and radical than himself and failed to fully comprehend the corrosive effects of the scramble for Africa. Crushed by a combination of ineptitude and bigotry he remains an inspiration. Hughes' long and close association with Mojola Agbebi and the independent Black African churches is testimony to his integrity, and the enduring influence of his students his abiding legacy. Davidson Don Tengo Jabavu was just one of the many inspired by Hughes at Colwyn Bay. On his return to South Africa, Jabavu, helped establish the hugely influential Native College of Fort Hare, where he passed the intellectual baton to his own students, one of whom, Nelson Mandela, later declared; 'Fort Hare and Professor D. D. T. Jabavu are virtually synonymous'. Through his students and his students' students, his influence lives on.

In a final letter addressed from 'The African Institute, Colwyn Bay', just before he was shuffled off into penury and obscurity, William Hughes begged of old friends and supporters, and perhaps of us today: 'Please do not forget to remember me.'

Bibliography, Notes and Acknowledgements

Newspapers
- *Weekly News & Visitors Chronicle*
- *Colwyn Bay & Welsh Coast Pioneer*
- *Llandudno Advertiser*
- *Seren Cymru*
- *African Times*

African Institute Publications
- Twenty-two Annual Reports of Congo House Training Institute for African Students from 1889 until 1911 (separate English and Welsh copies were published)
- *Reasons for Training the Most Promising of the African Converts in this Country* – Revd William Hughes, 1893
- *Sefydliad Colwyn Bay Wedi ei Brofi trwy Dan* – James Spinther James, 1894
- *Yr Amddiffynydd Cenhadol* – James Spinther James, 1895
- *Early Christianity in Africa* – A paper written and delivered by James Spinther James at the Ministers' Fraternal at Congo Institute, 4th October 1895
- *Besedi Ba Yehova* – Dualla Hymn Book (native language of Cameroon) compiled by Joshua, Alfred & Samuel Dibundu and James Spinther James, 1896
- *The Congo Institute, Colwyn Bay and John Greenhough, of Africa* – Anonymous, either William Hughes or James Spinther James, 1896
- *Short Biography of the late Katie H Hughes of the African Institute* – William Hughes, 1909
- *Pwnc y Dydd! Y Buddioldeb O Gael Cymdeithas Genhadol I Fedyddwyr Cymru* – Anonymous, edited by either William Hughes or James Spinther James, 1911
- *Third Visit of the Revd W Hughes, Colwyn Bay, to the West Coast of Africa* – William Hughes, 1917

General Publications
Bassett, T. Myrfyn, *The Welsh Baptists* (1977)
Bassett, T. Myrfyn, *The Baptists of Wales & the Baptist Missionary Society* (1991)
Bolt, C., *Victorian Ideas on Race* (1971)
Booth, John, *Africa for the Africans* (1897)
Dabydeen, Gilmore, Jones, *Black British History* (2007)
Fryer, Peter, *Staying Power; the history of black people in Britain* (1989)
Geiss, Imanuel, *The Pan-African Movement* (1974)

Grant, Kevin, *A Civilized Savagery: Britain and the New Slaveries in Africa, 1884–1926* (2005)

Murray, Jocely (ed.), *Cultural Atlas of Africa* (1981)

Packenham, Thomas, *The Scramble for Africa; the white man's conquest of the Dark Continent from 1876–1912* (1991)

Stanley, Brian, *The History of the Baptist Missionary Society 1792–1992* (1992)

Sundkler, B. & Steed, C., *A History of the Church in Africa* (2000)

Williams, Evans & O'Leary, *A Tolerant Nation? Exploring ethnic diversity in Wales* (2003)

Winder, Robert, *Bloody Foreigners; the story of immigration to Britain* (2004)

Young, Tom, *Africa: A Beginner's Guide* (2010)

Notes

Chapter One: Farm Boy to Visionary (1856–1882)

Capel y beirdd, Rhoslan is preserved in splendid order although the railway of Hughes' boyhood has long gone and Congo House (see chapter 3) stands anonymous and pebbled-dashed into obscurity. Llangollen Baptist College (also known as Bartholomew College after the day of its opening) can still be seen in Berwyn Street although the building now serves as a Post Office.

Hall, R.   *Stanley: an Adventurer Explored* (1974)
Parry, Gruffudd   *Crwydro Llyn ac Eifynydd* (1960)
Wheeler, B. R.   *Alfred Henry Baynes JP* (1951)

Chapter Two: Steaming up the Congo (1882–1885)

Hughes' few surviving African 'curiosities' may be viewed by appointment with Conwy archive. A variety of Elder Dempster shipping records can be consulted on-line or at Merseyside Maritime Museum Archive, Liverpool.

Bentley, H. M.   *W. Holman Bentley; the Life of a Congo Pioneer* (1907)
Hughes, William   *Dark Africa and the Way Out* (1892)

Chapter Three: William, Nkanza and Kinkasa in Wales (1885–1890)

Ebenezer Chapel, Llanelian and Tabernacl Chapel, Abergele Road, Colwyn Bay remain almost unaltered since Hughes' period as pastor. Congo House, Rhoslan and the Congo Guest House, Bay View Road, Colwyn Bay, survive but have been insensitively modernised. The grave of John Ystumllyn can be visited in the graveyard of Eglwys Cynhaearn, Pentrefelin near Portmadoc. The memorial englyn translates as: 'India [*sic*] was the land of my birth / but I was baptised in Wales / this spot, marked by a grey slate / is my cold, dark resting place'. Williams' daughter was formally registered as 'Katherine Hughes Hughes', an interesting echo of the old Welsh patronymic.

Davies, P. N.   *The Trade Makers: Elder Dempster in West Africa,
                        1852–1972*
Draper, Christopher *Walks with History; Colwyn Bay* (2000)
Eifion, Alltud   *John Ystumllyn* (1888)
Frimston, T.   *Bedyddwyr Canfref y Rhos* (1924)
Lewis, Thomas   *These Seventy Years (1883–1923)* (1931)
Thornley, F. C.   *Past and Present Steamers of North Wales* (1952)

Chapter Four: Early Days at Congo House, Colwyn Bay (1890–1893)

The original Congo House building, Myrtle Villa remains, largely unaltered in Nant-y-Glyn Road, Colwyn Bay. The adjacent extensions to the original Institute have been demolished. The title of the institution evolved over the years and was variously and inconsistently applied. I have echoed this informal approach throughout the book but as a general guide **Congo House** was the form initially adopted. From about 1892 the more grandiose and inclusive **Congo House Training Institute** for African Students was preferred. This was contracted to **African (Congo) Institute** in around 1896. From 1900 until its demise Congo House was officially titled the **African Training Institute**. That God-ordained anthem of imperialism, 'From Greenland's Icy Mountains' was written by Reginald Heber in Wrexham in 1819 in response to a request from the local vicar 'for something for them to sing in the morning'. Completed in just twenty minutes, the patronisingly offensive 'heathen' identified in the second verse was originally a 'savage'! Despite Hughes' enthusiasm for H. M. Stanley, even in 1891 he wasn't universally welcomed. Speaking in Sheffield immediately prior to his Caernarfon engagement, Stanley's meeting was disrupted by John Creaghe and John Bingham of the local Anarchist group, who distributed a pamphlet exposing the violence and racism integral to his 'heroic exploration' of Africa (*Commonweal*, 10 June 1891).

Davies, P. N.   *Sir Alfred Jones; shipping entrepreneur par
                        excellence* (1978)
Findlay, J. F.   *Dwight L Moody: American Evangelist* (1969)
Green, Jeffery   *Thomas Lewis Johnson (1836–1921): the
                        Bournemouth Evangelist* (1986)
Johnson, Thomas Lewis *Twenty-Eight Years a Slave* (1909)
Sankey, I. D.   *My Life and Sacred Songs* (1906)
Stoeker, Helmuth (ed.) *German Imperialism in Africa* (1986)

Chapter Five: Letters from the Dark Continent (June 1893–December 1893)

This chapter comprises Hughes' 1893 epistles from Gambia, Liberia, Sierra Leone, Ghana, Nigeria and Cameroon. To provide context for readers unfamiliar with African history I offer the following potted histories:

Gambia – a hundred stone circles survive as evidence of ancient civilisation along the River Gambia, and between the seventh and fifteenth centuries Gambia was part of a flourishing Muslim gold-trading empire that only declined after the arrival of the Portuguese in 1447. England supplanted Portuguese influence in the sixteenth century and established trading posts on the Gambia River controlled from Sierra Leone. In 1816 Captain Alexander Grant founded the city of Bathurst (Banjul) and in 1843 Gambia was declared a Crown Colony with its own colonial administration, based at Bathurst, and no longer ruled from Freetown. In 1889 Britain's imperial strategy prompted her to seek to swap Gambia with France in exchange for Gabon but no agreement was concluded.

Liberia – founded by the American Colonization Society as a homeland in Africa for liberated black slaves from the southern USA. The first settlers landed in 1822 and Liberia was declared an independent republic in 1847. A social and financial failure from the outset, African-Americans refused to integrate with Africans from the interior and continued to form a corrupt governing elite. This Americo-Liberian ruling class enjoyed a neo-colonial relationship with the USA which provided finance and arms to ensure the continued exclusion of the indigenous population. A coup in 1980 brought Africans to power for the first time since 1822.

Sierra Leone – inhabited for at least 2,500 years, agriculture was practised by coastal tribes a thousand years ago. After Portuguese exploitation in the fifteenth and sixteenth centuries, in the seventeenth century the British built forts and actively traded in the Sherbro and Tasso Island areas, with the first slaves in north America taken from Sierra Leone in 1652. In 1792 the capital, Freetown, was founded by the British as a home for 'Black Poor', generally African-Americans granted their freedom after seeking refuge with the British army during the American Revolution. In the early nineteenth century Freetown served as the residence of the British governor who also ruled the Gold Coast (Ghana) and the Gambia. British influence remained strongest at the coast although the government sought to agree treaties with inland chiefs in order to facilitate trade. Uncooperative chiefs were threatened with military intervention. In 1896 the territory was declared a British Protectorate but in 1898 the imposition of a 'hut tax' triggered a wide-spread insurrection which was ruthlessly suppressed by the colonial administration with mass executions.

Ghana – inhabited for at least 6,000 years, by the thirteenth century it comprised several African kingdoms, most notably the Fanti on the coast and the Ashanti further inland. The Portuguese arrived in 1471 and until about 1800 shared commercial trading, mainly in slaves and gold, with several other European nations. An increasingly expansive Ashanti disrupted trade and attacked coastal settlements until defeated by Britain and the Fanti in 1874. The coastal region was then declared the British colony of the Gold Coast and after further fighting in 1901 the Ashanti kingdom was annexed and decreed a British Protectorate.

Nigeria – inhabited since at least 700 BC, around the twelfth century highly-developed societies developed in both the Yoruba area and the Muslim north. From the fifteenth century Portuguese and British slave traders raided the region. In 1861 traders claimed to have bought Lagos from an African chief and in 1886 it was deemed a British colony and protectorate. Trade in the Niger River valley was developed by the United Africa Company, founded by George Goldie in 1879. The company's charter was withdrawn in 1899 when the government decreed two British protectorates, North Nigeria and South Nigeria, with the latter joined to Lagos in 1906. In 1914 Nigeria was formally united, creating Britain's largest African colony.

Cameroon – the Mandara kingdom, founded around 1500, erected magnificent fortified structures, but in the eighteenth century Islamic Fulani pastoral nomads from what is now Nigeria began to migrate overland from the north, forcing the indigenous population southwards. In the early nineteenth century British and American missionaries intervened and German influence began in 1868 when the Woermann Company of Hamburg erected a warehouse on the estuary of the Wouri river. British influence was curtailed in 1884 when Cameroon became the German protectorate of Kamerun, but for the local inhabitants the agreement meant little more than a shift from one form of colonial exploitation to another. In WWI the British invaded, with the last German fort in the country surrendering in February 1916. After WWI, France governed about 80 per cent of the area under a League of Nations mandate, with Britain administering the remainder.

Blunt A.	*Travel, Gender & Imperialism; Mary Kingsley and West Africa* (1994)
Davies, P. N.	*Trading in West Africa* (1976)
Dea, B.	*Mary Kingsley: Imperial Adventuress* (1992)
Hargreaves, John D.	*A Life of Sir Samuel Lewis* (1958)
Hayford, Mark Christian	*Mary H. Kingsley: From an African Standpoint* (1901)
Hayford, Mark Christian	*West Africa and Christianity* (1900)

Chapter Six: Days of Hope at the African Institute (1894–1899)

This was a defining period in Hughes' enterprise where he actively supported the emerging movement of independent native churches and attempted to fashion working relationship with Africans like Agbebi, Aboyami Cole and Kofi Assam. Readers wanting to examine this relationship further are advised to study the works of Hazel King cited below.

Brown, Hallie Quinn	*Homespun Heroines & Other Women of Distinction* (1926)
Fullberg-Stolberg, Katja	*African Americans in West Africa in the Late Nineteenth and Early Twentieth Centuries; Agents of European Colonial Rule?*
King, Hazel	*Cooperation in Contextualisation* (1986)
King, Hazel	*Mojola Agbebi – Nigerian Church Leader* (1986)
Ward, Andrew	*Dark Midnight When I Rise: the story of the Jubilee Singers* (2000)

Chapter Seven: 'Afric's Sons Welcome You Both' (Autumn 1899)

There are no secondary sources chronicling this curious episode. My own researches over many years included productive newspaper appeals for information on Bessie Hutton both in Wales and also around the Manchester/Ashton-under-Lyne area. Local newspapers (*North Wales Weekly News & Visitors' Chronicle*, the *Colwyn Bay & Welsh Coast Pioneer*, and the *Ashton Reporter*), of the appropriate dates, offer the most useful and accessible sources of information.

Chapter Eight: End of the Honeymoon (1900–1907)

In Colwyn Bay in April 1904 occurred the curious death of James Knofi, 'a native of the Gold Coast'. According to the local newspaper, 'It appears the deceased, who was only 18 years of age, and had been in England for about ten months, came to Colwyn Bay from Liverpool where he was studying.' Although Knofi isn't listed amongst students attending the Institute it is likely that his presence in Colwyn Bay was linked to Congo House. Intriguingly, in December 1901 a James Knofi donated a wristlet of the Ashante King Prempeh (exiled from Ghana by the British for resisting colonial domination) to Liverpool Museum.

It is likely that the 'proto-Pan-Africanist' Edward Wilmot Blyden visited the Colwyn Bay Institute in this period during his stay with Sir Alfred Jones on 14th and 15th September 1901 at his holiday home in Llanddulas, just along the coast. Blyden was in Britain to address the Liverpool Chamber of Commerce of which Alfred Jones was President.

Frederick William Bond's faithful service as printer and instructor at the Institute from 1899 to 1909 deserves particular recognition. Born in

Yeovil, Somerset in 1867 Bond followed his older brother, Walter, into the print trade in his very early teens. After employment with local printer and stationer, W B Collins, he worked at the *Western Chronicle*, Yeovil before taking up a post at the *Herald Printing Works*, Harrogate in 1894. From Harrogate, Bond moved to Liverpool before, in April 1899, accepting William Hughes' invitation to develop a printing department at Congo House. It was Bond's skill, enterprise and commitment that made the print department such a valued part of the Congo House training scheme as well as providing a resource for producing reports and publicity. Bond's 1909 departure is indicative of the Institute's dire financial position by then. He stayed on in Colwyn Bay, began a photographic business and kept a guest house, 'Yeovil', with his wife, Susan, in Hawarden Road.

A brass plaque acknowledging William Hughes' founding role remains a prominent feature of the foyer of Colwyn Bay library.

B. M. S.	*The Congo Question and the Baptist Missionary Society* (1909)
Emerson, Barbara	*Leopold II of the Belgians* (1979)
Hoschild, Adam	*King Leopold's Ghost* (1999)
Langworthy, Harry	*Africa for the African – the Life of Joseph Booth* (1996)
Morel, E. D.	*King Leopold's Rule in Africa* (1904)
Shephard, Ben	*Kitty and the Prince* (2003)

Chapter Nine: Young, Gifted and Black: Student Biographies (1882–1912)

The marked graves of Kinkasa (1888), Samba (1892), Nkanza (1892) and Joseph Emmanuel Abraham (Kobina Boodoo, 1909) and unmarked graves of George Steane (1894) and Alfred W Jackson (1894) can be visited in Old Colwyn Cemetery. Fragmentary biographies can be gleaned by consulting a variety of the Institute's Annual reports and various newspapers identified above.

Green, Jeffery	*Black Edwardians – Black People in Britain 1901–1914* (1998)
Killingray, David	*Africans in Britain* (1994)
Mandela, Nelson	*Long Walk to Freedom* (1994)
Mandela, Nelson	*Conversations with Myself* (2010)

Chapter Ten: 'Black Baptist's Brown Baby' (1908–11)

It is curious that no reference to the dramatic traffic accident suffered by Katie Hughes in her infancy appears anywhere in the thirty-page tribute published by her father to commemorate her early death. At the time it was reported that (see Chapter Three), 'The wheels passing over her chest undoubtedly caused internal injuries', yet the possible long-term contributory effects of the accident seem to have been entirely overlooked on her demise. Councillor William Hughes' specific contribution to meetings of Colwyn Bay Council can be identified in the comprehensive set of bound minutes available for consultation in Colwyn Bay Reference Library. Gorsedd stones commemorating the 1910 National Eisteddfod of Wales survive in situ at the Flagstaff Estate (now the Welsh Mountain Zoo), Colwyn Bay.

Bottomley, Horatio (Ed.)   'A Baptist Mission Scandal – I & II'
                                  (*John Bull Magazine*, 16 & 23 December 1911)

Chapter Eleven: Scandal and Disgrace (1911–1912)
Contemporary newspapers offer the most detailed reports of Hughes' various legal examinations although in several instances the relevant pages are missing! Clearly Hughes' supporters actively attempted to suppress news of the scandal but it is possible, by accessing a number of archives to eventually compile a comprehensive variety of accounts of the proceedings. The former grand home of Hughes' lacklustre solicitor, Soughton Hall, Flintshire, has been converted into a rather grand hotel.

Edmondson, Robert   *John Bull's Army from Within* (1907)
Hyman, A.   *The Rise and Fall of Horatio Bottomley: the biography of a swindler* (1972)
Symons, Julian   *Horatio Bottomley* (1955)

Chapter Twelve: 'Do Not Forget to Remember Me' (1912–1924)
Conwy Workhouse, where Hughes died in 1924, was demolished in 2005, despite the public protestations of the author. Only a portion of the original stone boundary wall survives. The graves of William Hughes and his family can be visited in Old Colwyn Cemetery. Mark Hayford's legal action is still cited by barristers and details can be found on the web by searching for 'Hayford v. Forrester-Paton, 17 June 1927'.

Cline, Catherine Ann   *E. D. Morel 1873–1924: the strategies of protest* (1980)
Draper, Christopher   *Paupers, Bastards and Lunatics* (2005)
Haliburton, G. M.   'Mark Christian Hayford: a non-success story' (*Journal of Religion in Africa*, vol.12, 1981)
Hobson, John Atkinson   *Imperialism* (1902)
Mandela, Nelson   *Conversations with Myself* (2010)
Maathai, Wangari   *The Challenge for Africa* (2010)
Scholes, T. E. S.   *Chamberlain and Chamberlainism* (1903)

Acknowledgements

Innumerable people contributed to this book. Some offered the fruits of original research, some permitted the reproduction of illustrations, some argued me out of intemperate judgements whilst my partner, Anna Jeffery, patiently read, re-read and improved numerous ill-punctuated drafts. I owe a particular debt of gratitude to Hazel King, who not only generously provided documentation but also offered invaluable insight into the faith that drove Hughes and Agbebi. The researches of Martin M'Caw, Jeffrey Green and the late Ivor Wynne Jones all helped enormously, as did the unique recollections of Dora Pearson, Benllech, concerning Bessie Hutton Hughes. Carole Dalton generously provided invaluable information and unique illustrations of her grandfather, the Institute's printer, Frederick William Bond. I would also like to take this opportunity to thank the archivists of Angus Library, Oxford (especially Emily Burgoyne); Conwy Archive, Llandudno; Denbighshire Archive, Ruthin; Flintshire Archive, Hawarden; Gwynedd Archive, Caernarfon; National Archive, Kew; Tameside Local Studies Library, Stalybridge; University of Wales, Bangor, for their assistance in making available for research a variety of original documents. I am grateful to my local (Penrhyn Bay) librarians Mair, Denise and Janet, for patiently tracking down and obtaining obscure text books from all over Wales despite constant threats of closure from self-serving politicians and their management minions. Family members of William Hughes, past and present, contributed precious memories, documents and pictures whilst John Lawson-Reay (ably assisted by Barbara Lawson-Reay) employed his professional expertise in ensuring my text, if not readable, was at least accompanied by interesting illustrations.

Index